COMRADE SAK

A POLITICAL BIOGRAPHY

COMRADE SAK

A POLITICAL BIOGRAPHY

MARC WADSWORTH

PEEPAL TREE

First published in Great Britain in 1998
This new edition 2020
by Peepal Tree Press Ltd
17 King's Avenue
Leeds LS6 1QS
England

ISBN 9781845235109

Supported using public funding by
ARTS COUNCIL
ENGLAND

CONTENTS

PHOTOGRAPHS
(between pp. 157-158)

ACKNOWLEDGEMENTS

Fellow Labour activist and author Vidya Anand introduced me to Sehri Saklatvala, the daughter of Shapurji Saklatvala, sparking my interest in him and the idea of writing a biography. But holding down a full-time job and being a political and trade union activist took its toll. After I failed to get my book written by 1986, the fiftieth anniversary of her father's death, Sehri herself started a labour of love and published *The Fifth Commandment: A biography of Shapurji Saklatvala* five years later. Furthermore, a communist academic, Michael Squires, also wrote a book, both works adding to the short, biographical volume published by Panchanan Saha in India in 1970. I would like to place on record that the now departed Sehri Saklatvala was kind and helpful to me when I was doing my research, for which I am most grateful.

Yasmin Saklatvala, for many years partner of the late Beram, Shapurji Saklatvala's son, lent me important private family material and gave great encouragement, as did the politician's grandson, Christopher Saklatvala. At the beginning of the project, journalist and film-maker Julian Ozanne, then an undergraduate at the London School of Economics and Political Science, helped with research. I am no academic, but have done my journalist's best to uncover Shapurji Saklatvala's life story. My gratitude also goes to Jeremy Poynting and Hannah Bannister, of Peepal Tree Press, the publishers, whose commitment to this project was demonstrated by the unreasonable hours they worked in the preparation of the original book and this new version, which Jeremy deftly edited. Peerless scholar and author professor David Dabydeen introduced me to Jeremy Poynting, who had to be persuaded to print his first non-fiction title. The film-maker Christopher Mitchell made available material, which was gathered during the production of his 1990 Channel Four Saklatvala documentary. He also read the manuscript and made wise suggestions, as did Keith Bennett and Arif Ali, of Hansib Publications. Kevin White, a Grassroots Black Left comrade, has done a masterful book cover. I must also give my gratitude to Battersea Labour Party for allowing me to use material from their archives. Others who rescued me from my ignorance of history include Iqbal Singh, who made extremely pertinent suggestions about the 'MP for India' chapter, Noreen Branson, George Matthews, Francis King, Andrew Rothstein and staff at the Marx Memorial Library for providing invaluable information about the Communist Party, as well as Tony Shaw, Sean Creighton, Michael Ward, Trevor Carter, Peter Fryer, Malcolm Deboo, Edward Stawiarski, Deborah Hobson and Rozina Visram.

I thank them all, and other people not mentioned, for their invaluable help and support.

To Sisko and George

PREFACE TO THE SECOND EDITION

In the twenty-two years since the original publication of *Comrade Sak*, I believe its subject has become even more relevant. This second edition updates my book in three ways. It includes new primary information that has come available since the first publication; it takes note of fresh perspectives on Saklatvala and his times in books published since 1998; and considers contemporary social and political contexts for the book, some of them personal.

Since MI5 papers, including files on Shapurji Saklatvala, were opened to the public in 2000, fresh information emerged about just *how* seriously the British state regarded him as a threat to the status quo, and about his deep involvement with revolutionary anti-colonial Irish politics. From another existing but overlooked source, Arthur Calder-Marshall's *Glory Dead* (1939), the account of a young British communist's visit to insurgent Trinidad in the aftermath of the workers' uprising of 1936-37, provides further evidence of Saklatvala's place at the nexus of a global network of anti-imperialist radicals in his collaboration with a young Trinidadian, Adrian Cola Rienzi; a relationship that further connected the Indian and Irish anti-colonial struggles.

Two books added hitherto unconsidered frameworks for thinking about Saklatvala's life. There was Kate O'Malley's revelatory *Ireland, India and the Empire* (2008), Francis Devine's correspondence about Saklatvala and Ireland in the journal *Saothar*, and Priyamvada Gopal's seminal book, *Insurgent Empire: Anticolonial Resistance and British Dissent* (2019). The latter located Saklatvala as a crucial figure in the history of opposition within the British Empire, from the time of the Indian uprising of 1857, and the terrible imperial acts of revenge that followed, to the appalling treatment – including hangings, torture and castrations – meted out to detainees in concentration camps during the Kenyan Mau Mau uprising of 1952-1960, which in 2012, after a long legal battle, resulted in surviving veterans winning an historic victory for compensation in the British courts. This was the first time in British history that victims of colonialism were given the right to claim compensation from the British government for the abuse and suffering they had endured.[1]

Gopal's book was an important element in what has been taking place in the national political discourse, in the written word, speech and action since the first publication of *Comrade Sak*. At the time of its original writing, I saw Saklatvala's career as a communist and anti-imperialist activist, who was actually elected as a Labour MP for two successive parliaments (the second time not endorsed nationally by the party), as a precursor to the activities of contemporary Black radicals. That included the author, as a founder member and leader of the Labour Party Black Sections (circa 1983-1991), and the concerted campaign they conducted. This was to persuade Labour not only to take seriously the issues of racism and the economic, social and cultural structural inequalities that restricted the lives of Black people, its most loyal voters, but to make space in the party, through Black self-organisation and self-determination, for them to be properly represented at all levels and have an active role in defining those issues that most affected them, and determining policy. Since then there have been advances, certainly in the number of British African Caribbean and Asian MPs, but whether these Black politicians are any nearer to playing a determining role in Labour Party policies is another matter altogether. I feel sure Comrade Sak would not have approved of decorative "Black faces in high places", as is the case with Boris Johnson's Conservative government that boasts an Asian chancellor and home secretary and African Caribbean party chair. They are not there to bring Black politics to the Cabinet table; for them, their bourgeois class is more important than their colour. These questions have been brought into sharp focus after the resignation of Labour's most progressive leader, Jeremy Corbyn, when the new party leader, Keir Starmer, seems bent on winning back socially-conservative white working-class electors by a Tony Blair-type display of managerialist, pro-capitalist *responsibility* that dares not raise issues of fundamental inequalities of race, class and gender.

What has opened up in the world outside parliamentary politics is a discourse concerning the long-term effects of Empire and colonialism on the British psyche and as a driver of the country's political attitudes. We have long been drawn to think that empire and colonialism happened 'over there', and that when former parts of the empire fought for and gained their independence – from Ireland in 1922/37, India in 1947, Ghana, 1957, Nigeria 1960 and the Caribbean islands and Guyana between 1962-1978 (though Montserrat is still an overseas territory of the United Kingdom) – that with the exception of Louise Bennett's 'Colonisation in reverse' of postwar migration, colonialism was over and done with, at least as far as Britain was concerned. Of course, the exposure by Amelia Gentleman of the scandal of the cruel and racist treatment of the 'Windrush generation' in *The Guardian* and her subsequent book, that began to surface in 2017-2018,[2] showed that this was very far from the case. There has long been an acceptance – to take the Caribbean as an example – of the fact that colonialism, with its roots in plantation slavery, has had profound and continuing limitations on the possibilities of economic independence and genuine sovereignty of the debt-burdened societies of the global south. Few would dispute that the economic and cultural hierarchies of class remain intermeshed with those of race and colour, and that in many parts of the old empire, new Black elites have simply stepped into the former masters' shoes. On the other hand, the recognition of the lasting impact of empire and colonialism on British society – beyond the presence and settlement in the UK of people of African, Caribbean and South Asian heritage – has been a much more contemporary focus.

It was a long overdue resumption of a conversation begun in Eric Williams's *Capitalism and Slavery* (1944), which argued, in broad terms, that capital drawn from the profits of slavery funded the British industrial revolution. That argument was built on by Walter Rodney's *How Europe Underdeveloped Africa* (1972) and in Joseph E. Inikori's *Africans in the Industrial Revolution in England* (2001) and has been continued at a much more closely documented micro-level in studies such as in Madge Dresser's very pertinent study of Bristol, *Slavery Obscured: The Social History of the Slave Trade in an English Provincial Port* (2001); in the work of Catherine Hall in *Civilising Subjects: Metropole and Colony in the English Imagination 1830-1867* (2002); in Nicholas Draper's *The Price of Emancipation: Slave Ownership, Compensation and British Society at the end of Slavery* (2009); in Madge Dresser and Andrew Hann's *Slavery and the British Country House* (2013); in the multiply-authored *Legacies of British Slave-Ownership: Colonial Slavery and the formation of Victorian Britain* (2014); and *Emancipation and the remaking of the British Imperial World* (2014) as well as in a flow of studies of family fortunes and the business, political, heritage and sometimes philanthropic dynasties based on engaging in the slave trade, financing it and producing slave-grown sugar. Here, among others, there have been studies of the Gladstones (by S.G. Checkland), of the Lascelles still at Harewood House outside Leeds (by S.D. Smith) and the Hibberts (by Katie Donington)[3]. On the making of whiteness and Westerness, there has been Saree Makdisi's *Making England Western: Occidentalism, Race, and Imperial Culture* (2014), which provided an incisive construct of how English identity can only be understood in the context of the relationship to empire. The persistence of such frameworks into the contemporary period are charted in Wendy Webster's *Englishness and Empire 1939-1965* (2005), in Paul Gilroy's *After Empire: Melancholia or Convivial Culture* (2004), and in Robert Gildea's *Empires of the Mind: The Colonial Past and the Politics of the Present* (2019). All these are books that tell us just how central slavery and empire was to the construction of what is taken for granted as Britishness in economic, political and cultural terms. There are, of course, many other books that continue to explore the Black British presence as a part of Britishness, such as *The Oxford Companion to Black British History* (co-edited by David Dabydeen, with John Gilmore and Cecily Jones (2007), but the focus on empire and white British attitudes is relatively new.

These works of generally academic research have been given wider public exposure in the BBC-platformed popularising work of David Olusoga in print and on television.[4] There's the Colonial Countryside project involving the National Trust, which is committed to truth-telling about the slavery and East India Company sources of wealth that funded the building or expansion of many much visited 'stately homes'. The involvement of older primary school age children is a welcome aspect of this project.[5] There has been a welcome though belated effort by several British universities, prompted by calls for reparations from academics in the Caribbean, to identify the sources of multi-million pound bequests they have received, paid for by slavery and colonial exploitation, and to seek to make some sort of redress.[6] For the past few years, several universities have been confronted by student demands (with some staff support) for the decolonisation of the curriculum. There are teachers, too, who have recognised that the small steps made in the 1970s and 1980s towards more 'diverse' lessons disappeared with the imposition of the national curriculum in the Education Act of 1988, and calls for the teaching of Black history have gained some traction, though resisted by the Conservative government.[7] All these, of course, have become rather more than the issues of "a moment", as Keir Starmer patronisingly suggested, through the militant activism of the Black Lives Matter (BLM) and RHODES MUST FALL campaigns.[8] The latter got the University of Oxford to at last agree the statue of its imperialist white supremacist benefactor Cecil Rhodes should be taken down. RHODES MUST FALL inspired mainly white BLM protesters to topple the statue of the slave trader Edward Colston in the British former slave port of Bristol in an iconic act of widely-applauded civil disobedience on 7 June 2020.

Even the BBC has engaged with the record of that icon of British/ English identity, Winston Churchill, in examining his leading role in the shameful episode of the Bengal famine of 1943 when up to three million lives of Asian British subjects were cynically sacrificed as worth less than white lives during the war effort.[9] Churchill remained a strident opponent of Indian self-rule, which he believed would bring about the downfall of the British Empire.

We should also recall that a year after the First World War, Churchill defended the use of poisonous gas against what he called 'uncivilised tribes' that included Iraqi Kurds and in Afghanistan as a means of spreading 'a lively terror'. His 1919 War Office Memorandum said:

> I am strongly in favour of using poisoned gas against uncivilised tribes. The moral effect should be so good that the loss of life should be reduced to a minimum. It is not necessary to use only the most deadly gasses:

gasses can be used which cause great inconvenience and would spread a lively terror and yet would leave no serious permanent effects on most of those affected.[10]

The squeals of outrage from British prime minister Boris Johnson downwards to this challenge to received conservative views of his hero and the UK's historical identity signal that a raw nerve has been touched.[11]

The continuing delusions of British sovereignty and exceptionalism that emerged in the Brexit debate were present for all those with eyes to see and ears to hear in the delusions of Conservative Brexiteers' Empire 2.0 and the hasty visit and absurd dancing exploits of Johnson's predecessor, Theresa May, in Africa. There used to be a right-wing and racist Conservative ginger group called the League of Empire Loyalists; it apparently never went away. One significant title here is Danny Dorling and Sally Thompson's *Rule Britannia: Brexit and the End of Empire* (2018). Not least pertinent is to note that little Englishness (including its Northern Irish and Scottish unionist allies) and the drive to leave Europe was not shared by Scottish voters, nor by the Republican and non-Unionists electorate in Northern Ireland, or by the 'native' Welsh (as opposed to English settlers in Wales). It was a reminder of older colonial relationships, much closer to home.

But the lingering effects of Empire and colonialism have not been solely a matter for Conservative England. One of the virtues of Gopal's book is the searchlight it throws on the record of the Labour Party, after the 1910-1936 period of Saklatvala's active political life, with regard to imperialism. As Saklatvala repeatedly charged, and is documented in my book, Labour in power frequently displayed attitudes and practices towards empire, colonialism and, frankly, in the racist immigration laws it brought in, that differed little from those of the Conservatives. Jeremy Corbyn was one of just six Labour MPs who had the courage to vote against the 2014 Immigration Act, which caused the Windrush Scandal. John McDonnell, Kelvin Hopkins, Fiona MacTaggart, Dennis Skinner and Diane Abbott, the only African Caribbean or Asian MP among them, were the others.

Saklatvala's principled, internationalist and socialist critique of empire was never shared by more than a minority of members of the Labour Party, with the exception, in the main, of small groups on the left, such as Fenner Brockway's Movement for Colonial Freedom.[12]

In the period when this second edition of *Comrade Sak* was being prepared, Labour was wracked by the charge that antisemitism was rife in its ranks, and the author was himself expelled from the party on those grounds, for allegedly abusing a Jewish Labour MP. At Labour's June 2016 launch of its report into antisemitism and racism, I called out an anti-Corbyn MP, Ruth Smeeth, whom I did not know was Jewish, after I spotted her in a cosy exchange with a reporter from the most right-wing organ of the daily press, the Conservative Party-supporting *Daily Telegraph*. The main thrust of my intervention was to raise the under-representation of African Caribbean and Asian people among those in attendance, about which I had been campaigning in the Labour Party for decades. This complaint was taken on board by Corbyn at the event, who admitted the party needed to do better, but was ignored by the journalists who covered the story.[13]

It seems even clearer to me that Saklatvala's quarrels with Labour and his at times anomalous position within the Communist Party of Great Britain had to do with his very clear position as an anti-racist, anti-imperialist fighter on behalf of colonised peoples. Gopal's book supports the case I made in the first edition of *Comrade Sak* about why his struggle was often a lonely one. Reni Eddo-Lodge's best-seller *Why I'm No Longer Talking To White People About Race* (2017) points to only limited improvements in empathy and understanding over the past ninety years.

It is a pity that Gopal's book does not include a discussion of the policies and practices of British governments, including Labour ones, towards colonial Palestine,[14] particularly because she is crystal clear on the malign conjunction of British imperialism and settler colonialism in Kenya. I think attitudes to empire and colonialism have been a critical dividing lines within the Labour Party concerning responses to the inexorable progress of settler colonialist Zionist governments in Israel from 1948 onwards,[15] the continued building of settlements in the occupied territories, declared a 'flagrant violation of international law' by the UN Security Council, and the present threat by Prime Minister Benjamin Netanyahu to annexe the occupied West Bank and continue the process of the ethnic cleansing of Palestinians and their imprisonment within apartheid-style Bantustans.[16] Generally, the Labour left, including several antizionist Jewish groups, have been clear about the nature of imperialism and colonialism. They have concluded that Zionism is a racially-exclusive philosophy that justifies settler colonialism and the establishment of the Israeli state through brutal land-theft, ethnic cleansing and the denial of Palestinian rights to self-determination. On the right (and centre) of the British Parliamentary Labour Party, there has generally been loyal and unquestioning support for the state of Israel, and any criticism of Zionism and its works has been cynically conflated with anti-Jewish hatred and denounced as antisemitism. The convulsion in the Labour Party came when the membership elected a leader in Corbyn who was a lifelong supporter of Palestinian rights. This upset the right-wing majority of Labour MPs, and in particular those Jewish organisations within the Labour Party, such as the Jewish Labour Movement (previously named Poale Zion) and Labour Friends of Israel, which are explicitly Zionist. I was to find out, to my cost, as collateral damage in Labour's internecine warfare, that Smeeth was one of their foremost activists.

Tariq Ali is among a number of prominent Corbyn supporters who argue that the Labour leadership self-harmed by not going on the attack over claims their party was antisemitic. It was a failure and as electorally damaging as the Labour leadership's lack of clarity over Brexit.[17] The two issues played a major part in Labour's crushing defeat at the 2019 general election. Ali told a Campaign for Free Speech in the Labour Party webinar in July, the following year, that Corbyn should have said: 'Yes, there is antisemitism in society. Yes, there may be some in the Labour Party. There's certainly more in the right-wing parties [like] the Conservative Party that [far right] Britain First members have been queuing up to join. But we are going to fight any attempt to stop us speaking on Palestine or being critical of Israel.' He added that the party should have firmly stated 'it is a complete slander and slur to say that the Labour leadership, Corbyn in particular, are either antisemitic or encourage antisemitism. I mean, a big fight could have been waged. We may not have won it but it would have been a much better thing to do than caving in.'[18]

The present leader of the Labour Party, Keir Starmer, has declared himself an unequivocal supporter of Zionism, the religious philosophy that justifies the foundation of Israel as an explicitly and exclusively Jewish state. With the death of a viable two-state solution, there remain stark choices: continuing an ever more brutal occupation that has the ultimate goal of ethnic cleansing, or a single secular state, as India was when it was founded, that embraces all its people. I raise the issue of the state of Israel in this book not just because I personally fell foul of an internal Labour Party argument, but because it is a glaring reminder that issues of active colonialism remain with us and that the largest party that purports to represent working people in Britain is no less split on issues of colonialism than it was at Saklatvala's time. On the evidence of Comrade Sak's contempt for the conservatism of Labour Party attitudes to empire, it is not hard to guess what his views would have been.

Labour and antisemitism aside, I hope this new edition of *Comrade Sak*, published coincidentally but appropriately in the centenary year of the founding of the Communist Party of Great Britain, will contribute the example of a brave and principled person to our current attempt to understand what it will take to decolonise British society in general, and specifically its labour movement.

CHAPTER 1

INTRODUCTION

Four years after the end of the First World War, an Indian nationalist and communist was elected a member of the British Parliament. Shapurji Saklatvala MP was a small, lean man with a cultivated manner and immense energy; an eloquent and charismatic speaker given to lively gestures with his right hand as he held his lapel with the left.[1] According to the *South Western Star*, he 'had lustrous dark eyes that have a penetrating quality, possibly some magnetic power' and a 'winsome lingering smile'.[2] An Indian journalist who met Saklatvala, Sant Nihal Singh, observed 'he had a trick of running his fingers through his black hair, rumpling it. The way it was brushed back gave him an immense forehead, which, in any case, would have been broad and high. Under the black, arched brows, his eyes were alive – afire – ever astir. The cheek bones stood out prominently. Between them was a long, firm nose. The way he screwed up his mouth reinforced the impression that his features in general conveyed of strength of character and fixity of intention.'[3] Even his opponents conceded that he was fun-loving and humorous. Although he was a member of India's wealthiest industrial family, he bridged class and cultural barriers with his powerful commitment to the revolutionary working-class cause. In a celebrated statement, he said: 'I am out for a revolution and am quite willing to be shot down.'[4] This fate did not befall him, but Saklatvala paid a price for his politics. He suffered police raids on his home; the security service spied on him by opening his post and doing round the clock surveillance. During the 1926 General Strike, Saklatvala was arrested and put in jail. He was also banned, for political reasons, from going to countries such as Egypt, the USA, Belgium and even from his native India. In particular, he paid for his beliefs with his health. Despite a heart condition, as the *Daily Worker* wrote: 'Night after night, year after year, in all parts of Britain he carried out his task of working-class agitation, education and organisation. No comrade ever did more of his work so uncomplainingly as Comrade Saklatvala. No call was ever made to which he did not respond.'[5] As his comrade Tom Bell observed: 'There is no doubt Saklatvala wore himself out before his time in an unselfish devotion to the cause of the colonial peoples and of communism.'[6]

Commentators described him as one of the most gifted orators of his generation. A contemporary in parliament, Philip Snowden, an aristocrat turned left-wing MP and Labour's first chancellor of the exchequer, spoke of Saklatvala's 'volcanic eloquence'. A journalist of the time, Herbert Bryan, said it was not a 'mock eloquence of the demagogic wind-bag but the deep sincerity of the man finding expression in flaming words'. Bryan went on to observe: 'His command of the English language is infinitely superior to the average Englishman.'[7]

Freely describing himself as an 'extremist', and an 'agitator' at the pro-Indian independence and trade union meetings at which he spoke, Saklatvala played the role of teacher, calling on young activists to go to agricultural and industrial areas to do the same hard and unpleasant work as rural and factory workers and share their precarious existence, but then lead them to self-assertion.[8]

While serving as an MP, Saklatvala wrote a ferocious article ridiculing the House of Commons. He clearly revelled in being a parliamentarian for the opportunity it gave him to almost sadistically exploit the contradictions of being in the belly of the capitalist, imperialist beast. He put himself forward as a parliamentary candidate at a time when few fellow communists thought it was a good idea. From Saklatvala's first days in the Commons, his biting wit and irreverence were unleashed. *The Times* of 28 February 1923 reported: '"As to the Indian Civil Service", Saklatvala said, "it was not Indian, it was not civil, and it was a domination and a usurpation. Barring those three great defects, the Service was all right".'[9] Referring to a debate in 1928, *The Manchester Guardian* wrote: 'No contribution to the debate had such a stirring and stimulating effect as Mr Saklatvala's, and for some hours afterwards the enquiry was everywhere made when two persons met within the walls of Parliament, "Did you hear Saklatvala?"'[10] He scored a parliamentary first when he addressed the Speaker as 'Comrade' and his rejection of the ruling class and their institutions, particularly the monarchy, was evident when he lampooned them. 'A few families supply monarchs to Europe just as a few biscuit factories supply biscuits all over Europe,' he told the Commons. In a debate about whether or not to allocate the Prince of Wales a £2,000 grant for a trip to Africa and South America, Saklatvala mocked the muted Labour criticism of the proposal. 'If they want an Empire and a "Royal nob" at the head of it, (Loud cries of "Order" and "Withdraw") Saklatvala, quipped: "The Royal head, I mean".'

He added, in the same spirited fashion, that he opposed any grant to the Prince of Wales on the grounds that it was 'the usual trickery of the minority, who were helping themselves at the expense of the majority.' When the Commons was told the Prince of Wales had received a cordial invitation to visit India, Saklatvala protested: 'The people of India said they did not want his Royal Highness there, and the Government of India had to empty out the gaols and pay money to spectators. (Ministerial cries of "Withdraw.")'[11]

His skill as an orator was all the more remarkable because he preferred to *ad lib* rather than write down his speeches. Those that were later reproduced in pamphlets, especially House of Commons speeches, demonstrate a brilliant marshalling of facts and figures. The number of his speeches, questions and interjections in parliament reached almost 500. They covered foreign, colonial and domestic issues from world revolution to cases of hardship and injustice faced by British and Indian workers.

For Saklatvala the battle against imperialist subjugation was just as important, wherever it was being fought: in India, Palestine, Ireland or Africa. In his extraordinary first speech to the House of Commons in 1922, which broke Parliamentary convention by being controversial, he stated: 'No Britisher would for a moment tolerate a constitution for Great Britain if it were written outside of Great Britain by people who were not British. In a similar way, the constitutions for Ireland and India and Egypt and Mesopotamia [Iraq] should be constitutions written by the men of those countries, in those countries, without interference from outside.'[12] This was a speech bitingly critical of the imposition of a partitioned settlement on colonial Ireland, which only offered self-governing dominion status, not full independence and, of course, excluded the northern six counties. As Chapter Four documents, Saklatvala had a long history of commitment to Irish independence, along with that of all subjects of the British Empire.

Further, in his uncompromisingly anti-imperialist first speech in parliament, he attacked the Foreign Secretary, Lord George Curzon (1st Marquess of Kedleston), for 'sitting in consultation' with Mussolini, the founding father of fascism in Italy, who had already taken power in his country by deposing King Victor Emmanuel III, who he kept on as a puppet monarch.

It is revealing of how little the causes for which Saklatvala fought have advanced in British society, but also heartening to recognise that something of his iconoclastic spirit survives, when, almost a century later, in 2019, a 26-year-old radical Labour MP, Zarah Sultana, gave a similarly uncompromising first speech. She recognised that the 'convention is for maiden speeches to avoid saying anything members opposite will find very disagreeable. I can't do that. Because my generation has only ever faced a future of rising rents, frozen wages and diminishing opportunities.' The new MP for Coventry South echoed the sentiments of Saklatvala when she added: 'I'm a working-class Muslim woman and I know Bullingdon boys[13] will never be on my side and they will never be on the side of shop stewards in Coventry, cleaners in Carlisle, migrant workers in Manchester or teachers in Tottenham.'[14]

The speech made headlines in the press because, while it was a critique of the neo-liberal economic policies implemented by former Conservative PM, Margaret Thatcher and her Conservative successors, it also suggested that the Tony Blair New Labour governments from 1997 to 2010 were responsible for pushing similar agendas.

Two weeks later, the new Streatham MP, Bell Ribeiro-Addy, who represented a south London constituency that takes in part of Saklatvala's old seat, also made her first speech. She said: 'While we spent years debating Brexit and... engaging in monumental self-harm, India surpassed the UK to become the fifth-richest economy in the world: India, a former British colony, where this country presided over a bloody partition, the Amritsar massacre and the Bengal famine.'[15] She added, with pride: 'Countries in Africa, such as Ghana, Kenya and Uganda, are among the fastest-growing economies in the world; countries that Britain deliberately underdeveloped, stole resources from and brutally enslaved their people.' She asked her colleagues if they were aware that 'in the mid to late 1700s, over fifty Members of this House represented slave plantations? Members of Parliament just like me enslaved people that looked just like me.' She said, bluntly:

> I recently discovered that after the slave trade, this country – our country, my country – took out a loan of the equivalent of £300 billion to pay off slave owners. We only finished paying off that loan in 2015. That means that for decades the descendants of the enslaved and the colonised have been contributing to paying their oppressors. That means that members of the Windrush generation who were invited here to work paid their taxes to pay off a debt to those who brutally enslaved their ancestors.
>
> For their troubles, some lost their homes and their jobs, were separated from their families, detained, deported and dehumanised, and are now being denied the dignity of a proper civil compensation scheme.

And, touching on another racism scandal that engulfed the Conservative government of prime minister Theresa May, Ribeiro-Addy said:

> Let us not forget the people of Grenfell Tower: 72 people dead and many more traumatised by the loss of their loved ones and the loss of their homes, a community scarred for generations. This Government failed them on their promise to rehouse them in the aftermath of the catastrophe and have failed to remove flammable cladding. They all need justice as equal citizens, and that means bringing those responsible to face the law.[16]

Saklatvala's attack on the Government of Ireland Act and his performances in parliament were only a small part of his activist life. If there is one thread that runs through his politics it was his forthrightness in tying together the fight for socialism in the British context and his internationalist anti-imperialism, his constant message that the exploitation of the African, Caribbean and Asian world damaged Black and white workers alike. He told a British audience that private enterprise, which was so much lauded in this country, had spread to India, with the result that its big dividends, low wages, and long hours were depriving thousands of workers in the cotton industry in Britain of their livelihood. He argued that 'Underpaid German and Continental labour is now added to the large mass of Asiatic and African labour purposely created by Conservative and Liberal financiers, more largely by Liberal financiers, with the object of gaining profits, and breaking the backs of British Trade union standards.' He said that Indians on the Assam tea plantations were earning half the wages of workers employed in British industry and explained:

> The Conservative financier says, 'I will exploit human beings in other parts of the world, using for my purpose the Union Jack and Armaments but he says, 'I will now put on a tariff duty at home, make everything costly for the worker and consumer, sweat them at wages and prices different from wages abroad, and thus earn dividends at home also!'
> The Liberal says: 'I will exploit the Negro, the Chinaman, the Indian in the same manner, but I will keep my door open, and when my own goods, produced by cheap labour, flood the markets of the world, I will propose to the British Worker to accept a reduction in wages'.[17]

As noted in the preface, Saklatvala's critique of the xenophobic stance of the main UK political parties could easily have been applied to the toxic UK Brexit debate, almost a century later, following Britain's 2016 referendum that resulted in a finely balanced vote to leave the European Union.

Inevitably, Saklatvala made Conservatives see red. One Tory MP, Colonel Herbert Woodcock, refused to be on an Inter-Parliamentary Union delegation to America with him, saying: 'I think all ex-service members will agree with me that a man whose delight is to drag the Union Jack into disrepute throughout the world is a man who is worthless to this country, and whose scheming and planning to bring disrepute on this great Empire must be sterilised.'[18] Fortunately, that was not the immediate view of working-class voters in Battersea, who twice elected Saklatvala to Parliament. Nor was it the view of other colonial radicals who sought him out when they came to London, to bring their struggle to the heart of Empire. Saklatvala's engagement with the Trinidadian radical Adrian Cola Rienzi is outlined in Chapter Four.

The forthright anti-imperialist dimension that Saklatvala introduced to British politics brought him into increasingly sharp conflict with the Labour Party. Even with the Marxist left there was not always an immediate meeting of minds. Saklatvala's devotion to his family and the Parsi customs he had grown up with caused conflicts with the Communist Party of Great Britain that exposed its Euro-centric limitations. There are clear connections with the phobic attitudes towards the Muslim community among sections of the British left that the Rushdie affair exposed, or with the stance of some of the French left to the wearing by Muslim women of the hijab scarf.

A Channel 4 television documentary and four biographies, including this one (and one by his daughter Sehri, whom I interviewed for this book), indicate a considerable interest in his life. During Saklatvala's time, the Labour Party was born and the first socialist government formed. There was the Russian Revolution of 1917 and the subsequent

establishment of the Communist Party of Great Britain, the General
Strike of 1926, the struggle for Indian independence and for an end to
colonialism throughout the world. Both in Britain and internationally,
Saklatvala was at the heart of debates that remain highly pertinent, such
as the interrelationship between race and class and the struggle for
socialism and the lasting reverberations of imperialism in contemporary
British political life.

This book differs in emphasis from earlier biographies, one of which
focuses strongly on his Indian nationalism, another on his role in the
Communist Party and within the British left, and the third, by Saklatvala's
daughter, Sehri, which is particularly insightful about his family life. My
contribution deals with all these aspects of Saklatvala's life, but focuses in
particular on the fact that he was an Indian in Britain, part of a very small
minority in his time, on the relevance of his life and political journey to the
African, Caribbean and Asian politics of our own era, and to contemporary
calls to decolonise British society from the hangover of its imperial
delusions and failure to face up to the shameful episodes in its past as a
colonising and imperialist power. These issues are explored from the point
of view of an author who is Black, has been active in national politics and
for whom the issues are of much more than academic interest.

Comrade Sak was written so that valuable lessons from the past are not
lost. Karl Marx warned in *Das Kapital*: 'Labour with a white skin cannot
emancipate itself where labour with a black skin is branded.'[19] Although
Saklatvala never described himself as 'Black' (in his day people of African and
Asian descent were politely called 'coloured', though the word 'Black' was
used to describe him by some of his opponents), he did identify himself very
strongly with the cause of 'coloured people' throughout the world. In the
post-colonial age, for 'people of colour' in Britain, the struggle has shifted
from national emancipation to Black liberation. Reading the political life of
Shapurji Saklatvala in the light of Marx's prescient words provides many
contemporary resonances. Surely Saklatvala and his Pan-Africanist ally, John
Archer, would have supported the pressing of a Black agenda on government
in general and the Labour Party in particular. It is not the least of the betrayals
of Tony Blair's now discredited New Labour that it turned its back on any
serious commitment to anti-racism. As the Black trade union leader Bill
Morris wrote to *The Guardian* before the 1997 general election:

> After the 1983 general election, the revisionist tendency in the Labour
> Party apparently concluded that there were no votes in anti-racism and
> that the Black community was another 'special interest group', listening
> to which might alienate White middle class voters.[20]

He went on to note, echoing Saklatvala's experiences in Battersea in
the 1920s:

Where Black people have shown any sign of seeking selection in winnable seats, Walworth Road [Labour Party headquarters] has acted to close down the local parties and suspend the democratic process. The result is that we go into the election with fewer Black candidates in relation to the Black population than in 1992 or 1987.[21]

There were ructions among some left-wing Labour activists in the run up to the 2019 British general election when they bitterly complained that the party's 'control freak' apparatchiks had parachuted in outside candidates favoured by the bureaucrats over local hopefuls. Black, particularly male African Caribbeans, lost out as a result.

It is a sad irony that I first became acquainted with the name of Saklatvala on the eve of the 1983 General Election when a Black comrade of mine, Russell Profitt, was selected to fight the 'safe' Labour constituency of Battersea North. Saklatvala's name cropped up as the former MP for that seat (then known as North Battersea). Perversely, the Boundary Commission stepped in and merged North and South into one Battersea seat. And, true to form, Labour dumped Profitt for Alf Dubs, the white MP for Battersea South. Today, Battersea is part of the Conservative's favoured borough of Wandsworth and has been wittily nicknamed 'south Chelsea' by the new middle classes who have moved there. In Saklatvala's time, it was a mini Red Republic with a communist MP and five communist councillors. It was to be more than half a century before another Black person became an MP, and then only after a bitter struggle by 'Black Sections' activists in the Labour Party, a group which was succeeded by the Jeremy Corbyn-supporting Grassroots Black Left. Marsha De Cordova, a registered blind Black woman, who also backed Corbyn, defeated the sitting Conservative MP to get elected to parliament in one of the upsets of the 2017 general election. Afterwards, as a congratulatory gift, the author handed her a copy of the previous edition of this book. De Cordova kept her seat at the 2019 general election.

Anyone who embarks on research into Saklatvala's life is hampered by the fact that he never wrote anything longer than a speech, newspaper article or letter and no collection of private papers, including his private letters, has been found. The author has included some of Saklatvala's published writings, including his monumental correspondence with Gandhi, in the appendices. The selection is inevitably a personal rather than an impartial choice. As indicated in the Preface, even though some new information has surfaced in MI5 files, Saklatvala's life must still be written as a record of his actions, and their significance seen within the historical context of times in which he operated. Sadly, there are no longer people alive who had first-hand knowledge of him, but, where possible, contemporary interviews from three decades ago, with those people who were able to shed valuable light on events, have been included.

The structure of this book is in part sequential, in part thematic. Chapter Two covers Saklatvala's passage from being the poor but favoured relation of the patriarch of India's wealthiest industrial, and hence modernising families, politically a liberal nationalist and a temporary resident in Britain, to the point where he is permanently settled, married to a working-class English woman and on the verge of joining the Communist Party. In the process, the book examines his formative relationships with the Tata dynasty and with the left-wing Independent Labour Party.

Chapter Three focuses on Saklatvala's adoption and election as an MP in the working-class constituency of North Battersea in south London. It examines how, though a member of the Communist Party, he came to be endorsed as an official Labour candidate. In a lurch to the right, the Labour Party then moved to exclude communists and disaffiliated its left-wing branches. The chapter gives a detailed portrayal of the Battersea constituency at the time and Saklatvala's relationship with people such as John Archer, Britain's first Black councillor and mayor. It deals with Saklatvala's imprisonment and political activity in Battersea during the General Strike, but also questions whether his concentration as an MP on Indian and international affairs may have in part contributed to his eventual rejection by his voters.

Chapter Four examines the central preoccupation of Saklatvala's political life: the contribution he made as an MP and activist in the British labour movement to the cause of Indian freedom and the author's more contemporary discovery of his role as a supporter of struggles in other parts of the British Empire, in particular the depth of his involvement with the Irish anti-colonial struggle and his position as a much admired advisor to radicals in other parts of the British Empire, in this case Trinidad. It gives an account of the impact of his political tour of India in 1927 and the subsequent action of successive British Governments, including Labour, to prevent him from ever again returning there. The chapter deals with the critical role Saklatvala played in influencing the Communist Party of Great Britain to adopt a non-sectarian approach to the role of the bourgeois-led Indian Congress Party in the nationalist movement for independence, but at the same time records Saklatvala's sharp disagreements with Gandhi for failing to accord the Indian labour movement a more central role in the struggle and for taking what Saklatvala saw as a backwards-looking attitude to industrialisation. This substantially revised chapter has provided the opportunity to make a fuller appraisal of the monumental correspondence in 1927 between the canny gradualist Mahatma and "impatient communist" Comrade, which the author unearthed three decades ago. There is also updated text following the 100th anniversary in 2019 of the Amritsar massacre.

Chapter Five gives a more detailed account of Saklatvala's break with the Independent Labour Party and his relationship to the Communist Party. It outlines his advocacy of the party's 'New Line' policy of unrelenting hostility to the Labour Party and the damage this sectarian approach caused the communists within the broader labour movement. It discusses the contradictions that Saklatvala faced between his acute analysis of 'Labouralism' and the failure of the broader labour movement to share his commitment to anti-imperialism, and the increasing marginalisation he suffered as a result of this unswerving stand. The chapter implicitly raises the question of how far racism can be implicated in the reluctance of the Labour Party and Labour voters to accept Saklatvala's position on empire.

Chapter Six discusses Saklatvala's life within the context of the role of African Caribbeans and Asians in British politics. It notes the activities and experiences of his two Indian predecessors as British MPs, Liberal Dadabhai Naoroji and Conservative Mancherji Bhownagree. It adds to that history the much earlier presence of an Asian British radical, David Ochterlony Dyce Sombre who was elected MP for Sudbury, Suffolk, in 1841, half a century before Naoroji.[22] The descendant of German and French Catholic mercenaries, a Scottish Presbyterian British army lieutenant, and their secluded Indian wives, David Ochterlony Dyce Sombre defied classification in the North Indian principality where he was raised. His father was Anglo-Indian George Alexander Dyce and mother Juliana Le Fevre, was also mixed-race. Made an army colonel and Indian prince by his adoptive mother, Zeb un-Nissa, David Ochterlony Dyce Sombre, was described by the London *Daily News* as a "half-caste Croesus". When Zeb un-Nissa died, Sombre suffered the indignity of having his rich fiefdom, north of Delhi, confiscated on extremely dubious grounds by the East India Company. After settling in England, Dyce Sombre succeeded in breaking through the ceiling of Victorian racism to become an MP, only for his election to be annulled months later by the courts, following an allegation he "bought the seat" through bribery. His marriage to the daughter of a prominent English viscount fell apart and her family had him declared insane and took control of his Indian fortune. He never succeeded in regaining most of it, despite alleging, from exile in Paris, that his unfaithful wife had bribed doctors to have him locked up so that she could seize his money.

The chapter records how racism combined with hysterical anti-communism in the contemporary media treatment of Saklatvala as both parliamentary candidate and MP. It also discusses his commitment to the Communist Third International in the context of the racism of European socialist parties affiliated to the Second International and argues that Saklatvala succeeded in pushing the Communist Party of Great Britain into giving higher priority to anti-imperialist and anti-racist activities. It notes the decline of such policy commitments as his influence within the party waned and explores its failure to accommodate Saklatvala's continuing attachment to his Parsi culture and Zoroastrian religion.

Chapter Seven focuses on the last seven years of Saklatvala's life. While the chapter traces his increasing political marginalisation, it also records a steadfast courage in pursuing his political ideals, despite increasing frailty, to the very end of his life, aged just sixty-one. The chapter concludes by attempting an assessment of Saklatvala's achievements and his continuing relevance to the understanding of radical African Caribbean and Asian politics in Britain.

Saklatvala was considered 'one of the most violent anti-British agitators in England' by the spies who monitored him.[23] He was a militant opponent of the British empire and therefore rejected gradualist reformism. In parliament, he chided fellow MPs: 'Between slavery and freedom there is no middle course, and a transition from slavery to freedom can never be attained by gradual measures.'[24]

His abiding theme was that resistance to empire was in the interests of both the Indian and British working classes. Where Labour Party leaders Keir Hardie, Ramsay MacDonald and other prominent fellow party members, who visited India during the *Swadeshi* years (the 'buy Indian' campaign that also involved a boycott of British goods) came back to make the case for reforms that might defuse the 'unrest', Saklatvala, by contrast, made a sustained case in parliament against reformism and 'liberal' approaches to colonial governance in India.

'Comrade Sak' crafted a unique political voice for himself, at once Indian and British, the 'consummate hybrid' as Gopal says,[25] speaking out candidly and passionately on many causes, but most especially against imperialism, which, for him, was inextricable from capitalism. Candidly, Saklatvala described himself as being a member of 'one of the conquered and enslaved subject races', adding, he was also 'representing the interests of the British electors who sent me'. He would tell his British audiences that 'he could not help it that his accent was a little foreign but his heart was not foreign'.[26]

Gopal remarks, 'it is this sense of him carrying a dual but intertwined representational responsibility – and his persistence in identifying common ground between the two sides – which makes Shapurji Saklatvala a figure of transnational significance in thinking about the relationship between colonial insurgencies and British anticolonialism in the interwar period.'[27]

For almost thirty years of his life, Saklatvala made a unique contribution to working-class emancipation and colonial freedom in Britain and abroad. He deserves to be in standard history books, as do other Black labour movement figures such as William Cuffay, William Davidson, John Archer, George Padmore, C.L.R. James, Claudia Jones, Olive Morris, Jayaben Desai, Dr Harold Moody, Rajani Palme Dutt and Krishna Menon, to name but a few.

CHAPTER 2

FROM SILVER SPOON TO RED FLAG

When an Indian Communist won a parliamentary election at North Battersea in 1922 his working-class supporters said they thought they would storm heaven next.[1] The victor was Shapurji Dorabji Saklatvala.

He was born in Mumbai (formerly known as Bombay) on 28 March 1874, the second of his parents' five children. The Saklatvalas were closely related to the Tatas, India's most renowned Parsi[2] family and pioneers of capitalism in the subcontinent. Jamsetji Nusserwanji Tata was revered as the 'Father of Indian industry'. It is not disputed that the Saklatvalas were Parsi merchants, but whether they handled serge-cloth, used to make the uniforms of British military officers or sailcloth[3] for the navy, is unclear. Whatever, they ended up with the name *Saklat-wallah*, following the Parsi custom of using their profession in the family name. They also use 'ji' or 'jee' at the end of a name to denote respect. Saklatvala used the less formal Shapur when writing to his family and friends.

Saklatvala's father, Dorabji, was a wealthy merchant who managed a cotton mill, and his mother, Jerbai, was the younger sister of J.N. Tata, whose father founded Tata Industries, India's largest industrial conglomerate. The Tatas' business was originally based on cotton mills but later branched out into iron, steel and even hotels. By 1925 they had an authorised capital of £4m (a quarter of a billion pounds today). They lay claim to having brought the industrial revolution to India. The founding of Air India was among later achievements and their turnover currently stands in billions of pounds. An official brochure states: 'At a time when the politics of empire dismissed the need for indigenous industry, Jamsetji N. Tata's revolutionary vision initiated an era of industrial growth which played a key role in the process of nation-building.'[4] Typically for a Parsi family business, from the start they prided themselves on their philanthropy. Currently, the Tata group is Britain's biggest manufacturing employer, with holdings in the car industry and steel.[5]

Shapurji, Saklatvala's paternal grandfather, also named Shapurji Saklatvala, was J. N. Tata's business partner. However, after the grandfather's death, no arrangement was made for his family to inherit his share of the Tata fortune and the Saklatvalas became the poor relations. Moreover, according to a cousin, Jamsetji Saklatvala, Shapurji's grandfather made a fortune out of contracts for rice, dal, ghee and spices during the Abyssinian war in 1868. But four years later, just as the distribution of the profits of Shapurji Saklatvala and Co. was to be undertaken, Shapurji died 'and the whole brunt of settling the accounts went into the shrewd hands and keeping of Naswanjee R. Tata and Naswanjee Vajifdar, the Cashier and Accountant of the Company'. Jamsetji Saklatvala contends that Shapurji's widow was short-changed.[6]

As a result, there were considerable family tensions, political as well as financial. Saklatvala's father held a lifelong grievance that his family had been swindled out of a fortune by the Tatas. Although Saklatvala's daughter Sehri quotes from a letter written by her father in later life, which speaks sharply of the 'cruel wrong done to my father',[7] Shapurji's relationship with his uncle was less strained than might have been expected. Since Dorabji, Shapurji's father, was away from home on business for most of Saklatvala's childhood, it appears that his uncle J.N. Tata became the paternal figure in his life. What is more, uncle Jamsetji was an unashamed nationalist. Indeed he joined the Indian National Congress when it was founded in 1885 and named one of his factories *Svadeshi*,[8] an Indian nationalist slogan of self-reliance, a year afterwards. His more conservative sons were quite different and Saklatvala's relationship with the eldest of them, Dorabji Tata, was particularly antagonistic. Like many prominent Parsis, they accepted British domination because it was good for their business. Saklatvala, when he was about fourteen, moved with his family to live in the Tatas' palatial home, Esplanade House in Mumbai; he supported his uncle's politics and was the old man's favourite. Thus favoured, Saklatvala might have become a multimillionaire businessman. Instead he chose a tough life fighting for socialist equality, as the unofficial 'MP for India', at the heart of the British Empire.

He went to the exclusive private school and college of St Xavier's in Mumbai, run by the Jesuits, its motto in Latin: *Provocans Ad Volandum* (Challenging to Fly). The Communist Party of India (Marxist) ex-chief minister of West Bengal, Jyoti Basu, attended a branch of the same school in Kolkata (formerly called Calcutta). Here the charitable values for which the then wealthy Parsi community is famous were converted into the concepts of social justice which motivated Saklatvala's actions for the rest of his life. At St. Xavier's he learnt about public speaking, helping to set up a debating society, the Gwalia Circle. His interests included English literature, religion, philosophy and mathematics, but not sport. There is speculation that while at college Saklatvala became a Roman Catholic, but he was later to deny this. Nonetheless, two of his children were sent to a convent school. He did though remain open-minded about religion all his life and at one point insisted that there was 'no essential difference between

Christianity and Communism'.[9] As discussed later in the book, he remained involved with his Parsi culture and the religion of Zoroastrianism, which insists on purity of thought, word and deed.

The rebel in Saklatvala surfaced when he was a student. Asked to write about the free-market economist, Adam Smith, he used the essay to argue what he believed to be the truth, not the 'generally accepted view'. Saklatvala's opinions came across as 'revolutionary' to his examiners and they failed him. He remarked that he was 'miseducated' at college when he studied law.[10]

As a 22-year-old, Saklatvala was active as a volunteer working with a pioneering doctor, Professor Vladimir Haffkin, in the plague hospitals and slums of Mumbai during an epidemic which began in 1896. For six years Saklatvala worked with Haffkin, a Jewish revolutionary who had been exiled from his native Russia because of his anti-Tsarist activities. Haffkin's influence could well have sparked Saklatvala's interest in communism, though if this was so, it was several more years before it took a solid political form. It was during his time with Haffkin that Saklatvala had another of his formative experiences when he was the victim of blatant racism at the hands of the British Raj. Many years later he described what had happened to his fellow MPs in the House of Commons:

> In 1902, a plague was having devastating effects all over India. It was to be taken in hand not merely as a grave problem, but as something to save human lives. There was a Professor Haffkin in those days, who was the first man, who, with some measure of success gave out an anti-plague serum for inoculation. His experiments were being conducted on a large scale. I was then associated as secretary with an important committee of welfare work. The Governor of Bombay immediately sent a telegram to Professor Haffkin to go to him with certain facts and figures because the matter was becoming of vital importance. Professor Haffkin asked me to go and assist him. I gave up my work in the office and I went to the place where he was staying, and that was his European club. People talk about my untouchability! Although I had facts and figures at my disposal, I was actually prevented from entering the white man's club. Ultimately, when it could not be helped, the messenger of the club, after telephoning to various government officials, took me to the back yard of the club, led me through the kitchen, and an underground passage to a basement room, where the professor was asked to see me because I was not a white man.[11]

Saklatvala also spent three years on family business in uncharted parts of the eastern Indian states of Bihar and Odisha (formerly Orissa), on the Bay of Bengal, doing exploration work for iron ore, coal and limestone, which aided the foundation of the mighty Tata Iron and Steel Works. Although his work contributed to the Tata fortunes, Saklatvala refused to hold shares in the business, insisting he should be no more than a salaried employee. It was a time of adventure for Saklatvala, travelling hundreds of miles on the back of an elephant and bullock-drawn carts, but also a time when he further developed his sense of social justice, though at this stage it could not be said that he was more than a liberal. He did, though, work closely with the labourers, and as his daughter Sehri reports:

> His experience both in the plague hospitals and in the jungle brought him into contact with the very poor... They slept with the bullocks. It was quite some time before they had tents. And, occasionally, they slept in the huts with the peasants.[12]

The pay of an Indian labourer at that time was 3d a day. Saklatvala paid 1s 3d, in spite of protests from the English sahibs – the military officers and superintendents – who complained in an all too familiar way that such action would ruin the country. He insisted, too, that, if it was good enough for Englishmen to rest during the hottest part of the day, then the Indians should also have a break from 2pm to 4pm. The result was that mines which had operated at a loss when run by the British, became profitable under the Tatas because the workers were much better cared for.

Saklatvala encountered a great deal of opposition, including from the corrupt local police who regularly extorted money from the workers. To get around this, he paid the men with credit notes which he got accepted by all the stores. On one occasion, the police responded by spiriting away all the labourers. Saklatvala's response was audacious. He got the men back by locking up an officer in the police station and refusing to release him until the labourers were returned.

During his time prospecting for the Tatas, Saklatvala became seriously ill. As a result of malaria, he had to use crutches for a time and despite recovering his health, he was to limp for the rest of his life. Because of the injury, Saklatvala wore shoes with thick rubber soles and these, later in his life, saved him from possible death. Despite the fact that the Tatas were responsible for the electrification of much of northern India, Saklatvala had no understanding of electricity. His wife one day had difficulty pulling out the plug of an iron from its socket. Saklatvala prised it out with a metal screwdriver and the shock flung him across the room.[13]

The tensions in the Tata household, particularly between Jamsetji's son Dorabji and Saklatvala were such that in 1902, a year after he had joined the family firm, Saklatvala left the Tata home and went to live with his mother and sister at Hornby Road nearby. The antagonisms between him and Dorabji worsened following the death of J. N. Tata in May 1904. To Dorabji's intense displeasure, Saklatvala's increasingly outspoken views on home rule for India had come to the attention of the colonial authorities. This was at a time, in 1905, when the pro-independence struggle was intensifying and the British were resorting to bloody repression in an attempt to thwart the growing militancy against them. So, in November that year, with the perfect excuse that the 31-year-old Saklatvala was suffering from the effects of malaria, which had been made worse by high doses of medicine, the Tatas sent him out of the way to England to recuperate.

In England, Saklatvala stayed at Smedley's Hydro, a world-renowned health spa at Matlock (which later became the headquarters of Derbyshire County Council). It was there he met Sally Marsh, who was born on the 10th of September 1888 and baptised Sarah Elizabeth, but always called Sally.[14]

The Marsh family lived at Gregory Yard, now known as Walston Close, at Tansley, Derbyshire, where they had the centre cottage of three with their own parents in the cottages at either side.[15] Life was tough for Sally. There always seemed to be a baby being born at her home and everyone had to help with the younger children. At seven she was baking bread and at 13 she was in service, as childminder to the baby of a publican and his wife.[16]

After a brief spell working as a factory hand at the Tape Mill, in nearby Lumsdale, Sally went to work at Smedley's Hydro. A number of 'water cure' hydropathic establishments were built in and around Matlock but the largest and most luxurious was Smedley's Hydro, named after a wealthy textile mill owner who built it on a hillside overlooking the place. By this time, Matlock had become well-known as a place to 'take the waters' and this attracted influential and wealthy people from all over Britain and abroad. They included Ivor Novello and Robert Louis Stevenson.[17]

As a couple, Shapurji Saklatvala and Sally Marsh could not have been more different. Saklatvala's background was Indian and privileged, while Marsh was a working-class young English woman, fourteen years his junior, who had left school at thirteen to go into domestic service. Sally was the fourth of twelve children, the daughter of Henry Marsh, a quarryman from the village of Tansley, two miles from Matlock, on the southern edge of the Derbyshire peak district. First, seventeen-year-old Sally worked in the pantry at the health centre. She enjoyed far better food at work than she was used to, according to her daughter Sehri Saklatvala. Sally 'blossomed in the unfamiliarly lavish surroundings', and soon graduated to the dining room, where she worked as a waitress.[18] Saklatvala had his eye on Sally for several months before he plucked up the courage to talk to her.

In a letter written much later, Sally gave her account of their meeting and what followed, as quoted in Sehri's biography of her father:

> He asked Maria Marsh who I was. She told me I was her cousin, so he asked her to call me over to his table and introduce me to him, which she did. With his beard, I took him for an old man. He gave me flowers almost every day and asked me to go for walks. I was too frightened to do so, but I kept saying I would just to satisfy him for the time being. Whenever I went out he would walk behind me. One afternoon I went

to Matlock Bath by bus; when I offered my fare, the conductor said a gentleman behind had paid. I gave a blind man a penny in the afternoon without knowing he [Shapurji] was following; afterwards he told me that he had given the blind man two shillings and told him what a lucky man he was, as he had been given a penny by the sweetest girl in the world.

One day I got a note from a shoe shop... would I go in and try on some shoes. There was a note inside a special pair of shoes which I was to try on from him, saying that he hoped to be able to buy all my shoes from now on.

The day he left the Hydro, he asked me to see him off on the 2:19 train. I said yes but had no intention of going... I had a phone message to say that he was on Matlock Bath station and he intended to remain there however long it was until I went to see him. I went at nine o'clock at night and said goodbye to him.[19]

Shapurji was clearly besotted. He wrote to Sally twice a day, and soon took the opportunity to visit again, just for the day. That September he went to Tansley for Sally's 18th birthday, when he saw Mr and Mrs Marsh for the first time and 'got them on his side', according to Sally. Finally, she accepted an engagement ring from Shapurji.

Early in the courtship Shapurji changed Sally's name to Sehri, a name of his own invention designed to combine 'Sally' with 'Sarah'; this was apparently because 'Sally' sounds like a swear word in his Gujarati language. 'He pursued her, wooed her and won her,' said their daughter Sehri.[20] It greatly helped that Shapurji's mother Jerbai liked Sehri.

At the time of the courtship, the Marsh family moved to Oldham, on the other side of the Pennines, in search of work. It was there that the wedding of Shapurji and Sally took place in the imposing eighteenth century St Thomas Church, at Moorside, Lancashire, on 14 August 1907. The couple lived for a short time at 730 Holloway Road, in north London, before moving back to the Greater Manchester area until 1912, where Saklatvala worked for the Tatas.

It was a marriage that made an incalculable contribution to Saklatvala's ability to conduct his political life. Contact with his wife's family gave him his first intimate relationship with the British working class, and despite their political and cultural differences, Saklatvala got on well with them. He had particular affection for his sister-in-law Hannah, who lived in Oldham, and was a Baptist like the rest of the Marshes. There was a family joke that she was a bit of a religious fanatic.[21] So, soon after his marriage, when it was wrongly stated by some people that Saklatvala tinkered with the idea of becoming a Christian, he sent her a postcard from France with the ironical message: 'Keep on praying – nothing like it. Love to all at home. Shapur.' Saklatvala's humour was less sympathetic when he wrote to Hannah from the Soviet Union many years later: 'Well no churches and no slums. No prayers and no unemployment. Few priests and few criminals.'[22]

It was a traditional marriage in which his wife Sally's role was to provide him with domestic and moral support, to stay at home looking after their large family, though she did go to political meetings with him when she could. Sehri, their daughter, says: 'Mother did all the cooking, all the shopping, all the looking after us, all the washing up, all the ironing. She even made our clothes. She was a very domesticated, full-time excellent wife and mother.' Sehri roundly rebuffed the author's suggestion that this sounded like domestic servitude: 'No, it's all rubbish this post-1945 modern outlook to say that it was a life of slavery. It wasn't slavery so long as you were doing it willingly and with love. And my mother did it willingly not only with love but as an expression of her love. It was her career, her interest... to be a devoted wife and mother is certainly not to be a slave. It is to be a very joyful, greatly-fulfilled person.'[23] Alice Jones, of the National Guild of Cooperators, paid a tribute to the contribution made by Sally Saklatvala to which time has added an irony almost certainly not intended. She said: 'He must have an ideal wife for him to have put his whole time for the workers...'[24]

Sally was a remarkable woman who kept the family together with her 'calm and strength'. This was to prove particularly important during Saklatvala's time in prison in 1926, described later. This was one of the few times when Sally Saklatvala, who never joined the Communist Party and probably remained Liberal in her politics, publicly expressed her support for her husband. Sehri writes that when Saklatvala refused to be bound over, even though this meant he would be sent to prison, her mother called out loudly, 'Hear! hear!'[25] Sally Saklatvala was devoted to her husband and adopted his pet name for her, Sehri, and would often wear a sari in public, which was quite daring for a Western woman at the time. 'She may not have fully supported his political views, but she supported his aims and objectives,' said their daughter Sehri. 'She was very proud of father and he was very much loved by her family.'

Living with Saklatvala was evidently not always easy. 'Our father travelled about a lot and had people home for breakfast, lunch and tea and Mum always coped,' said Sehri. On one occasion, he telephoned his wife at short notice to prepare a meal for the crew of the ship which had brought him back from the Soviet Union. His daughter writes that despite his frequent absence on political business that he was an attentive but strict father. He insisted his children should write regularly to relatives in India they had never met. What is more, he demanded that his daughters should wear their dresses below their knees. Among his family, Saklatvala had a reputation for being exacting to the point of eccentricity. He employed some workers to tile the kitchen but he was not happy with the result. 'Not like that,' he stormed, 'like this,' and he demonstrated what he wanted, taking a hammer and smashing the tiles to create a mosaic effect.[26]

Despite accepting such a gender-based division of labour at home with apparent equanimity (Saklatvala was a sincere supporter of the suffragette movement and a particular friend of Sylvia Pankhurst), he rued the way his domestic affairs were nonetheless affected. 'There were times in my life, when never mind a passage to India... It had become impossible even to take my children on a long bus ride on holidays. I started taking some members of my family... with me, when I was invited to go out on weekends for political propaganda. After a time, I was given a serious warning from my business superior [at Tata] that this might bring additional hardship, upon them.'[27]

At this stage, though, Saklatvala was still very much part of the Tata world and had no intention of making England his permanent home. But his political views, as a result of his contacts with British socialists, were beginning to develop in a leftward direction and this made it even more desirable to the Tatas that he stayed away from India. Initially, Saklatvala, who had arrived in England in the year before the 1906 Liberal landslide, had been close to the Liberals. This was certainly the Tata intention when they obtained for him life membership of the grand National Liberal Club in London, where Saklatvala lived for a few months after his arrival in England. But almost as soon as he had arrived in the country he expressed deep concern for the plight of working people and attended socialist meetings, including ones addressed by Johnny Clynes, later to become a trade union leader and Labour MP. By 1907 Saklatvala was a member of the Social Democratic Federation (SDF), a Marxist group founded in 1884 and Britain's first organised socialist party, headed by H. M. Hyndman. After moving from the north of England to London, Saklatvala heard George Bernard Shaw speak at his local SDF branch in East Finchley, and was much impressed, naming a daughter after one of the Irishman's plays.

Then, in November 1907, Saklatvala's mother Jerbai died in New York; her two younger sons had settled in the USA. Following tradition, Jerbai's ashes were buried next to her brother J. N. Tata's at Brookwood's Parsi cemetery, near Woking, Surrey, and the grief-stricken Saklatvala and his wife moved to the village to be near to her grave. There was no active SDF branch in the area, but that did not stop Saklatvala getting involved in progressive causes such as the campaign by women to win the vote. It is believed that Saklatvala first joined a political demonstration when he took part in a protest held by the women's suffrage movement in the summer of 1908, after he had met Sylvia Pankhurst.

He stayed a member of the Social Democratic Federation, later renamed the British Socialist Party, until they, along with several other small left-wing groups, established the Communist Party of Great Britain in July 1920. Saklatvala's daughter Sehri said he did not formally leave the Liberals until 1910 and some sources say that he even stood as a Liberal candidate in the local council elections. Sehri believes that though his name was put forward, he withdrew under pressure from the Independent Labour Party (ILP), which he had joined in 1909.[28] At this time it was not unusual for people to belong to more than one political group, but of the groups he joined, Saklatvala concentrated his efforts on the ILP, the largest of these socialist organisations. It was as a result of joining the ILP, an affiliate of the Labour Party, that Saklatvala became a Labour Party member in 1909.

Rajani Palme Dutt, a younger contemporary Indian Marxist based in Britain, explained why Saklatvala left the Liberal 'mausoleum':

> He speedily saw through the very limited outlook and snobbish hypocrisy, crossed swords with Morley, then Secretary of State for India, and turned from the liberal politicians to the working class. Travelling all over England, he saw the slums and unemployment, the ruthless exploitation of the industrial and agricultural workers... he came to realise that poverty was not just an Indian problem, but an international problem of the workers all over the world, and that its solution required the international fight of the working class against class society and for socialism.[29]

Lord Morley was a Liberal peer who fancied himself as a 'liberal' friend of India and liked to be known as 'Honest Jack'. As Secretary of State for India, he was co-author of the Morley-Minto Reforms of 1909, which were aimed at rallying 'moderate' opinion in India. This move sowed the seeds of communal division by introducing separate electorates for Hindus and Muslims. The eventual partitioning of Muslim Pakistan from India, after bloody conflict, was a tragic consequence of this 'divide and rule' policy.

After saying goodbye to Brookwood, the Saklatvalas moved back to London, where they occupied a modest bedsitter at 730 Holloway Road. Shapurji had by now largely given up working for the Tatas with the intention of becoming a barrister. He joined the Lincoln's Inn lawyers' chambers and took preliminary exams before changing his mind and joining the American Westinghouse Electric company, the UK arm of the American company which made generators, switchgear and other electrical equipment. Shapurji left his post at Westinghouse in 1909. It seems the firm had appointed him partly because of his involvement with the Tata family, potentially a very valuable business contact, before his estrangement from them became clear. Instead he joined a firm of consulting engineers in Manchester, and he, Sehri and their first born, Dorab, a son, moved to the nearby town of Ashton-upon-Mersey, five miles south of central Manchester. Sehri gave birth to a daughter there on her 21st birthday; she was named Jeyanbai Candida, the last name after the play by George Bernard Shaw; she became better known, as Candy. Next came the third child, Beram, named after his uncle, an outgoing and highly entertaining child who from an early age would often entertain the family with self-composed verse. Sehri describes Beram as the brains of his generation; he became a successful writer and had his paintings hung in the Institute of British Artists, as well as making a successful career with Tata.

It was here in Manchester, at the heart of industrial Britain, that Saklatvala first came to political notice. As well as joining the Independent Labour Party (ILP), he joined the socialist Clarion Club, which had its own influential newspaper. He was a lively debater who made spirited interventions on the subject of Indian independence, along with Bipin Chandra Pal, a fellow countryman who was one of the founders of the Indian nationalist *swadeshi (or, svadeshi)* movement about which more will be written later. Saklatvala attended meetings of the County Forum and spoke up eloquently for his beliefs.

In 1911, he was one of a group of people who agitated to get the British labour movement to take an interest in the formation of a General Workers Union in India. Others involved in this included his friend Johnny Clynes, the future president of the General and Municipal Workers Union (GMWU). This probably explains why Saklatvala became a member of the GMWU. He was also a member of the clerks' union and the co-operative movement. However, despite the overtures of Saklatvala and his associates, the British labour movement was not interested in creating trade unions in India to fight for its oppressed workers.

It was in Manchester, too, that Saklatvala first met Ramsay MacDonald, who in 1911 became leader of the Labour Party, and later the first Labour Prime Minister. Saklatvala did not support MacDonald for the leadership, believing he was not the right man for the job; instead he backed Johnny Clynes, who would become leader of the party in 1921. Clynes later wrote, 'We had very pleasant conversations, and as I learned later he gave me some credit for turning his views in the socialist direction'.[30]

In 1912, Saklatvala and his family left Manchester and again moved to London, where he worked as personal assistant to his older cousin, Sir Ratan J. Tata, an Indian businessman who had been knighted for his services to the British Raj. Good-looking, mustachioed, Sir Ratan affected the ways of a garden-party-throwing Englishman and lived at York House, a 17th century mansion at Twickenham, previously owned by the Earl of Clarendon, the Lord Chancellor, and before that a home of a Duke of York.[31] The sprawling Italian-styled gardens he had laid out were the size of a park and went right up to the bank of the River Thames. Tall, ornate cast-iron gates stood at the entrance of a long drive to the stately home that is now Richmond Borough Council's Grade II listed Town Hall. Saklatvala eventually became manager of Sir Ratan's cotton mills department.

Saklatvala went back to Mumbai in May 1912, taking his wife and their young children with him. He explained: 'After putting up with considerable hardship, I did succeed in convincing one of my family heads about my right to return and to re-establish myself in Bombay. I wound up my home in England altogether.' Back in India, Saklatvala worked as the manager of Mumbai's prestigious Taj Mahal Hotel, which was owned by the Tatas. But, evidently, his political activities were sufficiently prominent to attract the attention of the Indian colonial Government, and as he protested:

> ...within 12 months, to my bitter astonishment, I received a sudden notice to return to England with my family and to restart a home... I have never been allowed to know why this was done but my kindly-disposed cousin, who told me about it, had by his expression and moisture in his eyes, allowed me to understand that he was not doing it of his choice.
>
> After returning to England I had to pass through a period of extreme hardship having to live through the entire war period with a family of young children on £22 a month with periodical warnings and notices [about his political activity] from my English Superior in the London office.

Saklatvala recalls how his father, Dorabji, who was based in Manchester buying and selling mill machinery, remonstrated with the head of the family in Mumbai about these matters, but received a terse reply from India explaining that 'as my politics were displeasing to the Government of India, any improvement made in my condition would bring trouble upon their heads in their business and other activities in India, for which they had largely to depend upon and co-operate with the Government'.[32] Accordingly, in 1913 Saklatvala had to tell his wife to begin packing because the family were returning to England.

This did not, though, end his business relationship with the Tatas for whom he continued to work, even after his election as an MP in 1922. However, the fact that he failed to give up his £750 annual salary (today worth about £34,000) from the Tata company was a considerable embarrassment to the Communist Party. There were at least two occasions when Saklatvala stood up in the Commons to criticise the failure of both British and Indian firms to observe 'fair-wage' standards, repeating a Labour jibe calling Tatas 'the worst employers in the world', only to have gleeful Conservatives asking whether Tatas had observed the fair-wages legislation while he was still employed by them.[33] In his defence, Saklatvala had worked almost full-time for the Communist Party with no other income until he became an MP and, as he said, his parliamentary allowance of £400 a year (currently about £21,000, almost less than a quarter of what MPs are paid today) was not sufficient to keep his family. Quite possibly, Saklatvala's need for a reasonable income was influenced by his own privileged background, though his main motive was to ensure that his family did not suffer for his views. He sent his children to a fee-paying preparatory school at Twickenham, so that, among other things, they could learn French. Later, at Highgate, they were sent to a state school.

Saklatvala also had a taste for art, which might have raised eyebrows among the more puritanical communists, but they never publicly commented on it. He was particularly keen on classical Western art and bought some statues for his home at auction. One of the smears used against him during an election campaign in the 1920s, when he was accused of being a rich man who concealed his wealth and posed as a friend of the working class, was that he had installed an expensive marble fountain in his garden at Highgate. This was untrue, though he did have a fish pond the size of a rug.[34] The slander was laughed at, even by some staunch opponents in his constituency. A reporter from *The British Weekly* learned from 'ministers of religion' in Battersea, who opposed Saklatvala's doctrines, that they were nonetheless convinced he was 'sincere'. They were impressed that he had 'foregone a large fortune on account of his communist convictions'.[35]

Even if, as in the case of Marx's relationship with the wealthy socialist industrialist, Friedrich Engels, living off a rich benefactor was not unheard of among communist leaders, the mockery of his tormentors in the Commons and the abuse of the capitalist press labelling him a 'parlour Bolshevist', Saklatvala felt forced to give up the Tata salary in 1925. Even then the press still noted that his letter to what they described as the 'great Indian capitalist house' was couched in very friendly terms. (His letter of resignation on 16 September, ended with the sentence: 'In this step I assure you of the inseparable goodwill on my part towards all the members of the firm, and I am sure of the continuance of the same on their part.') More pertinently the *Daily Graphic* reported: 'Mr Saklatvala said he resigned because his attitude might injure innocent families in India, who gained their livelihood through the firm. "I shall suffer very heavily because of my action, but I must stand by my convictions. My family must not be persecuted because of my political opinions."'[36] As part of the deal, Saklatvala got an annual pension of £500 a year (just under £30,600) to help support his immediate family in England. But he maintained that a promised 'settlement' of £5,000 for his children's upkeep was withheld, at the instigation of the authorities.[37] One suspects that Saklatvala pursued the issue of a settlement from the Tatas not only for his children's sake, but also because he had a rankling sense of the original family injustice concerning his grandfather and because he was sure that he was being victimised for his political beliefs. He recalled much later how his friend Pandit Motilal Nehru, then the Opposition leader in the Indian parliament, had travelled to Mumbai in an attempt to unlock the outstanding money. But a Nehru aide wrote to George Lansbury in November 1925 that Saklatvala's relatives had told him they were helpless. They were acting under 'irresistible pressure of British financiers'.[38]

Saklatvala explained: 'The open and concealed persecution carried out by Government Officials against me was largely due to their desire that a Parsee taking part in a bona fide and unadulterated anti-imperialist Communist politics should be ruined to the finish to make an example to others.' He went on: 'All the above incidents definitely raised the siege of cruelty and hardship imposed upon me and my innocent family.'[39]

All this lay in the future. After living at Sir Ratan Tata's Twickenham mansion, the Saklatvalas moved to their own more modest home a mile away at 51 Lebanon Park, St Margaret's. It was a pretty, gabled five-bedroomed house a stone's throw from the River Thames. Today it is valued at almost three million pounds.[40]

Saklatvala went back to India, without his family late in 1913, returning to England the following year. After that, the Saklatvalas lived at Twickenham for the next nine years, before setting up a large family home at Highgate in late 1921, near the cemetery where Karl Marx is buried. From his four-storey house, there was a picturesque view of Parliament Hill Fields, where the Saklatvalas enjoyed walking.

Saklatvala's permanent move to England could hardly have turned out worse for those intent on marginalising him, because it was not until after his permanent settlement that his political development really began. In 1916, he joined the City of London Branch and within a couple of years he was gaining a national political reputation. Although he was perhaps ideologically closer to the British Socialist Party, it is evident that he worked in the ILP because of its broad base within the labour movement. Founded in 1893, the ILP played a part in the setting up of the Labour Party seven years later. The ILP were Labour's largest Socialist Society until they decided to disaffiliate in 1932, in disgust at the party's capture by the right-wing. Their first secretary was the left-wing leader Tom Mann, who had Battersea connections and with whom Saklatvala became good friends. By 1916 the ILP was an organisation which included both revolutionary socialists and reformists, anti-war pacifists and those who had enlisted in the army during the 1914-18 war. Joining the City Branch was important because it contained a high proportion of revolutionary socialists such as J. Walton Newbold, who went on to become a Communist MP, leading pacifist C.H. Norman and Arthur Field, a left-wing Battersea labour activist, who undoubtedly had a significant impact on the development of Saklatvala's ideas. At the same time, it is evident that Saklatvala himself was highly influential in the branch in raising the profile of its internationalist and anti-imperialist commitments. The editor of the Labour-supporting *Daily Herald*, who attended one of their meetings, was greatly impressed by Saklatvala's speechmaking. Thus in 1917, Saklatvala addressed the branch on 'Socialism and Racialism'[41] and in 1919 the branch held public meetings on labour conditions in India and invited members of the South African Native National Congress (the precursor to the ANC) to be speakers at another meeting. At a time when the British left was by no means committed to anti-imperialism, particularly with regards to Africa, the City

Branch was clear in its support of anti-colonial movements, whether in Ireland, India or Africa.

Saklatvala's position in the branch was recognised in his regular election from 1917 onwards as a delegate to the ILP's divisional and national conferences. At the 1918 National Conference, Saklatvala raised the issue of Indian independence and scolded the ILP on the need to be more internationalist. By 1919 he was undoubtedly a national figure in the ILP, writing regular articles in its newspaper, the *Labour Leader* (some repro-duced as pamphlets), and was much in demand as a speaker. Yet though the ILP leadership clearly valued his oratorical skills as a recruiter to the party and his tireless commitment to his party work, he was never elected to either a divisional or a national position. During this time, Saklatvala was said to be the ILP's most popular speaker, attending hundreds of meetings across the country. He was reported, for instance, while still working full-time for the Tata office in London, as having travelled to Leicester every evening during the 1919 election campaign to canvass for Ramsay MacDonald, whom he admired at the time for his pacifist activism during the 1914-18 war and his commitment to Indian freedom.

Saklatvala's failure to win any national position was due to two factors which, ultimately, led to his resignation from the ILP and to him joining the newly formed Communist Party. These factors were closely con-nected. The first was the divided response of the British labour movement to the 1917 Russian revolution that created the Soviet Union and the second was the movement towards a right-wing reformist position by both the leaderships of the ILP and the Labour Party. Saklatvala's unswerving position as a supporter of the 1917 revolution and as a prominent left-winger in the fight against the ILP's drift from being an alliance of Christian Socialists and Marxists to becoming an anti-Marxist party, and as a leading figure in the campaign within the ILP to affiliate to the Communist Third International, led to his failure to win any national position and to his eventual resignation.

Nevertheless, by 1921, Saklatvala had been adopted as Labour candidate for the seat of North Battersea. This was undoubtedly the result of the previous years of intensive work for the ILP, the recognition of his skills as a public speaker, his clear espousal of both the struggles of British workers and the worldwide anti-imperialist struggle, and the contacts he had made with leading Battersea Trades Council and Labour Party activists. The reason for the split with the ILP and how a communist came to be adopted as a Labour candidate are issues which are discussed in greater detail in the following chapter.

CHAPTER THREE

PEOPLE'S TRIBUNE OF BOLSHEVIK BATTERSEA

Why an Indian and a member of the Communist Party came to be elected as the Labour MP for North Battersea in 1922 needs some explanation. Saklatvala's rise to national prominence within the radical Independent Labour Party has already been discussed, but a major part of the answer lies in the nature of the constituency itself.

At that time, North Battersea comprised four wards: Church, Latchmere, Nine Elms and Park. It took in the whole of Battersea Park, with Clapham Junction on the south westernmost border, two and a half miles of land upstream, along the south side of the River Thames from the Houses of Parliament. The area's socialist rejection of British imperialism was not immediately apparent. There were several colonial connections. In Latchmere, roads named Khyber, Afghan and Cabul could confuse the casual observer. But for thirty-six years before Saklatvala was selected as the constituency's parliamentary candidate, the place had been in the forefront of radical British politics. *The Times* described it as 'one of the chief centres of the Socialist and Communist movements.'[1]

Local historian Sean Creighton described the scene: 'As Battersea developed, following the coming of the railway in 1838, into an urban industrial area with a large working class, four distinct strands of working-class organisation emerged: trade unions; cooperatives, radical and secular societies and temperance organisations.'[2]

Creighton observed: 'Battersea was a very exciting place to be in the early 1890s. The local labour movement was in the vanguard of the New Unionist explosion of trade union militancy and expansion led John Burns (1858-1943), Tom Mann (1856-1941) and John Ward (1866-1934). Burns and Mann were nationally prominent because of their leading roles in the Great Dock Strike of 1889.'[3]

The British Weekly, a Church of England publication, gave a Dickensian picture of Battersea in 1924:

> If we cross the river from Chelsea we first find a beautiful park, and fringing it a lofty cliff of most respectable flats... beyond that Hadrian's

wall of propriety and we find ourselves in Battersea Park Road. Smoke and dust thicken the flat, marshy air. Trams zoom along and 'buses rattle past, packed with men in caps and dungarees... acres and acres of grey streets, monotonous with dingy, low-browed little houses, the criminal legacy of jerry-builders – cramped, rickety and crowded. Recently the demolition of slums in Chelsea flung a fresh torrent of poor into Battersea which now shelters nearly 168,000 souls in its 14,000 houses and dwellings... The Medical Officer of Health would condemn scores of these homes but for the intolerable hardship to their packed inhabitants, who could find no other accommodation in the borough.[4]

Battersea's extraordinary politics were shaped by the people who worked for innumerable factories, which crowded the southern shore of the Thames. Several local industries had links with the colonies. These included Price's Candle Company, at York Place, the largest candle-makers in the world. They had a steam works in Ceylon (now Sri Lanka) where coconuts were crushed to produce oil for the Battersea factory where they employed almost 2,000 people on a 14-acre site. Price's also had branches in South Africa and China. Another company, Morgan Crucible, was a large engineering firm dealing with carbon-based products.[5] Then there was Bowley's, the chemicals firm, which operated on a huge site, with a river frontage, near Battersea Bridge. The company refined oil and made paint, motor oil and varnish. They had wide-ranging business connections throughout Britain and the colonies. There was armaments production at the Projectile Factory, Nine Elms, and one of the largest employers in the Wandsworth area was an engineering factory, Elm Works, at Summerstown, which employed 536 men and 300 women. A high proportion of the working population were railwaymen employed at Clapham Junction, the busiest railway junction in the world, and at Nine Elms.

Conditions were grim. People lucky enough to be in work rather than unemployed still had to suffer low wages and bad housing. It was not unusual for families to be cramped into one or two rooms in rented accommodation. Because they did not have basic amenities in their homes, the working-class population had to use public bath houses and laundries. According to government figures in 1924, hundreds of the houses were unsanitary. Companies like Price's built monotonous rows of terraced houses for their employees so that a ready supply of labour was right on their doorstep.[6]

While the factory owners lived secure and wealthy lives, their workers faced terrible health and safety conditions. At Bowley's there were many explosions, some causing serious injury. Indeed, on one occasion, the company set the river on fire. There were fatal accidents at the London Gas Light Company works, a huge plant at Nine Elms, with an output of gas unrivalled anywhere else in the country.

The workers of Battersea were not the passive victims of such conditions. As *The British Weekly* commented, given its social composition, North Battersea was a constituency 'predisposed to support anyone who prefixes his creed with 'anti'.[7] It is therefore not surprising that trade unionism was strong. In 1918, it was estimated that Battersea had between 5,000 and 6,000 trade unionists and at least 48 trade union branches operated in this part of south west London between 1918 and 1922.[8]

It was also an area with a large number of Irish residents, mainly settled in Nine Elms. According to *The Daily Telegraph*, the communists 'found, in the casual labourers who drifted into the district in large bodies and were subject to periods of fluctuating unemployment, the natural seedbed for extreme and alien doctrines, and this was developed until representation on to municipal bodies was attained by all sorts of extremists'.[9] In 1918 South Battersea Labour Party selected a former Irish MP, Colonel Arthur Lynch (1861-1934), as their parliamentary candidate. He had commanded the Irish Brigade during the Boer War and had been sentenced to death by the British for supporting the enemy. In the same year, feminist and Irish Home Ruler and friend of Eleanor Marx, Charlotte Despard (1844-1939)[10] was North Battersea's Labour candidate when women aged 30 and older won the right to vote, provided they met minimum property qualifications.

However, despite the concentration of industry, not everyone could find work and the area's high unemployment was a major local issue. Even before the start of the national campaign against unemployment in October 1920, when Saklatvala first became active in Battersea, street-corner protest meetings were regularly held there. Government concern about the political activities of the unemployed was at its height and the Special Branch closely monitored the situation. In their report on 15 September, the police listed meetings at Battersea attended by 400 people on 8 September; 500 on the 12th (with a further meeting of 100 at Clapham Junction) and 150 at Battersea on the 15th.[11] In the week which ended on 14 October, there were seven meetings at Battersea as well as at Clapham Junction and Wandsworth. There were more meetings of the unemployed reported at Battersea than anywhere else in the country. In 1921, the Battersea unemployed made national news when they took over the local Work House and defiantly hoisted the red flag in a dispute about 'outdoor relief' payments.[12]

It was this environment that produced working-class leaders such as the veteran Socialist John Burns, who, with Tom Mann, made his mark as a member of the Marxist Social Democratic Federation (SDF). The two men went on to become leaders of the Great Dock Strike of 1889. That year, the SDF successfully backed Burns as an independent labour candidate for the London County Council (LCC). The group founded the Battersea Workingmens' Representation Committee and then the Battersea Labour League, the first in a line of broadly-based coalition organisations supported by socialists, liberals, trade unionists and radicals. The Labour

League became the Burns machine and got him elected to parliament. This group set up the Battersea Trades and Labour Council (BTLC) in 1894. Another key person in the SDF, and Labour League, was the BTLC secretary William Stephen Sanders (1871-1941). He eventually broke with the SDF after rejecting Marxism and embracing the gradualism of the Fabians instead. In 1896, the SDF pulled out of an umbrella organisation called the Progressive Alliance, accusing Sanders of unprincipled dealings. Sanders was later to stand against Saklatvala as the official Labour candidate in 1929. All this splitting and fusing of smaller socialist groups into larger ones was a microcosm of what happened nationally in the creation of first the Labour Party, and then the Communist Party. Activists from Battersea helped found the Communist Party of Great Britain (CPGB) and some of them remained dual members of both parties for as long as that was allowed.

Battersea's radicalism was apparent during the Boer war (1899–1902) when it was one of the few places in the country to oppose the rampant jingoism stirred up by politicians and the press during the conflict. Opponents of the war drew large and supportive audiences at public meetings. The local pro-imperialist *South Western Star* newspaper reported one such event: 'Only in Battersea could there be held such a meeting... The people generally have refused them [Merriman and Sauer, two anti-war Boers] a hearing. On Sunday evening, it was demonstrated that Battersea, as in everything else, is unique... in the interests of free speech and equal rights 200 stewards... were got together... there was no need for the stewards. A more orderly and a more enthusiastic meeting has never been held in Battersea'.[13] The borough council passed a motion against the conflict, condemning it as capitalist and defiantly named Joubert Street, on their newly-built Latchmere housing estate, after a Boer general. It is a local left-wing joke that Reform and Freedom were also used as road names in the same area, but Reform did not lead to Freedom.

It was an area where significant sections of the working people manifested a strong socialist culture in their daily lives. The veteran socialist Harry Wicks (1905-1989), a one time close colleague of C.L.R. James, gives a vivid picture, for instance, of the role of women in the labour movement:

Memories flood in of the team of working women that devoted so much effort to building the influence of the party and helping the poverty-stricken working women on what was known as Irish Island. What a team that was, Mrs Hockley, Mrs Varron, Mrs Stone, Mrs Payne to name but a few. The local Labour Party was firmly implanted in those mean little streets over the Dogs Home Bridge. At the sixpenny Socials and Dances that were a regular feature of our activity in those days, those women in between teaching us to dance used to man the refreshment tables where tea and home-made cakes were sold to supplement ward funds...[14]

John Burns, who was the North Battersea MP from 1892 to 1918, held meetings in Battersea Park, attracting up to 5,000 people, attacking the war. Burns made history when he and Keir Hardie became the first Labour members of parliament. Henry Broadhurst (1840-1911), a stonemason and leading trade unionist, represented various Midlands seats as a Liberal-Labour MP between 1880 and 1906. Broadhurst was appointed a junior minister by the 1885 Liberal government of William Ewart Gladstone. But Burns is celebrated as the first working-class man in Britain to achieve cabinet rank when he became minister for local government in 1908, though, like J. Ramsay MacDonald after him, there was controversy over the way he later joined the coalition Liberal Government.[15]

Labour supporters in Battersea were initially a part of the Progressive Alliance, which brought together organisations such as the Battersea Labour League and Trades Council and put up slates of candidates for elections. The group was broad enough to unite revolutionary socialists on the one hand, and liberals on the other. A coalition of trade unions, liberals, and socialists, they took control of the Battersea Vestry, forerunner of the borough council, in 1894. Then, with the establishment of the borough council in 1900, they ran this new seat of local government. The Progressives' control of the borough council saw the implementation of a pioneering municipal socialism. But, given the breadth and looseness of the Alliance, they were susceptible to damaging internal disputes as a result of which in 1909 they lost power to the Tories.

The defeat occurred as a result of the Labour Party coming together as a quite separate electoral force.[16] That year, Battersea's working-class voters were presented with a triple choice: Progressive (Liberals), Labour or the Social Democratic Federation (Marxist). Because the vote was split, most of the Progressives lost their seats, and the Municipal Reform Party (Conservatives) won in all but two wards. The Progressives, aided by Labour, had to wait until 1912 to regain control of the council. During the First World War of 1914-1918, the Progressive Alliance, of which John Archer was a member, finally fell apart. By this time, the Battersea Trades Council and Labour Party was strong enough to gain control of Battersea Borough Council without the help of the Liberals, who were part of the Alliance.

But Battersea was not only the location of radical trade union and working-class politics, it was also the first place to witness the development of Black British local government politics when, in 1913, John Richard Archer (1863-1932) was elected as Britain's first Black mayor. Archer was a professional photographer who represented Latchmere ward. He was born at 3 Blake Street, near the Liverpool docks. His Barbadian father, Richard, was a ship's steward. Little is known about his mother, Mary Theresa, formerly Burns, except that she was Irish. Archer is said to have travelled the world during his early adulthood, and during this time met his wife Bertha, a Black Canadian. They came to London from Merseyside in 1880 so that Archer could study medicine, something he did not pursue for long, and settled in Battersea.[17]

Journalists poured into the area when they got wind that Archer, a Black man, was about to become mayor. As if surprised, *The Daily Chronicle* reported his 'well-groomed appearance' and the fact he 'was a man of wide sympathies and interests'.[18] Archer was a friend, for instance of Samuel Coleridge-Taylor (1875-1912), a pioneering Black composer in Britain. At the council meeting where he was elected to the post on 10 November 1913, he beat his opponent, a local tailor, by one vote. A large crowd gathered outside the Town Hall to hear the result and Archer addressed them: 'It is a victory such as has never been gained before. I am the proud victor. I am a man of colour.' He told the council: 'My election tonight marks a new era. You have made history. For the first time in the history of the English nation a man of colour has been elected mayor of an English borough. That will go forth to all the coloured nations of the world. They will look to Battersea and say "It is the greatest thing you have done. You have shown that you have no racial prejudice, but recognise a man for what you think he has done".'[19]

The leader of the Progressives used the event to claim that racism was 'not recognised' at Battersea. Archer knew otherwise. He said: 'Many of the things that have been said about me... are absolutely untrue. I have a brother, but I should have to have had several for us to be born in as many places as we have been said to be born in.' During Archer's speech at the Town Hall a councillor interjected: 'Where were you born?' The new mayor replied: 'I think that at least you ought to show me, after my election, the same respect as you would show a white man. I have been charged with not being of the superior race, and it behoves you now to show that you do belong to the superior race... I am the son of a man born in the West Indian Islands. I was born in England... My mother... she belonged to one of the grandest races on the face of the earth. My mother was an Irishwoman. So, there is not so much of the foreigner about me after all.'

Archer gently mocked the journalists who had treated him as a curiosity. 'I must compliment the Press on the manner in which it has conducted this campaign. There has not been a single word to which I could take exception. They have said I am a man of colour. I am. I am proud to be. I would not change my colour if I could.' But he was angered by a racist letter printed by his local paper the *South Western Star*. The writer claimed to represent the majority of people of Battersea, yet did not have the courage to identify himself beyond the 'nom de guerre' of 'True Progressive'. He wrote that 'White men should not be governed and controlled by a man of colour. It has always been that the white man has ruled,' the writer said, 'and East is East and West is West and never the twain shall meet.'

Archer, a staunch Catholic, replied in a religious vein: 'And God hath made of one blood all the nations of the earth... Is it true that "East is East and West is West and never the twain shall meet?" Why, not so long ago you (Britain) were breaking your necks to put the wedding ring on the finger of the East – to have an alliance with Japan, and you only enter into alliance – not with inferiors – but with people you think your equals. I have to pay the same rates and taxes as you. My critic probably calls himself an imperialist... That kind of man is an imperialist when he wants more land; but when an Indian or a Negro comes over here he ceases to be an 'Imperialist', and becomes a 'True Progressive'. I shall be glad to know if a man born under the Union Jack, whoever he be, has got the same rights as the white man. The colour of the skin cannot alter the affection of the heart.'[20]

Archer was prominent in a delegation sent to Liverpool to discuss with its mayor the outbreak of racist attacks on Black people, mostly involving demobilised soldiers, which had resulted in the death of a Bermudian stoker, Charles Wooton. He had been chased by a white mob and drowned in Liverpool dock. There were similar events in Cardiff and Archer was involved in protests to the government about the lack of protection afforded the Black population.[21] The government's response was racist, with blame for the troubles put on Black people and repatriation proposed as a solution. Only the reluctance of the colonial authorities in the Caribbean to go along with the policy prevented it from being implemented.

Archer's Pan Africanist activities outside the town hall also brought him into prominence. When the African Progress Union was formed in 1918, he was chosen as their president. The union saw themselves as a 'Pan-Negro club linking Afro-Americans and Afro-Peoples with other African peoples.' In 1919, Archer went to Paris as British delegate to the first Pan-Africanist Congress.

In the same year, in Battersea, the Progressive Alliance, to which Archer belonged, finally fell apart. By this time, the Battersea Trades Council and Labour Party was strong enough to gain control of Battersea Borough Council without the help of the Liberals. This was the Battersea into which Saklatvala came – to the disgust of the local conservatives.

As Municipal Reform Party Battersea councillor A. P. Godfrey complained to an MP friend of his, in a typed six-page letter, Saklatvala 'first came into the district in 1919 at the invitation of that section of the local Labour Party which was closely associated with the activities of the Irish malcontents'. Godfrey added: 'The Battersea and Wandsworth district has always [been] a nest of the most extreme members of that movement. Mr Saklatvala quickly allied himself to this group and championed their cause locally and in the country'.[22] Godfrey betrayed his bigotry when he said

Saklatvala would like to feel he is the parliamentary representative of 'all the unruly and lawless elements of the East, and the disappointed and disgruntled elements of this country'.[23] According to Godfrey, who was never elected to parliament himself, the Communist MP suffered from 'an overweening vanity' and was 'in his element, when, during a period of strike or political agitation, he can march at the head of the Battersea contingent of strikers or unemployed'. But Godfrey had to grudgingly concede Saklatvala was a 'stupendous worker, and takes infinite pains to help those who think they have a claim against Government departments or local authorities. He has surrounded himself with the most loyal and enthusiastic workers, and being quite a wealthy man, he pays most generously'.

The author could find no evidence to corroborate Godfrey's assertion Saklatvala's supporters had got 'hundreds of minor jobs and [union] posts', including for two election agents, as a result of his influence.

When Labour took full control of Battersea council, the ruling group comprised 10 trade unionists; 21 members of the Labour League, including Archer; two women and 13 politicians who were described as 'socialists', among whom four figured on the Special Branch list of five communist councillors they were monitoring in 1922.[24]

We do not know exactly how or when Archer met Saklatvala, who was 10 years his junior. Archer, as chairperson of a session of the second Pan African Congress in London in 1921, introduced Saklatvala to the delegates. He also worked for Saklatvala's selection and election between 1921 and 1922. A. P. Godfrey described him as 'Saklatvala's most loyal and doughty champion'.[25] Godfrey claimed Archer gave up his council seat in November 1922, to campaign for Saklatvala, not returning to office until three years afterwards. Sean Creighton says: 'His backing [in 1921] of Shapurji Saklatvala as North Battersea's Labour Parliamentary candidate fits with his political approach that black (and Asian) people in Britain could demonstrate through their public activities their people's right to rule in their homelands. He may have decided that the most fruitful course of action was to link his Pan Africanist and Battersea labour interests through supporting Saklatvala.'[26]

Throughout his political life, in addition to Pan-African and anti-racist issues, Archer actively campaigned for better health and education. His achievements included helping to secure a minimum wage of 32s. a week for council workers, while serving on the Wandsworth Board of Guardians, a pre-welfare state local government body. Like Saklatvala, he spoke up for the Irish, comparing their position to that of Black people in the colonies. Archer was active in the support the council gave in 1919 to the call for the withdrawal of British troops from Ireland.

Nineteen-nineteen was a landmark in Battersea radicalism because

Labour left-wingers won control of the council. Two men, who were to become leading communists, were elected to represent the North Division of the borough on the London County Council (LCC). They were Alfred Watts, a printer, and Joseph Butler, Secretary of the Royal Army Clothing Department Employees Union. Both of them were re-elected in 1922, just after Saklatvala won the parliamentary seat. At least three other communists served on the borough council and the party controlled the Trades Council, with one of their members, R. C. Kiloh from the Amalgamated Engineering Union, serving as secretary. All this Bolshevik success in SW11 won the area the nickname 'Bolshie Battersea'. The Communist Party made the most of this in 1922 by holding their Congress at Battersea Town Hall. Harry Wicks observed: 'From 1920-22 onwards, the Labour movement in Battersea was particularly left... even the Labour Party reflected that... The Labour Party swept the board in the council elections of November 1919 and from that point they adopted very progressive policy which was out of step with national Labour Party thinking.'[27]

Saklatvala found in North Battersea a congenial home, both in terms of its activists' commitment to anti-racism and anti-imperialism, as well as the willingness of its elected local representatives to take on the government of the day. Saklatvala represented North Battersea during the first flowering of municipal socialism. *The British Weekly* said the borough council deserved 'high praise for its efforts in regard to housing, public baths and libraries, open spaces and the well-equipped and flourishing Battersea Polytechnic, maternity and child welfare centres, and the care of defective children. These useful activities are carried on by socialists...'[28] The Labour Council was also responsible for the introduction of trade union wage rates, and extending the electricity supply.

However, some explanation is still needed as to how Saklatvala, as a communist, fought three campaigns as the official candidate of the Battersea Trades Council and Labour Party (formerly the Battersea Trades and Labour Council, but reformed as the BTC&LP in 1918) and was officially endorsed by the Labour Party in the first two of these. One reason was the important contacts he made in his ILP days and later through the Communist Party. Influential Battersea socialists Arthur Field and Clifford Allen had belonged to the same ILP City of London branch. Arthur Field and London Trades Council Secretary, Duncan Carmichael, who was a left-wing Battersea Borough councillor in the 1920s, joined forces with Saklatvala in 1919 to issue a statement to Parliament's Joint Committee on Indian Reforms. Furthermore, the Battersea Herald League and Battersea Socialist Society were both represented at the Communist Party's founding Unity Convention. Activists such as Alfred Watts, Joseph Butler and Jack Clancy were also there. Watts, the CPGB's first treasurer, like Butler, represented Battersea on the London County Council. Part, no doubt, of the decision to adopt Saklatvala was the result of the powerful impression he made when he spoke at Battersea Town Hall in 1921 in support of striking South Wales miners. The miners themselves were impressed and sent the BTC&LP congratulations on their choice of candidate.

At this stage, there were no proscriptions on individual communists having membership of the Labour Party and Saklatvala fought the 1922 election under the banner of 'Labour's United Front' and put forward an election manifesto which was an uncritical version of Labour's national, and quite radical, manifesto. This included commitments to nationalisation, state housing, welfare benefits, full adult suffrage and women's rights. There were, though, considerable reservations in the Labour Party leadership about endorsing Saklatvala as an official party candidate. The minutes of the party's executive committee referred to his association with the Communist Party, his attack on the policy of the ILP in continuing its association with the Labour Party and his attempt to form a secessionist ILP group favourable to the Third International (discussed in more detail in Chapter Five). But on the condition that Saklatvala accepted the Constitution of the Labour Party and took the Labour whip if elected, his candidature was sanctioned, the first and only time the Labour Party endorsed a Communist Party member for a parliamentary seat.[29] Tom Bell (1892-1944) also records in his book, *Pioneering Days* (1941), that in fighting for official Labour Party recognition, Saklatvala so wore down the General Secretary Arthur Henderson that 'the latter gave up in sheer despair.'[30]

It is probable that the Labour leadership did not expect Saklatvala to win the election, and it was reluctant at this stage to take on the powerful Battersea labour movement. In fact, Saklatvala won comfortably, getting 50.5% of the vote against the 41% for the National Liberal candidate, Henry Hogbin. He was aided by the fact that a dissident Liberal, Vivian Albu, stood as well as Hogbin, but Saklatvala more than doubled the vote the previous Labour candidate, Charlotte Despard, had received in 1918 (although it must be pointed out that she was standing against a combined Conservative and Liberal coalition candidate) and took more votes than the two Liberals combined. He wrote in *The Communist* how all sections of the Battersea labour movement '...the comrades of the ILP, the comrades of the Battersea Labour League, the comrades of the Trade Unions and the Labour Party Wards, and the Irish rebels stood solid as a rock without one woman or one man in the active Labour ranks making an exception.'[31]

Some of the old people the author interviewed in a Battersea nursing home still remembered the election. One sang for him an election song, 'Vote, vote, vote for Saklatvala, kick old Hogbin out the door. For Sakky is the man who will give us bread and jam and we won't go hungry anymore' and recalled that children called him 'sack of bananas' because it rhymed with his name. Mary Ecclestone, who worked as a clerk at the Bowley's paint factory in the 1920s, recalled that 'he was an outstanding local figure. We hadn't had a coloured representative in parliament before'; and Richard Peach, a factory worker at the time said, 'The majority voted for Saklatvala because he was for working people. Hogbin was a conservative and they've never been well-liked in Battersea.' Another factory worker, Rachel Annells recalled: 'He spoke up for people – the poor class. I remember crowds of people flocking to see him speak at Latchmere baths, because he was a new man to the borough. They wanted to find out about him. He was a good speaker.'[32] It was Saklatvala's speaking skills at the election meetings that Minnie Bowles, then a member of the Young Communist League and Harry Pollitt's secretary, remembered:

> Sometimes he was a bit late arriving at a meeting and the audience was getting a little edgy. He would come in at the end of the hall and walk right down the central aisle, and the whole audience would rise and applaud. He had the most beautiful speaking voice which had the crowd quiet in seconds.[33]

The speeches were evidently not mere rabble-rousing; as Harry Wicks recalled, they were 'lessons in economic geography and imperialism'.[34] And one of his longtime opponents, Godfrey, attested vividly to Saklatvala's powers of communication in a newspaper interview he gave in 1936:

> [He would] turn up at a street corner meeting on the coldest of nights and, by sheer personality and his wonderful eloquence, would rivet the attention of the audience so completely that they soon forgot their discomfort. One of the great secrets of his success was the humility of mind he displayed to the humblest member of the audience... He knew how to time his arrival at a meeting to the minute and, with a few witty sentences and excruciatingly humorous remarks, very quickly had his audience spellbound by his oratory...
>
> ...His rage on the platform could be frantic in its expression if he found himself discussing any piece of legislation hostile to his ideals. Every fibre of his frail body seemed to quiver with overwhelming indignation which, irresistibly, seemed to transmit itself to his audience...
>
> He attacked his opponents with skilful rapier thrusts, but the point of the rapier was always protected by the button. He never indulged in personalities nor did he ever hit below the belt.[35]

Godfrey noted Saklatvala's skill as a propagandist. 'He is a great believer in the frequent broadcasting of handbills and pamphlets, like the *Voice of the workers of the East*'. Saklatvala contributed to his local newspaper the *South Western Star* which carried a weekly report of his parliamentary and other speeches. According to Godfrey, Saklatvala visited Battersea at least every second Sunday, and kept in 'regular and close contact with his constituents'.

But Godfrey was not averse to xenophobic references to Saklatvala. In his reports to the security services he was much less guarded. He wrote: 'To anybody outside the constituency it is difficult to explain why it is that

Saklatvala has been able to completely mesmerise a constituency of thoroughly English character, there is no foreign element in Battersea, and to
induce a British audience' into a 'white heat passion by his fanatical oratory,
answer to his question "Are you Britishers" to immediately shout "No. We
are internationalists!" "Do you want the Union Jack!" "No! We want the
Red Flag, down with the Union Jack!" Then the proceedings would be
interrupted by the whole audience standing seriously to attention and
singing that doleful dirge "The Red Flag"'. Godfrey continued:

> I hardly thought it possible that Englishmen could be so completely
> entranced by the fanatical oratory of this little wizened Easterner. He
> employs ingenious methods to create an atmosphere. When he particularly
> wants to focus attention on some political incident in India, e.g. the
> Agra episode [an Indian rebellion], he will pack his platform with
> beturbanned Lascars from the docks or picturesquely gowned Indian
> women. The open mouthed crowd, composed of a rather ignorant type,
> absorb his clap-trap propaganda, and easily become receptive to the seditious
> and subversive doctrines, which he so insidiously tries to inculcate. You
> may ask, do I consider him a dangerous man. I do, most emphatically.
>
> He openly admits on public platforms that he is in direct communication
> with the leaders of unrest in India and Egypt, and his messages to the
> 'Workers of the East' are construed by fanatics in those countries as an
> encouragement to go the whole length of the bomb and the revolver.[36]

In complete contrast, Minnie Bowles, a Battersea member of the Young
Communist League, talked about Saklatvala's humility and naturalness.
She recalled going canvassing with him on the Guinness Estate, now
demolished, off Battersea Park Road. A woman came running from an
upper storey of an ugly tenement building, crying out for Saklatvala to deal
with a domestic fight in which a man was beating his wife. Bowles says she
followed Saklatvala to the flat where the row was taking place:

> Sak stood inside the door and said, quietly, "Now why do you beat your
> wife. She is not your enemy. You have real enemies. Think of the landlord
> who charges you rent for this slum; or your boss who pays your wages,
> hardly enough to keep you alive." And he went on in this quiet way
> until the man was weeping, and the wife was comforting him.[37]

The next election came quickly in 1923 when the Conservatives dissolved Parliament on the issue of trade protection. If Saklatvala was a model
of fair play to opponents, as Godfrey acknowledged, this was far from the
case of his opponents. In this election, there was increased and scaremongering emphasis on Saklatvala's communist membership in both the
national and local press. In particular, the Liberal candidate made the quite
bizarre and almost certainly wholly unfounded allegations that his life was
being threatened by gangs of Irish republicans and continental and Russian
communists, and that his meetings were being broken up by Saklatvala's
thugs. Such headlines as 'Battersea Reds – Terrorist Tactics – Free Speech

Denied' and 'Terrorism in North Battersea' appeared in the *South Western Star*.[38] Saklatvala shrewdly set out to undermine these claims by offering his rival a platform at one of his election meetings. Despite this, Saklatvala lost the election by 186 votes, even though he substantially increased the size of his vote. Whether this was the result of Hogbin's tactics or because the rival Liberal candidate Vivian Albu did not stand in this election, can only be surmised.

The very next year, Labour, which had formed a minority government after the 1923 elections, called a further general election because of the lack of Liberal support. Saklatvala was again endorsed unanimously as the BTC&LP's candidate, but by this election his position in relationship to the Labour Party had changed. At the 1924 Labour Party Conference that started on 7 October, the decision had been taken to expel communists. Saklatvala spoke at the conference in favour of affiliation as a delegate from his local St Pancras Labour Party and Trades Council. Communist historian James Klugmann noted: 'That the Labour Party had been founded precisely as a federation in which revolutionary *and* reformist socialists could unite on a common limited programme with the trade union organisations, was, of course, an embarrassment to the right-wing. That the old S.D.F. [Social Democratic Federation] and later the British Socialist Party had been affiliated was something that, so far as possible, they tried to conceal.'[39]

However, the 29 October general election came too soon after the conference to force the BTC&LP to change their candidate. Saklatvala was not, though, endorsed nationally as a Labour candidate, so he stood as a Communist supported by the BTC&LP. Despite new levels of anti-communist hysteria and reports of 'extremist ruffianism', Saklatvala got a bigger vote than before, with an increased turnout, and beat Hogbin by 542 votes. In the spirit of the highly imaginative reporting which seems to have characterised the output of *The Daily Graphic*, Saklatvala himself was reported to have been the intended victim of attempts 'To Kidnap "Red" MP'. The newspaper claimed to have learnt of plots by extreme communists in Yorkshire to 'gas' the mines in the event of the introduction of 'blackleg' labour, and of a counterplot by 'Anti-Reds' to kidnap Saklatvala. This was apparently leaked to the 'Communist Camp' with the result that Saklatvala was well protected by the 120 activists mobilised by the Communist Party.[40]

There have been attempts to see this result at the 1924 general election as the high point of Communist Party electoral fortunes, but the truth was more that the North Battersea working-class voters supported Saklatvala because he was the candidate of the BTC&LP and was backed by all the major Labour figures in the constituency. The activism of Communists was undoubtedly important, particularly in Saklatvala's election campaign, but it was chiefly influential as an integrated part of the broader labour movement. At the time of Saklatvala's adoption in 1921, there was no local

Communist branch. Communists put their energy into being members of the Labour Party, although there was an active Battersea Young Communist League in the 1920s. Individual Communists continued to represent the BTC&LP on the local borough council and there was no attempt to keep their membership of the Communist Party of Great Britain secret.

For as long as possible, the BTC&LP ignored the Labour Party conference decision and allowed communists to remain members of the organisation. Then in 1926, just before the General Strike, the Labour Party disaffiliated the BTC&LP, though this was not enforced until after the defeat of the strike, principally because of the popularity of the communist activists involved in the Battersea Council of Action which co-ordinated local support. The London Labour secretary, Herbert Morrison, described by the ruling right-wing in the party as 'our chief witch-finder', had Battersea comrades at the top of his hit-list.[41] Saklatvala denounced Morrison's action by saying: 'Here we have an example of the lengths to which the official clique are prepared to go in their efforts to show the bosses that the Labour Party wishes them no harm.'[42]

The period of the general strike was undoubtedly one of the high points of revolutionary activism and communist influence in Battersea. There was a high degree of organisation. By the middle of the strike, the Council of Action had a membership of 127 representing 70 organisations. During the first few days, while the Council of Action was being formed, picketing of local work places was sporadic and often ineffective. It was not until the mass picketing of Clapham Tram Depot on Friday, 7 May, which was successful in spite of police baton charges and many arrests, that the Battersea labour movement took a firm grip on the situation. During the strike, all the large factories in the area, including Morgan Crucible, Carson's Paint, Garton's, Farmiloe's and St. Ivel's were closed down. By the 12th of May, Jack Clancy, the Chair of the Council of Action, reported to the TUC that 30,800 people were 'signing on' at 10 centres throughout the borough. Three picket centres were operating, while picketing itself was 'being conducted most efficiently and in the best possible spirit'. On May 8th, thousands of workers came onto the streets and blocked the roads to prevent the passage of Government organised food lorries. Some of the Battersea churches allowed the use of their halls for meetings, and collections from their congregations were even contributed to the strike fund. The Council of Action was in almost permanent session in Battersea Town Hall and published two and a half thousand of its own daily strike bulletins. However, in an era before widespread access to telephones and long before the invention of fax machines, and in a time of much Government misinformation on the radio, there was poor communication between the labour movement in different parts of the country. Activists in Battersea were thus astonished and at first disbelieving when the news reached them that the strike had been called off. Despite attempts to prevent the local industrial action from crumbling, there was a dispirited return to work and much demoralisation.

During the period of the strike and in its immediate aftermath, Saklatvala had been removed from involvement by his imprisonment in Wormwood Scrubs. Just as the strike began he had been arrested following a speech he made in Hyde Park. There was a May Day procession that Battersea's labour movement took part in, with many other activists from all over London. The main rallying point was the Embankment, with participants stretching from Temple train station to Blackfriars, a mile and a half away. More than a thousand people marched the four miles from Battersea Town Hall to Hyde Park, with a band playing the 'Red Flag' at the front, and a brake containing the 'Women of Today', 'wearing red mob caps and sashes' bringing up the rear. The procession moved off along the Wandsworth Road, as the *South Western Star's* reporter put it, 'like a trail of flame'.[43]

The Times reported 'the strongest contingents were from the coopera-tives societies, the trade unions and the Independent Labour Party. The Communist Party was also represented, several of its members appearing in red shirts'. The organisers said the event had attracted one of the largest crowds ever, perhaps more than double what the police told journalists it was. *The Times* observed: 'Its number was estimated at not less than 25,000.'[44] One of the last groups to reach the park that afternoon was a delegation from the Indian Seamen's Union.[45]

Despite the colourfulness of the event, most people present were all too aware of the seriousness of its purpose. The day before, George V had signed a Proclamation declaring a State of Emergency and at that very moment the government was in the process of activating the 1920 Emer-gency Powers Act. What was not yet known was whether the TUC had taken the decision to call the strike. When Saklatvala gave his speech, in the knowledge that he was liable to prosecution under the Emergency Powers Act, he spoke of the role of the armed forces:

> We tell the Government that the young men in the forces whether [William] Joynson-Hicks [the Home Secretary] likes it or not; whether he calls it sedition or not to soothe the financiers and his rich friends, we have a duty towards those men to say to them that they must lay down their arms'.[46]

No immediate action was taken against him. But, on Tuesday 4 May, he was arrested at his home, by a Chief Inspector Parker, and charged with incitement and breach of the peace (prematurely since the Emergency Powers Act had not yet been activated). Such were government fears over the political implications of the state taking legal action against a high-profile MP, and how this might be framed as an attack on free speech, was evident in the discussions between the Metropolitan Police commissioner, the attorney general, the director of public prosecutions and the chief magistrate at the court where Saklatvala was due to appear. The DPP advised postponing the arrest 'pending further consideration'. A Keystone Cops-like farce then followed. Despite a messenger being sent by a frantic police commissioner to Parker to stop him making the arrest, it was too late. He had already jumped the gun and done it, forcing the hand of government hawks who wanted to make an example of the Communist Party's most charismatic and effective advocate.[47]

At first, he was released on bail, with Independent Labour Party MPs George Lansbury and Ben Spoor, the latter who had a special interest in India, putting forward sureties of £100 each, along with Saklatvala's own £100.

The North Battersea MP also agreed not to make any public speech before the next hearing. Two days later, at Bow Street Police Court, where the public gallery was packed with Saklatvala supporters, including his wife, he appeared before magistrate Sir Chartres Biron. This was a judge who had agreed the warrants to arrest the entire executive of the Communist Party in October 1925. Biron told Saklatvala:

> In this case, there is no dispute as to the substantial accuracy of the speech, which has been called into question. As proved (I have read it carefully through) I have no doubt in my mind, and no reasonable man could have any doubt, that it is a seditious speech, calculated to promote public disorder. It is the more mischievous considering the circumstances under which it was delivered. At such a moment as this, to inflame public opinion by such speeches is an act of criminal folly.[48]

Saklatvala was bound over to keep the peace in the sum of £500, being required to find two sureties of £250 each or go to prison. Defending himself rather than use a lawyer, Saklatvala refused, telling the magistrate that he would not be silenced except by *force majeure*. According to *The Times*, he addressed the court 'for nearly an hour', saying 'it was never his intention to incite to disorder or encourage a breach of the peace'. *The Times* added that Saklatvala said: 'All his speeches were directed to showing how an orderly method could be adopted of carrying through the aims of the [Communist] party he represented. They were inflammatory only from the point of view of those who did not attend his meetings but preferred to stand criticism from outside'.[49]

The official court record revealed 'Saklatvala admitted the fairness and accuracy of the police report of his speech'.[50] He was quoted as saying: 'The position in which I stand is one to which I cheerfully submit... intended for the public good and I don't look upon it as a personal prosecution.' But, referring to being bound over, the court report added 'it was hardly a mode of life for every body [sic] to be bonded citizens. [...] Having regard to the present propaganda and political outlook he considered he should not be bound over any more than the prime minister should be bound over for his speeches against a section of the community'. Saklatvala 'urged that in the present stage of political development the magistrate should not take the view the speech was seditious'.[51]

Faced with this defiance, Biron sent Saklatvala to prison for two months. There appears to have been a specific targeting of Saklatvala since George Lansbury, the left-wing Labour MP, was reported as making an identical appeal to the military, but was not charged and a Battersea trade unionist, Noah Ablett, who said he was prepared to say the same thing about troops as Saklatvala, was prosecuted and found guilty but simply bound over to keep the peace. It was characteristic, though, of Saklatvala to be completely unbowed.

Prisoner number 4472 wrote letters from his Wormwood Scrubs prison cell to aristocrat home secretary William Joyson-Hicks, a Conservative viscount known for his authoritarianism and class hatred of communism, and the Speaker of the House of Commons, J. H. Whitley, the last Liberal to serve in that role. He sought 'the Speaker's judgement on Members' imprisonment, not for actual breach of law or peace or illegal use of definite words, but for refusal to be bound over vaguely and indefinitely for political speeches'. Saklatvala wanted to be released early. The Speaker refused to intervene in what he said was a judicial matter. And Saklatvala got short shrift from the home secretary to whom he cheekily appealed for permission to be released for a day to speak in parliament, to dispel what he claimed were untruths about what he had said in the May Day speech that landed him in jail. Saklatvala exclaimed: 'Breaches of peace, crimes of violence, promotion of disorders are not my aim or work, and never arose from one single of easily over 1,500 of my meetings – including the delicate period of war – through my studied care, and, believe me through my excessive forbearance and endurance (shared often by my innocent good wife).

He added: 'The artificial atmosphere of bitterness against me, is raised by outsiders [the word underlined by Saklatvala] who broadcast a false version of my meetings or speeches framed in an adverse setting, and the present [prison] sentence is entirely undeserved by my character, my aims, or my actions.'[52]

Saklatvala said a report of his May Day speech in the *Morning Post* of 3 May 1926 'invents words re: destruction of Union Jack [sic] never used by me'. However, *The Times*, published the same day, was clear that among his remarks was 'the Union Jack had for hundreds of years harboured and protected fools and rogues, and it was high time it was torn down'.

The establishment's newspaper reported that: 'On the arrival of Mr Saklatvala, a huge crowd escorted him across the park to the wagon of the Young Communist League.' After voicing his support for the striking miners, Saklatvala went to say the workers should not buy the mines, the railways and 'other great industries'. Instead, 'the proper thing to do was to go ahead and take them [into public ownership]'.[53]

After serving all of his two-month jail term, with only one visit from his wife and children allowed despite his appeal to the home secretary to be allowed to see more of them, Saklatvala was making a speech in the Commons within a couple of hours of his release from prison.[54]

The Wormwood Scrubs log of 24 June 1926 recorded: 'Governor instructed he will be discharged about 10.30 am tomorrow'.

Even before the general strike, Saklatvala had been the specific target of state attack. In the autumn of 1925, the Special Branch had launched a raid on his house as part of their big purge against the Communist Party. (They had raided Saklatvala's previous home at Twickenham, searching for material they could use to prosecute him for sedition, in a similar operation five years earlier.) The Special Branch reported:

> Bulk of the property seized are pamphlets. There are 158 different kinds of pamphlets of which 90% are Bolshevik propaganda. Some in bundles ready for distribution. Bundle attracting most attention is 400 copies of leaflet 'Explanatory Notes on the 2nd International versus the 3rd International. The Soviets and the dictatorship of the Proletariat' signed by British Bolshevik sympathisers including Saklatvala.[55]

Saklatvala reported that the raid was conducted by military officers accompanied by a uniformed soldier in their car, '...all sorts of ordinary pamphlets, Labour Party newspapers (in those days there was very little Communist literature in existence) was taken away. This was followed afterwards, on my request, by a harmless and almost comical interview with two high army officers in uniform. I was fully convinced... this was an irregular procedure carried out without any *bona fide* suspicion against my activities.'[54]

In the same period, Saklatvala was banned from entry to America (as he was later to be prevented from entering his native India). The Secretary of State, Frank Kellogg claimed that while 'I do not believe in curbing free speech, nor do I believe in making this country the stamping ground for every revolutionary agitator of other countries.'[56] He quoted selectively from Saklatvala's public statements, for instance his speech to the National Minority Movement in August of 1924. Saklatvala had said, 'I am going to America as a friend of the working classes. British imperialism ought to crumble in the dust. I am out to work for a revolution and for the day when workers will control the whole world. But before this comes you will have to face cold steel.' Conservatives such as Sir Robert Horne, the leader of the Inter-parliamentary Union delegation which Saklatvala was supposed to be on, were delighted at the ban. They made maximum political capital out of the situation. 'I hope, indeed, that this will be an object lesson to our people, and that this incident, which has been embarrassing many of us in the last few weeks, may produce a beneficent result. It will do so if it brings home to the minds of the electors in North Battersea what a disgrace they bring upon themselves and upon the whole of their fellow subjects by electing as their representative in the House of Commons such a notorious person as Mr Saklatvala.'[58]

In America, Saklatvala's ban from being on the October 1925 six-day trip to Washington DC was challenged by civil liberties groups, the labour movement and even by a Republican Senator, William Borah, chairman of the Senate's Foreign Relations Committee. A conservative from Idaho, Borah nonetheless took an interest in native American and Oceanic affairs and deplored what he saw as the prejudiced treatment of Saklatvala. Borah, having read one of Saklatvala's disputed House of Commons' contributions, said: 'I think anyone who read the speech will come to the conclusion that Mr Saklatvala's crime is that of discussing conditions in India.' The *Baltimore Evening Sun* mocked the decision:

> He [Saklatvala] has a seat in the very midst of England's lawmakers; and not one of them has been discovered mysteriously murdered, not a single powder keg has been found in the Buckingham Palace coal bin... The American people, it would seem, are looked upon by their hired servants as just so many sheep to be led astray.[59]

The American Civil Liberties helped organise a big demonstration which greeted the British delegation when they arrived in New York without Saklatvala. Even the *New York Times* was moved to protest that the US Government had displayed 'too much zeal' in barring the Communist MP. *The Daily Worker* made the point that Saklatvala's views were 'the result of his country, India, being under the domination of Britain, a domination of which the mass of the American people strongly disapprove'.[60] According to US academic J.A. Zumoff, Saklatvala's exclusion drew attention to 'the racist nature of American political discourse in the 1920s and the connection between racial and ethnic discrimination and political repression in the United States'. For historians of South Asian radicalism, Zumoff saw the affair offering 'insight into an important period in the development of anti-imperialism and Communism in [America's] South Asian diaspora'.[61]

After the General Strike the attempt to silence Saklatvala continued. The Emergency Powers Act was still in force and he found that meetings at which he was invited to address workers – there were many invitations from miners among whom his popularity was never higher – were banned at short notice. However, what was the most serious attack on Saklatvala's influence came from the Labour Party.

In the period following the end of the General Strike, the Labour Party moved against the BTC&LP by disaffiliating it and establishing two new divisional Labour Party branches. Locally, the right-wing of the Battersea Trades Council and Labour Party regrouped and were able to capitalise on the mood of demoralisation within the labour movement. The disaffiliated BTC&LP continued to operate for some time and the two organisations

competed for members. Although at a by-election for the Borough Council a disaffiliated candidate won a narrow victory over the official candidate,
personal factors were undoubtedly influential, the candidate being Jack
Clancy, the popular chairperson of the Battersea Council of Action. But in
the longer battle the official Labour body was successful. It caused considerable embarrassment for Saklatvala that the *South Western Star* published
on 2 July 1926 the text of a confidential letter written by him the previous
year to the British Communist Party leadership. The letter had been seized
by Special Branch police when they raided the party's headquarters. At the
time, Saklatvala was publicly accepting the support of the BTC&LP. But,
behind their backs, he was advocating to the Communist Party a policy of
'merciless measures to fight the Labour Party' and of inviting trade union
branches to affiliate to the Communist Party rather than Labour. This sort
of underhand behaviour confirmed to his old champion Archer, by then
the secretary of the reconstituted North Battersea Labour Party, and other
Battersea Labour leaders they were right to finally accept their national
party's ban on the Communist Party and its members.[62]

By 1927 Saklatvala was faced with an official Labour candidate who had
been adopted to oppose him. Saklatvala bitterly described his rival, William
Sanders, an ex-army recruitment officer, as a 'Jingo Labour Warmonger'.[63]
Thereafter, the Communists, and Saklatvala himself, put the seal on the
collapse of his position in Battersea. As discussed in more detail in Chapters
Five and Seven, by this time the Communist Party, with Saklatvala himself
an enthusiastic proponent, was putting forward an aggressively anti-Labour
position, the 'new line'. Relationships with the non-Communists within the
disaffiliated BTC&LP became antagonistic and many resigned. As a result,
Saklatvala's remaining support within the constituency crumbled.

The question has to be posed, too, as to whether Saklatvala adopted the
wisest strategy as an MP, both while holding the Labour Party whip and as
a Communist Party member. There were matters of principle which no
doubt antagonised mainstream Labour voters, when Saklatvala on several
occasions went into the Conservative lobby to vote against the Labour
Party. There was also the issue of whether he paid enough attention to
Battersea issues, particularly those relating to social reform. The latter was
undoubtedly much more of a preoccupation for many who had voted for
him than Indian or anti-imperialist matters. Though in reality, Saklatvala
did campaign on some Battersea issues, interviews he gave to the local *South
Western Star* indicated otherwise. That paper was only too pleased to express
surprise that Saklatvala should tell them before the 1924 General Election
that 'he is not concerned with local interests. He will not devote himself to
the welfare of the local cricket club, for example. Local affairs, he holds, are
for local bodies. Parliament's concern is that of nation and empire.'[64]

The evidence is that, perhaps more outside parliament than within,

Saklatvala did campaign hard on issues of social reform, against the slum housing and the appalling wages and conditions faced by his working-class constituents. In May 1924, it was reported that he had managed to cajole the aristocratic MP for South Battersea, Viscount Curzon, into coming with him on a visit to slum housing in Stainforth Road. It was there that Saklatvala made an outspoken attack on the capitalist system which allowed 'father, mother and three or four children to live in the same room.' On the visit Saklatvala was heckled by someone who yelled: 'It's a Labour Council.' To which he replied: 'Even a Labour Council without enforcing a pure socialist system cannot remedy it.'[65] On another occasion, he clashed with Viscount Curzon in the Commons. The latter had attacked Battersea Council for paying over the odds for land it had bought for an electricity showroom. Saklatvala used the opportunity to extol the virtues of the Council who were, he said, selling electric current at half the price of neighbouring boroughs.

In April 1927, he urged the Government in the Commons to support women pieceworkers at the London Nut and Food Company in Battersea who were on strike over poor wages. A month later he was raising the issue of the insanitary conditions the women working in this factory faced, and managed to get the Home Secretary to send in government inspectors who saw to it that facilities were improved.[66]

He was even reported on occasion performing local duties of a distinctly public relations kind, attending the award of the challenge shield for the Lifeboat Essay competition won by a child from Battersea, and paying tribute to 'the British spirit'.[67]

However, though he was clearly an industrious MP, making almost 500 interventions during his parliamentary career, an analysis of these as listed by Hansard does indicate that though there are many significant interventions on British trade union issues, the Emergency Powers Act in force during and after the General Strike, unemployment, housing conditions and Ireland, the bulk of his speeches related to India and other anti-imperialist issues.

This focus was undoubtedly Saklatvala's most valuable contribution to Parliamentary life, raising matters which would otherwise have gone unchallenged and unreported. But the imbalance did make him vulnerable to the accusation, discussed in Chapter Seven, that his constituents had got an MP for India rather than an MP for North Battersea. It is possible, too, that while Saklatvala's stance on national and international issues over local ones was the norm for all MPs when he was first elected, by the end of the 1920s, voters were expecting a much greater emphasis on constituency matters. Certainly, Sanders, his official Labour Party opponent at the 1929 election, made considerable play on his position as a 'Battersea man for Battersea'.

CHAPTER 4

ANTI-IMPERIALIST MP FOR INDIA

Number 2 St Albans Villas in Highgate Road was the unofficial London home of the Indian independence movement. Many of the political activists involved in the fight for Indian self-government visited Saklatvala there, a stone's throw away from the cemetery where Karl Marx was buried. Among the visitors was the great Bengali orator, Bal Gangadhar Tilak (1856-1920), in 1910 a guest at the ILP's annual conference where a resolution was passed urging that the Indian people be granted the right to lawful association and freedom of speech. Tilak, known as 'the Father of Indian unrest', was the first Indian leader to approach the British people through working-class organisations and newspapers. Other visitors included Mohammed Ali, a Muslim member of the Congress Party. Despite the deep political differences he had with them, members of the Congress Party described Saklatvala as India's greatest fighter for independence abroad.[1] Exiled from India by the Tatas at the behest of the Indian colonial Government, and later banned from entry by the British Government, Saklatvala seized every opportunity to wage his struggle at the heart of empire.

During the first decades of the century, the upsurge in Indian nationalism was brutally suppressed by the British. Perhaps the most infamous atrocity occurred on 13th April 1919 at Amritsar, Punjab state, where, according to some commentators, close to a thousand unarmed Indians were murdered. The British claimed the official death toll was 379 people whose lives were lost in the Jallianwala Bagh massacre, on the site of the festival of Vaisakhi, in the Golden Temple complex, Sikhism's holiest shrine.[2]

The slaughter happened during the tenure of the Irish-born, Oxford university-educated lieutenant governor, Michael O'Dwyer, as the Punjab's British ruler. His repressive policies and actions are considered to have triggered the Gandhi-led rise of the Indian 'non-cooperation' independence movement. O'Dwyer brought in oppressive martial law in the Punjab on 15 April 1919, backdated to 30 March, clamping down heavily on protests. He was acting in support of the British army Colonel Reginald Dyer's order for his troops to open fire on unarmed Indian demonstrators that resulted in the Amritsar massacre. O'Dwyer called it a 'correct action'. In 1940, the killings were avenged when O'Dwyer was shot dead in London by Indian Sikh revolutionary, Udham Singh, a member of the Indian diasporean nationalist Ghadar Party and Hindustan Socialist Republican Association.

The massive nonviolent protests against the massacre, organised by the Indian National Congress all over the country, were being met with harsh repressive violence by the British. Thousands of people were thrown in prison where they were flogged and chained.

At the time, it seems that little of this horror reached majority British public consciousness. As Rozina Visram states:

> The overwhelming majority of the British people were not only apathetic but ignorant of the true nature of British imperialism. They still entertained a romantic notion of Britain's civilising role... And the British government's propaganda machine both fed on and helped to sustain this image of colonialism. The Indian national struggle for independence was largely unknown and unrecognised in Britain... The Indian National Congress was made out to be a bunch of discontented troublemakers, a mere 'microscopic movement', in Lord Dufferin's words. Government propaganda was on a massive scale and it gave most Britons a totally false picture of India.[3]

It was against this background that Saklatvala agitated inside and outside parliament to drive home the truth.

From Saklatvala's earliest years in Britain, there was a dossier on him compiled by the Criminal Intelligence Office. One of his former colleagues records how in 1909 Saklatvala was sitting in a London café with other Indian nationalists, talking loudly of plotting terrorist outrages in India, whose object was 'to kill as many Englishmen as possible'. Saklatvala's daughter Sehri insists that this was just flippant, half-joking hyperbole, but the subtlety might well have been lost on a State informer.[4] Government files reveal that from as early as 1910 that 'his propaganda on behalf of the Indian nationalist movement' first attracted official attention. In 1911 these files noted that he kept in touch with radical Indian nationalists like Madame Bhikaji Rustom Cama and Bipin Chandra Pal, and showed 'considerable interest in the extremist movement'.[5] Saklatvala also belonged to Annie Besant's reformist Indian Home Rule League, which towards the end of the First World War was able to get support in trades councils and ILP branches in Yorkshire and South Wales and in some of the larger industrial towns elsewhere. It is evident, though, that while Saklatvala sought allies where he could find them, he was not impressed by the likes of Besant, C.F. Andrews and Mirabehn (Madelaine Slade)[6], once describing them as 'white men and women' who 'pass as India's friends and pretend to be almost Indianised.' It is evident that while Saklatvala had close and lasting white friendships, he was in no way impressed with whiteness, and concentrated on those Indians who could define and carry forward the struggle for an independent, socialist India. For this reason, the secret service named him as 'one of the most violent anti-British agitators in England'.[7] None of this harassment resulted in him losing his humanity. One winter, when he knew there was a detective outside his house, he told the man, 'I know you are watching me, so why don't you come into the house for a coffee and watch me in the warm'.

Before Saklatvala was elected as an MP, and while the Labour Party still had only minority representation in parliament, he attended a meeting of Indians at Caxton Hall in London and explained why they must support the Labour Party: 'In this country no political progress can be made except through the channels of one of the existing parties...' Indians must also stand for parliament, he argued, because: 'The first thing that a member can do is to advertise better from the House of Commons than from anywhere else.' He gave a good example of what he meant in a parliamentary debate in 1927 when he said, 'today I can speak... as one of the conquered and enslaved subject races. Let me assure the House that I bear no malice to any persons in this House or outside this House, but I always prefer, when I give expression to the faith and feelings of those who are crushed and those who are oppressed, to speak in plain, blunt language.'[8]

But as revealed earlier, Saklatvala, although he made the struggle for Indian freedom his particular focus, was always concerned to put that struggle into the widest international context. He said that one of his most important tasks was to voice the need for solidarity among the oppressed. Indians must stop asking 'What have other people done for us?' They must begin to ask: 'What have we done for the Irish, the Egyptians, the Russians?' and throw themselves into 'the world movement of the Labour classes'.[9]

Was Saklatvala a nationalist? The crude answer is yes. But his politics were more complex than that. This is how he explained his position: 'The healthy life is the international life, provided national rights are preserved.' But, when 'power is abused in order to take away the products of a country for the sole use of those who took them, then the people of that country have the right to fight for their rights; a national fight is then justifiable'.

Some nationalists asked Saklatvala if he was in favour of a boycott of British goods as a weapon in the war for Indian independence. He replied that he supported the tactic, but it should not be used 'in an indiscriminate way'. Again, Saklatvala's overriding internationalism dominated his message. Indian workers must 'not starve the spinners in Lancashire or the miners in Wales'. But neither should the onus of solidarity be one-way.

British workers had a responsibility too. The labour movement had the power to 'send or stop sending munitions and weapons of murder into India'.[10]

When he was finally allowed into India, Saklatvala told a meeting in Madras he was not an enemy of English people but of English capitalism which was 'producing unemployment, underemployment and misery in the homes of millions of British workers'.[11] He set out his case in more detail by explaining: 'The Dundee jute workers do not yet realise the urgent need of making the Bengal jute workers as well as the Bengal jute growers, a part and parcel of the British Jute Workers' Federation, demanding a six-hour day and £5 a week minimum wages, whether the factory be in Dundee or Calcutta. The wages in Bengal jute factories are registered by the Government commission at 14s a month up to 38s. a month in some departments.' He further pointed out that the Dundee jute workers, in order to maintain this low-wage competition against themselves, had to contribute not only by their taxes towards the maintenance of the British Navy, but even in the supply of men – those who joined the Scottish Highlanders sent to India to terrorise the jute growers, as well as the jute workers in Bengal, and to teach them 'obedience to a law and order which insists on maintaining the right of the masters to extract 200 per cent and 300 per cent dividends from the misery of the people.' It was his contention that: '...the neglect of effective working-class solidarity abroad has reacted ruinously on the home position of the workers.'[12] For him, the workers' revolution was a truly international struggle because Indian and British Labour were bound together by economic ties. 'If by any chance continued unwisdom [sic], apathy or arrogance on the part of British Labour drives the Indian Labour or mass movement into open hostility against them, British Labour will have to be prepared for evil days.' In the short term, the success of the Indian Labour movement would depend on the amount of support they could get from British workers. But 'very shortly afterwards the united and full strength of the organised Indian masses will play no small part in the British Labour struggle for its economic emancipation and independence'.[13]

From very early in his political life, Saklatvala was also totally committed to the view that independence for India was only meaningful if it radically improved the quality of the lives of the workers and peasants. In this he anticipated the insights of Frantz Fanon and no doubt would have been saddened by not surprised by the direction taken by bourgeois nationalism and its caste of rulers and exploiters. Conscious that in India, before the turn of the century, there was no large-scale peasant or working-class organisation, he saw the building of trades unions as a top priority. He argued that this process had been held back in India by the Congress leadership, influenced by the 'hypocritical' British Liberal Party, who had downgraded the importance of organised labour. He was sorry that, 'At a certain period the Indian National Congress officially prided itself in being the representative of the aristocracy of wealth and talent'.[14] It was his view that Congress failed to involve those who could really effect major change: 'If the full organisation of the Labour movement were in operation things would be different. If there were shop stewards, if the miners could decide who their manager should be, if the railway porters elected their station master, the board of directors in London would be paralysed.'[15] He thus enthusiastically welcomed the beginnings of industrial struggle in India during the first decades of the twentieth century when key unions were formed, such as for print and postal workers, and when workers staged a number of strikes in Bombay mills, and there was industrial unrest on the railways, especially Eastern Bengal State Railways. In 1918, the Madras Labour Union was formed. Although its members mainly worked in textile mills, it also included tramway men and rickshaw pullers. He was supportive of the emergence among the leadership of the Indian National Congress of those such as Jawaharlal Nehru and Subhas Chandra Bose who were prominent trades unionists, both serving as presidents of the All India TUC, which was formed in 1920.

Even though he could not take an active role in the internal struggle, Saklatvala's external contribution to it was evidently perceived as a threat, as the reactions of his opponents testified. Although the Conservative under-secretary of state for India, Lord Winterton, attempted to belittle Saklatvala by claiming that 'No one takes him seriously. I have good reason to know that he is regarded with suspicion and dislike by the majority of the Labour Party, though he is naturally a *persona grata* with extremists like [J. Walton] Newbold [MP.], the Communist...', the truth was that successive Governments, including Labour, not only kept a close eye on his activities, but actively sought to suppress his influence. As the Eton College educated, Irish aristocrat Winterton continued, 'On the whole I think this dangerous man is safer as an MP than he would be otherwise, since his activities can be more easily watched'. J.W. Hose, senior civil servant in the India Office, revealed that the government was seriously committed to trying to undermine Saklatvala from the time he first set foot in parliament. Hose wrote to a British colleague in the Bombay Government, 'No opportunity has yet been afforded for a disclosure in the House of Commons of his real nature and personality because there has been only one Indian debate, in which it would not have been possible to deal with him personally; moreover, practically none of his violent speeches outside have been reported in the Press, and of course, it would be impossible to quote your police reports. If, however, he ever became really objectionable in the House itself, there is a certain amount of "stuff" which could be used.'[16]

In January 1924, Labour formed a government supported by the Liberals (although Labour won less seats than the Conservatives, their combined strength with the Liberals gave them a 34-seat majority). Prime Minister Ramsay Macdonald, whom Saklatvala had admired in earlier ILP days for his then commitment to Indian independence, took personal charge as foreign secretary. In July of that year, Saklatvala submitted a detailed 11-point blueprint of what he thought the policy of the Labour Party and Trades Union Congress should be on Indian labour issues. (It is reproduced in Appendix 2.) The document proposed a substantial pay rise for government employees, the abolition of forced labour, trade union rights and judicial reform, including trials by jury. Saklatvala's advice went unheeded and this experience undoubtedly increased his bitterness towards Labour. By November the government had fallen and the Conservatives won the general election in the same month.

In parliament, Saklatvala was a one-man party, waging a solitary opposition to all the other parties, able to rely only occasionally on the support of Labour left-wingers, mostly the Scottish ILP members. James Klugmann, the Communist Party's official historian, felt able to write that in Saklatvala: 'Marxist, trade unionist and anti-imperialist groups in the colonies and semi-colonies began to see that they had a real ally within the fortress of British imperialism, waging a common struggle, transcending colour and transcending race.'[17]

That internationalism was seen most clearly in Saklatvala's tireless support of the cause of Irish independence, the first of the anti-colonial, anti-imperialist struggles to begin the downfall of the British empire, if not the networks of global capitalism that continues to exploit much of the former colonial world. In 1920 and 1922, Saklatvala was a guest speaker at the Irish Labour Party and Trade Union Congresses (ILP&TUC).[18] In a letter he wrote to Irish history publication *Saothar*, scholar Francis Devine called Saklatvala '"The Red Tiger" hero of his father', who had served in India during the Second World War. Devine noted Saklatvala brought greetings from the All India Trade Union Congress and Workers' Welfare League of India to the 1922 ILP&TUC meeting in The Mansion House, Dublin. Saklatvala told delegates:

> Imperialism has been the emblem of starvation, misery, distress, degradation of womanhood, the breaking of the life and moral strength of innocent children. It is duty, it is humanity, it is religion, it is safety, it is interest, it is everything you may call it, that we should, everywhere and anywhere, stand up against it.[19]

But Saklatvala spoke bluntly when he said not all Irish in India were supportive. Some were 'red-hot Imperialists' despite the fact that 'when here [in Ireland] they are members of the Trades Unions' and protest about 'the oppression of the master classes'. But 'when they get the whip hand they employ coolie [Indian] labour, and pay them badly, 'working them 12 hours a day'. He called for the ILP&TUC to issue a 'National Manifesto' declaring it a 'shame and a disgrace for workers, whether in China, Peru, Dublin or Belfast, if he ill-treats another worker'.

Saklatvala argued that organised labour in the East would undermine labour in the West unless joint policies could be agreed, and that there was a particular need to organise agricultural workers.[20]

In 1925, meetings were held to promote the Irish Workers League, formed two years earlier by his comrade James Larkin (1876-1947) as an attempt to establish an Irish Marxist party, which the CPGB supported. Saklatvala also travelled to Dublin with other CPGB leaders Willie Gallagher and Bob Stewart to campaign for James Larkin in the 1927 Irish general election in which Larkin won a seat for the Irish Worker League. Saklatvala returned for the 1932 general election to do the same. The *Irish Times* reported that, on polling day, 'a vociferous army of youngsters, plentifully bedecked with red sashes and red jerseys and carrying red flags', paraded through the streets in support and Saklatvala accompanied him on a tour of the polling stations.[21] But this time Larkin, running as a Communist, lost.[22] Saklatvala was invited to one of the polling stations and got a reception fit for an international celebrity. Devine notes: 'A crowd, led by the Fintan Lalor Pipe Band and the Fife & Drum Band of the WUI (Workers' Union of Ireland) Dublin No.1 Branch, paraded on 19 April to welcome 'Saklatvala MP, The Voice of India'. More than 10,000 people turned up to hear him speak in O'Connell Street.[23]

In his speech, Saklatvala said he was 'cheered' to see so many people had gathered but that numbers were not enough 'until we learn to do things ourselves and not leave the winning of freedom to a few leaders, we will simply be a lot of hopeless mugs'. He added, as a poignant reminder to his Dublin audience, 'if the men of 1916 [Ireland's Easter Rising against the British] were right then', it was 'the duty of workers to do the same and keep on the path to freedom'. He said Irish workers should refuse to co-operate in the suppression of India and Egypt.[24]

There was a hysterical backlash to Saklatvala's visit from what the *Irish Worker*, the James Larkin-founded Communist newspaper, described as 'the gutter press of Dublin', which 'vilified' and 'falsified' what he had said in his speeches. The *Independent* claimed the Communist 'Red Menace' threatening to take over countries like Ireland was backed by 'millions of pounds from Moscow', despite the Bolsheviks 'reducing Russia to famine and starvation'. The *Irish Worker* hit back in defence of Saklatvala, saying the right-wing *Irish Times* was 'blind to the degradation and misery, premature death and degeneracy occurring in the MP's country of India'. It said both the *Irish Times* and *Independent* attempted to 'kill and smother' Saklatvala's anti-imperialism, knowing the danger should 'oppressed people, black, white and yellow' come to understand his message and bring down the 'bloodiest Empire the world has ever known'.[25]

Devine's and Kate O'Malley's scholarship and the release of MI5 files since the last edition of *Comrade Sak* has revealed the extent of Saklatvala's involvement – in Battersea, in parliament and in meetings with the highest level of Irish nationalist leaders, including Éamon de Valera, holding a secret meeting under cover of darkness, with the future Irish head of state, at his Highgate home. He also met Irish Free State leader Michael Collins in London.

Perhaps it was no coincidence that ninety per cent of Saklatvala's Battersea electorate (this was before women aged over twenty-one had won the same right to vote as men), were Irish, and he fearlessly went into battle for them in his first parliamentary speech, saying: 'In reference to Ireland, I am afraid I will strike a jarring note in the hitherto harmonious music of this house.' He then went on at length to speak about the Anglo-Irish Treaty of the previous year:[26]

> As a House, we may say that we are giving this Irish Treaty with a view to bringing peace to Ireland, but we know that it is not bringing peace. Either we are accentuated by the motive of restoring thorough peace in Ireland or we are doing it as partial conquerors of Ireland. Everyone knows that the Treaty has unfortunately gone forth as the only alternative to a new invasion of Ireland by British troops... the people of Ireland have a right to say that the very narrow majority which in Ireland accepted the Treaty at the time, accepted it also on this understanding – that if they did not accept it the alternative was an invasion by the Black-and-Tans of this country... As in 1801 England gave them a forced Union, so in 1922 England is giving them forced freedom.'[27]

Here, Saklatvala was going against the Labour Party line in his outspoken criticism of the Irish Free State Constitution Bill. But, as Irish historian Kate O'Malley says, in doing so he was 'taking the bull by the horns' and 'cementing UK based Indo-Irish bonds'.[28]

Saklatvala said he was putting forward the views of his electors who were 'Irishmen', who, like others of their countryfolk resident in Britain, had, by a huge majority, voted against the Irish Treaty.

Labour Opposition leader Ramsay MacDonald had offered no resistance to the parliamentary bill, meaning its passage was a *fait accompli*. Undeterred, Saklatvala tabled an amendment, saying: 'I realise the unpopularity of what I am courting in taking this step, but it was distinctly understood between my electors and myself that they did not want me to back up a Treaty which was based upon coercion, and was signed under duress.'

The amendment was rejected and the bill became law. Saklatvala kept up his brave resistance, vigorously defending British nationals of Irish parentage deported to Ireland as suspected members of the Irish Republican Army. Among them were his friend Art O'Brien. Saklatvala and his left-wing parliamentary allies, including George Lansbury, took up the case with Home Secretary William Bridgeman.[29] Bridgeman defended the arrests, saying there had 'lately been a progressive increase in Irish Republican activity here [in Britain]. We are in possession of material clearly indicating the existence of a quasi-military organisation'.[30]

Saklatvala managed to get letters of protest sent to Bridgeman, from internees on 'C' wing of Dublin's Mountjoy Prison, published in the left-wing *Daily Herald* under the headline: 'Deportees Challenge Home Secretary. Imprisoned Men Say Statements Are A Deliberate And Contemptible Falsehood.' Afterwards the deportations were ruled illegal by British courts and the UK government was forced to ask for the return of the internees 'with the exception of [those] …against whom criminal proceedings are contemplated'.[31]

Saklatvala continued to support the Irish anti-colonial cause through the many political organisations with which he was involved throughout the 1920s and 1930s. In November 1924, with his friend and fellow Battersea socialist, Arthur Field, he revived a moribund society, which had been active during the First World War called the East-West Circle. Its aim was to 'bring East and West together, and use efforts to thwart the imperialist spirit… so flagrantly apparent in England.[32] It was primarily a Communist-run group, with Saklatvala as president and Field its secretary. Art O'Brien was an active member and his influence is apparent from pamphlets appealing 'for subscription to a "Special November Collection of the Irish Language Fund" and a "Connemara Relief Fund"'[33] Kate O'Malley thinks 'it is more than likely that money raised for these particular collections ended up with Sinn Féin [the political wing of the Irish Republican Army].'[34]

O'Malley writes: 'Saklatvala by now had acquired a bit of a name for himself as an Irish supporter. In 1926 during a "mysterious two days visit" to London under an assumed name, Éamon de Valera was to attend a secret late-night meeting held at Saklatvala's home.'[35] This was shortly after the formation of the Fianna Fáil party in Ireland, and de Valera had been making increasing efforts to travel abroad and fundraise. MI5's Major Phillips told Scotland Yard about the meeting, about which one of their spies had told him.[36] Saklatvala's Irish political work was now not just at the grassroots but had reached an elite level.

One radical from another part of the colonial world who made contact with Saklatvala in 1924, in an association that linked India, Trinidad, Ireland and Britain, was a young Indian, Krishna Deonarine, who was then, at eighteen, the president of the San Fernando branch of the Trinidad Workingman's Association, which later became the Trinidad Labour Party. Deonarine was the grandson of a rebel who had taken part in the Revolt of 1857, and who had fled to Trinidad as an indentured labourer to escape the British vengeance then in progress.[37] Deonarine, who later renamed himself Adrian Cola Rienzi (1905-1972) after an Italian patriot of the renaissance (in part, perhaps to signal a departure from his brahmin status, perhaps to move more easily among African Creoles in the nascent working-class movement in Trinidad, or perhaps to enter the USA where he might pass as Spanish) wrote to Saklatvala. Later, he told the visiting British communist, Arthur Calder-Marshall, that they had engaged in a correspondence that swung him 'more to the left'.[38] Rienzi, while working to unite the ethnically divided working class in Trinidad, remained a staunch enthusiast for the anti-colonial struggle in India and was an office-holder in the Trinidad East Indian National Association. Committed as he was to inter-ethnic working-class unity, Rienzi was also concerned to bring a then educationally, economically and politically backward Indian community forward into the national mainstream in Trinidad.[39] It is easy to see why Saklatvala's dual commitments to the Indian national struggle and to working-class world revolution appealed to him.

In 1930, at Saklatvala's encouragement, Rienzi crossed the Atlantic, where he entered Trinity College, Dublin, to study and matriculate in law. In Ireland, Rienzi was active in the League Against Imperialism and deeply involved with abstentionist Sinn Féin; he toured Ireland drawing large crowds for his message of solidarity between colonised peoples in the anti-colonial struggle.[40] While in Ireland, Rienzi, according to Calder-Marshall, on Saklatvala's advice, applied for permission to visit India, but this was refused on the recommendation of the British Secret Service. In 1931, Rienzi entered Britain, where he met Saklatvala in person for the first time and according to his interview with Calder-Marshall deepened his friendship with him.[41] Rienzi remained in Britain until 1934, when he returned to Trinidad. In this period, on the evidence of Special Branch reports, Rienzi and Saklatvala were both involved in the League Against Imperialism (LAI) and jointly set up an Indian Independence League, which seems to have been chiefly concerned with Indian and Irish affairs. Rienzi was also connected to fellow Trinidadian George Padmore (1903-1959) in the activities of the Inter African Service Bureau [IASB][42]). In the year of Saklatvala's death, Rienzi played a crucial role in the trade union, working-class uprising in the oil-belt of South Trinidad, particularly when the oilfield workers' African Trinidadian leader, Uriah 'Buzz' Butler, had first to go into hiding and was then arrested and detained.[43] Later in life Rienzi returned to his Indian roots and also became a considerably less radical politician.[44] Nevertheless, his relationship with Saklatvala suggests that there are further areas of research into anti-imperialist connections in Britain worth investigating.

But if there was one cause to which Saklatvala constantly returned it was India. In parliament, he worked hard to express his views in ways that were pertinent to the Commons, highlighting the contradiction between the parliamentary myths of individual liberty and what was happening in India, or drawing attention to the stark contrasts between the privileges of MPs and the misery of mass Indian poverty. He ridiculed MPs when he told them:

> We are talking of the Indian Empire just in the same strain of common agreement, with that very placid attitude of mind and phraseology of speech as if we are discussing some matters relating to the renewal of furniture in the library or cooking utensils in the kitchen of the House of Commons... We are debating here as if the Bengal Ordinances were never promulgated, as if the shooting of Bombay operatives during the cotton strike had never taken place, as if a great strike by thousands of railway workers is not even now going on in the Punjab, with men starving... Is there a single man or woman today, is there a person in any country in Europe, in any of the backward countries, in the Balkan states, in any of the small nations which are not yet so fully developed as Great Britain, who would tolerate for one day a power so despotic and arbitrary as the Crown, under the Imperial system, is insisting upon enjoying in India?'[45]

A year later, Saklatvala again lashed out at British imperialism in the Commons: 'Your doings in India, which are of a hideous character... are going to be continued... getting hold of citizens and keeping them in prison without trial and without charge, holding them in bondage, ruling people under the name of civilisation and exploiting them industrially on miserable wages...'[46]

Palme Dutt recalled: 'On one occasion... when Gandhi was conducting his agitation against the salt tax, and it was the height of summer with MPs enjoying their favourite refreshment on the terrace, Saklatvala took the occasion to explain to them: "Salt is not like strawberries and cream; no-one wants to gorge on it', and this brought home to them how bitter must be the poverty in which a tax on salt becomes a deadly burden on living conditions".'[47]

In 1926 Saklatvala decided to go on a political tour of India, to coincide with increased communist agitation in the country. He explained, in a letter to the *Daily Herald*: 'I'm not going on any idle holiday. I am going to make another great effort from the Indian end to pull the two working-class brotherhoods together.' He appealed to the labour movement for active help: 'Every ounce of goodwill and encouragement from individuals and organisations of all types in the British labour movement is needed, and I appeal to you all to send me a word of support, a voice of encouraging good cheer for the poor downtrodden Indian worker from every trade union and socialist branch...'[48]

The British government were very uneasy about Saklatvala's proposed visit. They delayed issuing his passport on the pretext they were 'consulting the government of India'. It was only after a strongly-worded letter from the MP to the prime minister, Stanley Baldwin, that his passport was released. Saklatvala demanded that Baldwin should stop interfering with the 'legitimate functions and duties' of a Member of Parliament, who happened to belong to a party which 'your party may even hate or dread'.[49] It was an interference which smacked of the occasion in 1925 when he had been refused entry to the USA as part of an Inter-Parliamentary Union delegation of 41 MPs.

Saklatvala's visit to India finally began when he arrived in Bombay aboard the P&O steam ship *Razmak* on 14 January 1927. He had an enthusiastic welcome from most sections of the Indian nationalist movement. In a symbolic gesture, he laid all the welcoming garlands he received on arrival in Bombay at the statue of Dadabhai Naoroji, the first Indian MP in the British parliament. While many people in the Congress leadership were hesitant to become involved with Saklatvala because of his prominent communist affiliations, Indian nationalists in general saw him as a symbol of their beleaguered country's prestige. He was a member of the British parliament fighting for them. So, when he arrived he was praised to the skies as a great anti-imperialist champion.[50]

However, as part of the communist current that believed in radicalising and orientating Indian nationalism leftwards, Saklatvala's presence greatly alarmed the authorities, especially the British government who, at the time, were obsessed with what they perceived as the communist threat. Reports on communist activity were a common feature at cabinet meetings. The Foreign Office wanted the government to devise a way of banning all communists from entering India.[51] Some still slipped into the country, most prominently the British communist trades unionists Philip Spratt and Ben Bradley, who played a key role in setting up the Communist Party of India. Both were among those prosecuted in the famous Meerut Conspiracy trial discussed in more detail below.[52]

According to the Indian news magazine *Blitz*, Saklatvala was pursued by the secret police during his stay in India, though they did not dare to hinder him.

Lord Birkenhead, the secretary of state for India, sent the following revealing message to the viceroy on 3 February: 'While I was away Saklatvala was given permission to go to India. I do not quarrel with the decision to grant him a visa for India, but I do hope you will not scruple to act at once if his activities become really mischievous.'[53] There was another frantic telegram from the secretary of state to the viceroy a month later complaining that reports of Saklatvala's speeches were 'giving rise to opinion here that he has greater license in India than he would be allowed in this country. The secret dispatch went on: 'I hope you are watching closely and will not hesitate to act if you think possible. I have already assured you of my full support.'[54]

The main focus of Saklatvala's speech-making was the need for trades unions and for a peasant organisation. He used every opportunity to spread the word about communism, a dangerous thing to do in the light of recent criminal prosecutions of activists in India by the British government. Only a few years earlier the first Labour government had authorised the prosecution of some communist leaders in the Kanpur Bolshevik Conspiracy Case,[55] and in 1924 three men – Shripad Amrit Dange, Shaukat Usmani and Muzaffar Ahmed – were each jailed for four years.

The fear of the colonial authorities over the spread of communist influence in India was compounded by their knowledge that the country was regarded as a key location for the spread of world revolution by the Soviet leadership. Not long after the Russian revolution, a top Soviet propagandist, K. Troyanovsky, had written that, 'if Russia is justly considered the citadel of world revolution, India can definitely be called the citadel of revolution in the east'.[56] Lenin, too, had written that the colonial and semi-colonial countries had become 'an active factor in world politics and in the revolutionary overthrow of imperialism… British India stands at the head of these countries, and there the revolution is growing in proportion, on the one hand, to the rise in the industrial and railway workers' proletariat and, on the other, to the increase in the bestial terror of the British.'[57]

According to historian E. H. Carr, 'the importance attached to India in these early pronouncements was due partly to the fact that it appeared to be the Achilles heel of the most powerful capitalist country, but partly also to profounder causes. India was the colonial country where native capital, stimulated by European tuition, had advanced furthest in the process of industrial development.'[58]

Given that he spoke so plainly, it was not surprising that Saklatvala's presence was not welcomed by those Indians who had accommodated themselves to British rule. Thus, though Saklatvala was treated to civic receptions by several of the big municipal corporations, the vote to accord him such an honour was frequently hotly contested. In several municipalities, including his home town of Mumbai, Saklatvala was denied an official welcome by a vote of the municipality. In Mumbai in particular, the influence of the English and subservient Anglo-Indians was strong. It was only after Saklatvala's death that the Bombay Municipality saw fit to honour him by closing their businesses for a day as a mark of respect. Nonetheless, on his 1927 visit, a group calling themselves Bombay Citizens issued a touching welcome on 24 January: 'Brother, though you were born in wealthy surroundings, you have been from your very youth a true friend of the poor, the suffering and the sorrowing.'[59]

But while Saklatvala called for the primacy of the workers' struggle within the movement for Indian independence, his position was far from sectarian. He made a heartfelt appeal for communal unity between Hindus and Muslims and urged the left to work within the Congress Party. This was consistent with Lenin's advocacy of an alliance of communists with bourgeois-nationalist movements in the oppressed nations, but it put Saklatvala in direct conflict with the Comintern's most influential person on India, M. N. Roy, himself an Indian. The British Communist Party indeed received a complaint from Roy who said Saklatvala was hobnobbing with all sorts of Indians who were not revolutionaries. But nothing was done about it because, following the adoption of Lenin's arguments, the Comintern had made the Indian National Congress the focus of their policy for India and Roy was eclipsed. In this respect, Saklatvala's attitude to Congress was very similar to his earlier ILP position on the British Labour Party – that communists should get inside it and win over the best elements to socialism – rather than to his eventual position of unremitting sectarian hostility to the Labour Party, as discussed more fully in Chapter Five.

The truth was that Saklatvala was anything but uncritical of the 'bourgeois Congress leaders', among whom he included lawyer Mohand Karamchand Gandhi, who had eliminated from the party the revolutionary politics of his friend B. G. Tilak, a leader of the left in Congress. During his 1927 tour of India, Saklatvala declared himself, at a meeting in Mumbai, 'a Tilakite extremist'. What he wanted was the communist way. 'Workers of the world, let us unite together and break our chains and do not let Round Table Conferences and peace conferences; and imperialist conferences add stronger links to the chains round the workers and peasants.'[60]

Saklatvala chose a Congress mass rally in the Gujarat State capital of Ahmedabad to boldly criticise the programme of the party: 'Awake your peasantry from slumber,' he urged those present. He outlined the history of Congress and said the party had made a grave error, from its inception, of not setting a definite goal. The result was that everyone was defining *swaraj*, the movement for national independence, in their own way. The Congress must now embrace workers, peasants and villagers. They must tell them about their political rights and thereby create a peasants' party. He told them:

> You will never get freedom if you do not work with the village folk...
> If Gandhiji had taken the help of labourers and peasants, the boycott of foreign cloth and titles would have been successful... Awake your peasantry, your labourers and you will get a new strength, new vigour and you will find out a way which will bring your freedom and thus you will attain your goal for which you are pining for years.[61]

On the eve of his departure from India, Saklatvala made perhaps the most controversial speech of his tour. In it he called for the peasants and workers to rally round the Congress. He said his trip to India had convinced him that, despite the confusion and differences which existed, Congress was the best way forward.

> All must get into the Congress whatever might be their differences and exchange their views with one another. It was stupid to remain aloof and grumble... We should have a strong and united National Congress, representative of all the classes and interests. Nothing can be national in India if the peasants and workers are not in it for they form the largest majority.[62]

The left-wing Indian historian, Panchanan Saha, who wrote a short biography of Saklatvala, notes that his 'open appeal to the newly-emerged radicals to work inside the Congress was not accepted by many leftists. Unfortunately the leftist circle was then suffering from sectarianism.' Saha records how one veteran leader, Hasrat Mohani, claimed Saklatvala had become a 'Congress victim'. Mohani said:

> The very fact that he had begun to address as comrades the Ali brothers, who had recently exposed themselves as anti-proletariat at Gauhati, and Mahatma Gandhi, who thanked God, because of whom the independence resolution in the Congress was defeated, was sure proof that he was being all through deceived by a cleverly hatched up conspiracy of so-called leaders of the Congress which today had gone into the hands of those who did not care a bit to better the conditions of those whose sole cause Saklatvala stood to espouse... Saklatvala says the swarajist programme was the best for the country. Saklatvala must know only if he took care to meet those who worked with the masses that the swarajists were far removed from any activity really beneficial to the masses.[63]

This was a caricature of Saklatvala's position, which was rather that maximum unity was necessary in the struggle against imperialism and this could best be achieved through the Congress. But, at the same time, an ideological struggle had to be waged in that party for communism.

Just how little Saklatvala was a 'Congress victim' can be seen from the correspondence he began with Gandhi during his visit, a correspondence which is reproduced as an appendix to this book. Saklatvala began this debate when he published an open letter criticising the Mahatma's policies. They then exchanged several letters between March and July 1927. The correspondence began in a friendly vein but became increasingly bitter. Saklatvala wrote on 8 March 1927: 'We are both erratic enough to permit each other to be rude in order to freely express oneself correctly, instead of getting lost in artificiality of phraseology.' Gandhi acknowledged that Saklatvala's sincerity was 'transparent', but began with the frank reply on 17 March 1927 that: 'We do stand at opposite poles'.

Saklatvala insisted that the 'Great Mahatma' should abandon his opposition to the industrialisation of India as symbolised by his advocacy of *khaddar,* the spinning of cotton by self-reliant peasants. Gandhi should also support strikes and mass demonstrations against colonial rule. Saklatvala's view was that *khaddar* was 'only a supplementary economic weapon not a political weapon'. Furthermore, Saklatvala took the orthodox communist view of the time that Gandhi's notion of class harmony, that there should be a consensual arrangement between the different classes, was no more than a policy of 'class collaboration' which would be to the disadvantage of workers and the poor.

Gandhi replied by saying that *khaddar*, apart from being able to feed India's villagers, was a revolutionary idea because it was based on peasants organising together. For Gandhi the important thing about such peaceful organisation was that it involved millions of people in a traditional cooperative activity. In his view, it was not possible to give calls for strikes and mobilisations on the streets in each of India's individual states. What was needed was a network of alignments all over the country. For him, *khaddar*, based on villagers scattered all over India, was that network. He argued that, 'if cooking required this kind of organisation, then I would say cooking is the most revolutionary method of struggle'.

In keeping with other international communists, Saklatvala was particularly critical of Gandhi for calling off the mass non-cooperation movement in the same year it had been launched. The pretext for the climb-down was an explosion of violence at Chouri Choura in 1921 when a mob set fire to a police station. Leftists viewed Gandhi's action as the Indian equivalent of the TUC General Council calling off the General Strike in 1926. But the Mahatma defended the decision. He said that if he had not withdrawn, the state would have been stronger and used even greater repression. Instead, the state was weaker because of the tactical retreat and his movement could live to fight another day.

Saklatvala and Gandhi met at Nagpur. The *Amrita Bazar Patrika* publication reported:

Saklatvala declared himself against charkha, the spinning wheel, and khaddar – both of them representing a symbolic opposition to industrialisation – but the Mahatma advised him to go to England with a charkha to educate public opinion on India. Saklatvala, naturally, could not agree with this but the Mahatma insisted. Saklatvala wanted Gandhiji to help in organising the workers and peasants in the country. But Gandhiji replied that the first need for swaraj was a more liberal use of khaddar and charkha.[64]

Saklatvala's analysis of what was needed betrayed a simplistic belief that European Marxist theory, based on the need to mobilise industrial workers against capitalism, was applicable to an overwhelmingly peasant country like India. As the Indian academic Bhagwan Singh Josh has argued, most revolutions in the 20th century have occurred in backward countries where the state was rooted not in any kind of parliamentary framework but in authoritarianism. According to Josh, this applied to Russia, China, Cuba and Vietnam. Anywhere where the state was rooted in a form of constitutional democracy, the communists have remained on the periphery. Josh argues, contrary to Saklatvala's perception of India, that:

> ...the British colonial state in India was much closer to a European kind of state, rather than the Soviet absolutist state. And, in this regard, it was a state rooted in limited civil liberties... rooted by a parliamentary democracy and managed from Britain...
>
> Now this is the point which Gandhi constantly emphasised, the British state in India rules the country not only with the help of arms and the police, it rules with the help and consent of the Indian people. And there, so long as the Indian people's consent is not withdrawn from the state, the state cannot be fought with the help of arms...
>
> And Gandhi's reading was that this kind of state, which is the most modern bourgeois state form, cannot be smashed with the help of arms... This is the state in which, if you use armed opposition to it, you give an opportunity to the state to crush it.
>
> So, neither the state can be opposed through constitutional means, because it will absorb any movement by making concessions to it; neither can the state be smashed directly the way the Russian revolution was organised, because the state is too powerful – armed to the teeth and bound to crush such a movement... Therefore he put forward a new strategy, what he called non-constitutionalist and non-insurrectionist... based on a mass movement. And the key role of that strategy was non-violence'.[65]

Perhaps there was in Saklatvala's failure to see the logic of Gandhi's strategy in building a 'non-violent' movement based on 'non-co-operation', an impatience with the moral/cultural dimensions of Gandhi's appeal to a traditionally-minded peasantry. Saklatvala clearly regarded much of the symbolism of Gandhi's crusade as backward-looking. He mocked, for instance, Gandhi's scantily-clad asceticism: 'You are not teaching people to wear more clothes than before, your own example would rather lead them to wear less. At the same time you are teaching more people to produce clothes...'

Gandhi was just as scathing in response: '"Comrade" Saklatvala swears by the modern rush. I wholeheartedly detest this mad desire to destroy distance and time, to increase animal appetites and go to the ends of the earth in search of their satisfaction. If modern civilisation stands for all this, and I have understood it to do so, I call it satanic, and with it the present system of government, its best exponent.'

The Black Marxist C.L.R. James, with the advantage of hindsight, had a clear view of who was right and who was wrong in this dispute over tactics. He wrote: 'Gandhi introduced a new dimension into the technique of mass struggle for national independence and perhaps for more.' James described Gandhi's 'genius' as 'one of the greatest of our time'.[66]

What emerged from the Gandhi correspondence was that it was the Mahatma not the Comrade who had a more sophisticated view of the Indian state. Saklatvala, like Roy, suffered in his political judgement as a result of having lived away from India for a long period. Saklatvala's revolutionary vanguard strategy could only have worked if the British colonial administration had been universally detested, and it was not. Some consent and much collaboration were the cornerstones of the Raj. So the system, contended Gandhi, could only be defeated by a complex network of non-cooperation. This was the gradualist approach loathed by socialist revolutionaries. By contrast, Saklatvala envisioned a volcanic eruption of the working class which would destroy British rule.

Yet if Gandhi's view of strategy was subtler, Saklatvala's analysis of the way 'class collaboration' suited the interests of the big Indian landlords and business class has surely been borne out first by the nature of Congress rule in the decades after independence and more recently by the emergence of the Modi-led populist-capitalist Bharatiya Janata Party (BJP) with its street lieutenants in the quasi-fascist Rashtriya Swayamsevak Sangh (RSS) and the abandonment of state secularism for an exclusive Hindu nationalism.

If, too, a little envy crept into the bitter exchange between the two politicians – according to his daughter Sehri, Saklatvala would have liked to have had a following the size of Gandhi's – Saklatvala's letters are not without insight into Gandhi's deficiencies, particularly the mystical cult of the Mahatma. He chided Gandhi: 'If your purpose is to give your share in the national and political work, your approach to the people should be on terms of absolute equality... From this point of view you must stop allowing people to address you as Mahatma.' (Mahatma was translated as the 'Great Soul' or 'Saintly One', as an honorific title for a person revered for outstanding spiritual qualities.) Saklatvala added: 'You are preparing the country not for mass civil disobedience but for servile obedience and for a belief that there are superior persons on the earth and Mahatmas in this life when in this country the white man's prestige is already a dangerous obstacle in our way.'[67]

Three years later, in an article, titled 'Who is this Gandhi?', Saklatvala stepped up his attack. He accused the Mahatma of recruiting Indians for the British army during the Boer War and First World War. He said, '…at a Recruiting Meeting at Kaira in 1916 he exhorted every Indian to join the British Army, and he openly declared that India's liberty was to be won on the battlefields of Belgium murdering the Germans.'[68] Was this true? Saklatvala meant it as a damning indictment both of the 'non-violent' Mahatma and of the contradictions in his attitude to the Empire. Certainly Gandhi offered the services of the Indian community in England to the government at the outbreak of the First World War to 'share the responsibilities of the membership of the Empire'. As a result, the Indian Voluntary Aid Contingent was formed to support the war effort in England. But the purpose of the group was not combat. As Gandhi protested: 'Nor do I consider it to be wrong to have offered during the late war services of my companions and myself, under my then convictions, as ambulancemen.'[69]

According to Saklatvala, Gandhi used 'revolutionary phraseology and religious slogans' to advance himself, but was 'really shuddering at the thought of a Communist State. His ideal is a Dominion under British guns with Gandhi as the new 'General Smuts' (the South African Boer leader who collaborated with the British). As an example of how Gandhi had neglected the 'revolutionary side' in his campaign against the salt tax, Saklatvala claimed:

> He does not call upon millions of Indian villagers to expel the Salt Police from their villages and he does not call upon his own friends, the big Indian salt manufacturers, to refuse to pay the taxes and to go to prison. He does not call upon his propertied and mill-owning friends to refuse to pay income tax and have their property confiscated. He does not support the railway strikers and textile strikers who were shot down, and his Congress Committee has not got a word of praise for the Indian troops at Peshawar who practised true non-violence and refused to shoot down innocent people wanting their liberty from a foreign occupier of their country. By knowing the past of Gandhi… we shall… be able to guess his future activities.
>
> …Some people think that because Gandhi and some of his followers are put in prison, and because they use strong words, therefore they will never again become friends of the British Empire. This is all nonsense. British Imperialists have been able to win back in the past much stronger fighters, such as General Botha and General Smuts…
>
> …There is a great warfare, more cruel than that waged with firearms and bullets, between rich and the poor all over the world. Almost all of our leading politicians, including Mr Gandhi, do not care for Indian labourers.[70]

The references to General Smuts connect to Saklatvala's criticism of Gandhi's role as a lawyer in South Africa and the charge that he pursued only the interests of Indians and expressed views about the African majority that were racist, a charge that is further explored in Chapter Six.

Back in England, Saklatvala had the ironic experience of being attacked by some people who would not normally have had a good word for Gandhi – for his criticisms of the Mahatma, which, they said, had made him widely unpopular. Yet it is evident that the authorities felt the trip had made a big enough impact politically for them to want to ensure nothing like it happened again. After Saklatvala's return to Britain, he was banned from ever going back to India. The Foreign Office wrote to him: 'With reference to the endorsement of your passport granted on 21 December 1926, I am directed by Sir Austen Chamberlain (the foreign secretary) to inform you that the validity of your passport for India has been cancelled.'

Confidential correspondence shows the Government was nervous about the potential backlash against their brazen move. Minister for India, Lord Birkenhead wrote to the viceroy: 'There was some difficulty in persuading the Foreign Office to issue the letter, their hesitation being based upon the apprehension that the action proposed conflicted with the principle, which is generally accepted, that no country can refuse to accept back one of its own inhabitants if his nationality is not in doubt.'[71] The government used the spurious argument that Saklatvala had had 'no connection' with India for nearly twenty years and regarded himself as a 'fully domiciled British subject' and the Foreign Office conceded to granting the ban, chiefly because of Saklatvala's behaviour during the tour. He had earlier been refused entry to Egypt en route to India. That was because of his support for the Egyptian national liberation movement.

When the Labour Party returned to office in 1929, it might have been expected that the ban would be lifted. But, to their shame, William Wedgewood Benn, secretary of state for India (the late Tony Benn's father), and Arthur Henderson, foreign secretary and Saklatvala's Labour Party adversary, made sure it stayed in place. The Indian National Congress had invited their London Branch to be represented at their Congress in 1929 and Saklatvala was selected to be the representative. He wrote to the new Labour foreign secretary, 'I imagine that the cancellation of the endorsement has now been rescinded, but I wish to be quite sure about this and perhaps you will arrange for me to have an official confirmation'.[72]

Five days later, the Indian National Congress (London Branch) wrote in similar terms to Henderson. The reply they received should not have been a surprise, given Labour's actual policies on India when they were last in power. The Foreign Office passed the buck to the India Office who informed the Congress: 'I am directed by Mr Secretary Benn to state that he is not prepared at the present time to agree to the grant of an endorsement for India on Mr Saklatvala's passport.'[73]

C.V. Vakil, an officer of the London branch of the Congress, wrote back in strong terms:

> Your letter in the first place gives us a clear proof the present Labour Government's policy of repression and suppression is a faithful continuity of the old Imperialist policy of your predecessors, regardless of any consideration of human rights or fair play... The present political situation has been created by your Government working in close unity with Mr Baldwin, Lord Irwin and the European Association of Calcutta on the one hand and Mr Lansbury, Mr Brockway and Mr Maxton [left-wing MPs] on the other playing a dramatic party game as if there is a fundamental difference between your policy and that of your predecessors.

This prompted a curt response from the Foreign Office. 'I am directed by Mr Secretary Henderson to state that the decision conveyed to you... must be regarded as final.'

Saklatvala continued the war of words in a letter of 18 November, 1929 to Henderson:

> This matter raises important political and personal considerations which I think I ought to put before you in some detail, having regard to the startling decision of a Labour Secretary of State. In the first place, there is no doubt, in the control of passports and visas, a weapon in the hands of governments to rid themselves of persons whom or whose views they do not like. That control has long been the subject of serious criticism by the Labour Party and even more by the Party of which Mr Wedgwood Benn was recently a member [the Liberals].
>
> This control has in the past exceeded any fair or reasonable limits but it has never, so far as I am aware, been used to prevent a man from visiting his own country and being practically kept in exile... I have relatives in India whom I have always been anxious to visit... While I have been in this country some of these have died – expressing regret they have not seen me; others are still alive – some in advanced years and are anxious to see me... Upon these perhaps sentimental, but nonetheless human grounds, this embargo is a monstrous inhumanity.[74]

There were also protests from the labour movement, but they fell on deaf ears. The reaction of the Birmingham City branch of the ILP was typical. They sent the following resolution to Henderson: 'That the refusal of the Labour Government to grant permission to Mr Saklatvala to visit his native land – India – is an outrage on the principles of political liberty.'

In parliament, a leading Liberal, Sir Geoffrey Shakespeare, who had been David Lloyd George's private secretary, demanded to know whether the Secretary of State for India would withdraw the Saklatvala ban. He asked, pointedly: 'Does not the Right Honourable Gentleman think it extremely harsh to prevent an ex-Member of Parliament going back to his native land, and is he not rebuked by the echoes of his own speeches on the subject?' Wedgwood Benn replied: 'I do not like doing it at all, but I have to consider a very delicate situation in India.'[75] His son, Tony Benn, told the author that his father was a passionate advocate of Indian and Irish independence, 'But he was caught up in a ghastly imperialist mode.'

Saklatvala had encountered similar difficulties earlier in the year. He was detained at Ostend and refused admission to Belgium in January on his way to a meeting of the League Against Imperialism in Germany.

Despite the obstacles put in his way, there was no let up in Saklatvala's work for the cause of Indian independence. The British Government was using every device it could think of to thwart independence. One of these was the notorious 'Simon Commission'. The Viceroy of India, Lord Irwin, announced its formation on 8 November 1927. The commission's brief was to look at possible 'reforms'. But the choice of a right-wing Liberal, Sir John Simon, as its president was not a good sign. The former Liberal home secretary and attorney general had already earned his anti-working-class credentials, pressing the government in 1926 to rule that the General Strike was 'illegal'.

Saklatvala's chief opponent in parliament, the government's minister for India, Lord Winterton, on 25 November, moved the resolution supporting the appointment of the 'Indian Statutory Commission'. In the Commons, Saklatvala said the commission was 'a farce':

> The issue is perfectly clear: Is Great Britain determined to carry on an antiquated, savage system of rule of another country and another people, or is Great Britain prepared to let the people of every country manage their own affairs in a friendly way or even a hostile way if they choose so to do?
>
> The early appointment of the Commission does not get rid of the belief that the only purpose of the Government is to put a hypocritical cloak on the system of a tyranny that exists in India – a tyranny which, in the name of commonsense and Justice, ought to be abolished as quickly as possible.

Saklatvala suggested instead the appointment of 'an independent Commission composed entirely of Indians'. He said: 'Let those Indians come over to this country and cross-examine you and listen to your witnesses and advise this House as to what is the exact position.'[76] But though the *Daily News*, *Manchester Guardian* and *Westminster Gazette* took up Saklatvala's point about the non-inclusion of Indians, the Simon Commission went ahead to general British political approval. The parliamentary Labour Party, led by Ramsay MacDonald, failed to support Saklatvala, not for the first time in defiance of the position taken by their National Executive Committee. MacDonald's capitulation handed the Government a gift because they had admitted privately that they would not go ahead if Labour withdrew from the commission. Nevertheless, a handful of left-wing MPs such as George Buchanan, Josiah Wedgwood, Richard Wallhead and Ellen Wilkinson spoke in favour of Saklatvala's stand. Wedgwood said, 'the use to which they (the Government) intend to put this measure is likely to do more harm to Anglo-Indian relations than anything... (the) Government have yet done'. He added, 'we should do much better in refusing to appoint any such Commission to go into affairs in India until we have sure and certain knowledge that Indian representatives in their Assembly welcome this change in the Government Act of India'. Buchanan, who seconded Saklatvala's amendment despite Labour's 'almost unanimous wish... that the Bill should be passed', suspected the Government wanted 'its friends... its lackeys' on the Commission.[77] Saklatvala's amendment read: 'That the House resolves to invite Pandit Motilal Nehru to the Bar of the House to explain Indian sentiments and guide the House as provided in the preamble of the Government of India Act 1919, before concurring in submission to His Majesty, of the names of persons.' The amendment was overruled by the Speaker without discussion and Winterton's motion passed.

The future prime minister Clement Attlee represented Labour on the Simon Commission. At the party conference in October 1927, George Lansbury proposed a motion in favour of 'dominion' status for India.[78] Though this did not go far enough for Indian leaders such as Nehru and certainly not for Saklatvala, Labour considered themselves quite radical when they passed it.

In India, two months later, the Congress Party held their annual meeting in Madras. Its president, K. Iyengar, got the conference to pass a motion in favour of boycotting the Simon Commission. A resolution proposed by Nehru which demanded full Indian independence – a rejection of dominion status – was also successful. Just as significantly, delegates resolved that India should not be a part of any future war involving Britain.

In 1928, the year after Saklatvala's three-month speaking tour of India, there was a massive strike by textile workers in Bombay who were refusing to take a wage cut. The strike ended in victory, but in March 1929, at the behest of the Bombay Government, which wanted to crush the emergence of strong organised labour, 31 people were arrested, including the leaders of the Girni Kamgar (Mill workers) union involved in the strike. Since the government was anxious not to be seen as anti-trade union, thereby risking further demonstrations, they presented the case as being about communist insurrection. As mentioned above, they held the trial of the 31, including two British Communist Party members, Philip Spratt and Ben Bradley, at Meerut – hundreds of miles from Bombay. The case became an international *cause celebre*. In Britain, Meerut Defence Committees sprang up and

Saklatvala played a leading role promoting them. The League Against Imperialism, the Worker's Welfare League of India, the Meerut Trade Union Defence Committee and the Meerut Prisoners' Release Committee all had Saklatvala as a prominent speaker, and his daughter Sehri records his tireless activities in travelling throughout the country addressing meetings and raising money for the Meerut defendants. Even after losing his parliamentary seat, there was no let-up in his activities or in the demand for him as a speaker. In 1932, as the trial was coming to an end, The League Against Imperialism held a rally attended by more than 500 people at which Saklatvala was one of the main speakers. At the end of the trial savage sentences ranging from transportation to life for one of the union leaders, Muzzafar Ahmed, to three years rigorous imprisonment were handed down. This was a trial that took place while a Labour government was in power and Saklatvala wrote an article published in the *Sunday Worker*[79] which accused Labour MPs of continuing 'the time-honoured Tory policy of British imperialism, accompanied by all its bloodshed and murder, through political and economic strangulation, but all done in the garb and cloak of Socialist benevolence...' When the verdicts were announced, Saklatvala said:

> By savage and appalling sentences after a monstrous trial, the British Raj in India has proclaimed, to her 350 million conquered slaves, that henceforth the study of the mighty triumph of Communism in the USSR, which in seven brief years has put to shame the inhuman results of a hundred and fifty years of British rule in India, will be visited upon the heads of Communists in India with a revengeful ruthlessness.[80]

After the trial a worldwide campaign against the sentences continued and in 1933 all the sentences, though still severe, were much reduced. Saklatvala was present at Victoria Station to welcome back Ben Bradley, one of the British defendants, after his release.

Although Saklatvala never ceased in his active support of Indian independence, after he was banned from returning and was no longer an MP, his influence began to wane even within the communist movement. A contemporary, M. R. Masani noted: 'his special position *vis a vis* India was undermined and Rajani Palme Dutt emerged as the rising star in the firmament'.[81] Palme Dutt[82] has been described as a chief theoretician of the British Communist Party from their foundation. From 1919 to 1922 he was international secretary of the Labour Research Department, an influential left-wing think-tank. He had been a member of the ILP, but left it to form the Communist Party. In 1921 he started the party's theoretical journal, *Labour Monthly*, which he edited for more than fifty years. From 1936 to 1938 he was editor of the party's official organ, *The Daily Worker*.

He was elected to the Communist Party's central committee in 1922 and continued to serve on it until the mid-1960s. He rose to vice-chairman of the party and head of their international section. From the time the Indian Communist Party was founded in 1925, Palme Dutt performed for it the same role of chief ideologue as he did for the British party.

It is suggested there was rivalry between Saklatvala and Palme Dutt, who was twenty-two years Saklatvala's junior – each one wanting to be the party's principal voice on Indian independence. Some people believe that it was this rivalry that resulted in Saklatvala being dropped from the central committee by supporters of the much more powerful Palme Dutt in 1929. But whatever the disputes, Palme Dutt praised Saklatvala highly after he died, as quoted in Chapter Seven.

CHAPTER 5

SAKLATVALA AND THE THIRD INTERNATIONAL

In 1921 Saklatvala broke with the Independent Labour Party and joined the newly-formed Communist Party of Great Britain. It was a major turning point in his political development. He left behind him the belief that liberal reformism could free working-class people in Britain and India. For Saklatvala, the ILP was a failure because it did not live up to his internationalist vision of a political party.

Yet it would be a mistake to suppose that Saklatvala leaped to join the newly-formed Communist Party. In fact, although he was for the 'rapid establishment of a strong Communist Party in Great Britain' he was strongly opposed to the actions of those who left the ILP to join it on the ground that the left-wing in the ILP could 'ill afford to give away our fighters'.[1] What he wanted was a broad revolutionary movement united through its affiliation to the Third International (the Moscow-based worldwide organisation of communist parties who adhered to the Bolshevik model). However, though Saklatvala's City of London branch of the ILP and, initially, the Scottish and Welsh divisions were in favour, and though the 1920 ILP National Conference voted to withdraw from the discredited Second International and begin to negotiate over conditions for entry to the Third International, the insistence of the Third International's existing leadership on absolute acceptance of its twenty-one principles was always going to be a barrier to ILP membership. These principles included commitment to the Soviet system, the central role of armed struggle in the overthrow of the capitalist state, and the dictatorship of the proletariat – principles which were anathema to the ILP's reformism, pacifism and commitment to democratic forms. At the 1921 National Conference, not only was the motion for affiliation to the Third International crushed by 521 to 97 votes, but the left was heavily defeated in elections for National Council positions. In the debate, Saklatvala said the ILP was being hypocritical. How could they ask the British government to 'enter into closer political and trading relations with the Russian government when they said that for socialist purposes their own representatives must not sit round a table with the Soviet representatives or enter an International with them?'.[2]

At this point, according to the communist leader Willie Gallagher, Saklatvala left the party 'at the head of a group of determined revolutionaries'. [3] This was not quite true, for though some ILP left-wingers, perhaps two hundred, immediately left to join the Communist Party, Saklatvala was not among them, though the Police Special Branch papers also assert that Saklatvala was the leader of the group leaving to join the communists. They also claimed that he had received '£50 from Theodore Rothstein', Lenin's representative in Britain to force a change in the Executive of the ILP.[4] Was this their idea of Moscow gold? For a time Saklatvala continued work in the City of London Branch, proposing that it dissolve itself and reform as the City of London Socialist Society. This was defeated and when at a later meeting his much more limited proposal (to suspend payment of affiliation fees to the National and Divisional bodies of the ILP until negotiations with the Third International were resumed) was defeated, he regretfully resigned saying that it gave him 'considerable pain to cut myself off from the associateship of the comrades of this branch.' Even then it was not until some three months later that Saklatvala joined the Communist Party. At this stage, at least, in his political journey, and as his activities in Battersea indicate, Saklatvala appears to have been concerned with avoiding any slide into sectarian politics. He made it clear in a letter he wrote to the ILP newspaper, *The Labour Leader*, published on 10 June 1921, that his reasons for leaving the party were not merely upon the issue of their refusal to join the Third International. It was more. He wrote:

> I fail to see any resolution carried there [at the 1921 Southport Conference] as any measure of Socialism... It also appears to me that this was not a chance voting at a single conference, but it is the new life on which ILP members are launching out, namely of seeking municipal and parliamentary advantages at the sacrifice of true Socialism...[5]

The split was bitter. The Labour Party maintained its attachment to the Second International, which embraced Social Democracy, and, as discussed in the next chapter, under pressure from German, American and South African socialists had reactionary policies on Black rights and anti-imperialism. These divisions affected even those who shared the same international commitments. Thus Fenner Brockway, the Indian-born English pacifist who was to become the ILP leader, though an avowed anti-imperialist and Indian home-ruler, never worked with Saklatvala. He said later: 'I think it's possible that, as an office-bearer of the ILP, I held back under the influence of those among the leaders of the party who didn't want close association with the Communists. It was then an issue of intense emotion in the ILP.'[6] Nonetheless, in a tribute to Saklatvala, one member of the ILP described him as 'a very brave and unconventional spirit... an incomparable orator,'[7] and left-wingers who stayed on as members of the

ILP tried hard to get Saklatvala to break with the Communist Party. One of them told his wife: 'Perhaps, had I been an Indian, I should have seen in Moscow an ally whereas, being British, I recognised in the latter only an implacable enemy to be fought to the finish! I never thought of him (Saklatvala) as, and always used to chaff him that he was, no real Communist. He was a great Indian patriot, a proud bearer of a great Oriental tradition, a true Asiatic.'[8] It was, though, for this very reason that Saklatvala wanted a political base where he would get total support for the cause of Indian self-determination. His criticism of the ILP was that, though it fought on behalf of British workers, it did not attack the root of capitalist exploitation and failed to link the British working class with their counterparts abroad. Saklatvala observed sagely many years later: 'Imperialism is the acid test for all leaders and presumptive representatives of the working class. It is on the rock of imperialism that your so-called Labour leaders and ILP Socialists split.'[9]

Throughout his life he argued that India's oppression was clearly connected to British capitalists and their ability to exploit Indian workers through their privileged position within British imperial rule. He saw in the Russian revolution of 1917 a model for ending that dominance. According to his Indian biographer, Panchanan Saha, he saw the revolution as a precursor to a 'new civilisation – a new social order' which would, in the end, bring liberation to the exploited millions living under the heels of capitalism and imperialism.'[10]

Karl Marx had already made this connection in his analysis of the relationship between the fight for Black civil rights and the workers' struggle for socialism. One of the main reasons why V.I. Lenin broke away from the Second International was because he saw it as an organisation defending the privileges of white workers and the bourgeoisie against the colonies and Black people.

Saklatvala's view of communism, which he outlined in an address to the Battersea electors in 1923, had the same kind of moral basis: 'The fact is that individual ownership and control of industrial wealth is unnatural, is inhuman and has been grossly abused. All the religious founders and teachers of the East and West have warned the Nations against the worship of gold by individuals.'[11]

As discussed in Chapter Three, initially the break with the ILP and move to the Communist Party was not an obstacle to Saklatvala's work within the broad left-wing of the labour movement, or his adoption and election as an MP. In the period following the end of the 1914-18 war, the Labour Party, some of whose leaders had opposed the First World War, rode on the crest of a wave of working-class disenchantment after the Armistice. Demobbed soldiers, returning home from the war, had been promised a 'land fit for heroes', but the reality was very different. Poverty, bad housing and unemployment, which in December 1921, according to the government's own statistics, stood at 16.2%, was what awaited many of them. This percentage disguised the real figure, since it recorded only those covered by unemployed insurance. Many hundreds of thousands of people had to seek 'outdoor relief' from the Poor Law 'Guardians'. The peak figure was 1,065,000 in June 1922, and some were refused relief. Many conflicts erupted between socialists in local government and their national government opponents. In September 1921, for instance, thirty Labour councillors at Poplar in East London, including George Lansbury, were jailed for refusing to levy a rate for central bodies such as the police, in order to divert more of their resources to helping the unemployed and destitute.

In this climate, at the 1918 general election Labour challenged the Liberals as the main opposition party. A year later they made sweeping gains in the municipal elections. A police special branch report to the cabinet noted '…the danger lies in the fact that so many elected men and women are secretly pledged to smash the whole machinery of capitalism.'[12] The election of Labour MPs was frequently greeted by the singing of the Red Flag, and Mr Fred Shaw, for instance, who was returned for Huddersfield, stated that he was a 'Bolshevik without apology'.[13]

With the value of currency collapsing, capitalism appeared to be in deep crisis. The employers' response was to launch an attack on wage levels, against workers who were vulnerable as a result of the high levels of unemployment. Coal miners were the first to face an ultimatum from the employers in 1921: 'Take a drop in pay or lose your jobs'. They went on strike. As noted in Chapter Three, Saklatvala gave a rousing speech to a mass meeting at Battersea Town Hall organised in support of the miners by the local Trades Council, a few months before his selection as parliamentary candidate. He asked whether 'the masters [were] to be at liberty to treat employees as vermin and dirt', who could be controlled by ultimatums? The men expected their leaders not to produce explanations and excuses, they wanted results. They wanted to be led to victory. If they failed in that it was time they made room for others. [14] But the miners were not supported by the rail and transport unions, fellow members of the 'triple alliance', and they had to return to work defeated. Food was being rationed and there were hunger marches. There was an angry mood of disillusionment among the working class and in this situation the Marxist belief that capitalism was about to collapse had considerable support.

There was certainly alarm in the capitalist press. *The Times'* headlines screamed: 'Bolshevik Agents At Work Inciting the Unemployed in London', and went on to claim: '*The Times* have received confirmation that the turbulent minority of the unemployed in this country is being deliberately

exploited by the Third ('Red') International of Moscow (which is practically identical with the Soviet government), through the agency of a small
though very active group of agitators whose names are now known to the
police authorities in London.'[15] There was alarm, too, within the social
democratic wing of the labour movement. Right-wing Labour leaders,
including Herbert Morrison, raged against the likes of Lansbury for
'breaking the law'. In turn, aware of the uphill task they faced as a result of
the unending flow of hostile state propaganda, communists established the
People's Russian Information Bureau in 1918. Their aim was to help win
public support for the Soviet Union. As a founder member, Saklatvala was
an energetic propagandist for the bureau.

The Communist Party's 'united front' approach to the Labour Party and
the latter's non-revolutionary commitment to parliamentary democracy
was outlined in a letter Saklatvala was sent 10 months before he became an
MP. It was written by the acting national secretary of the Communist Party
on 10 January 1922, and it said: 'At the meeting of the Executive Committee
held last weekend, the question of the position of members of the Party
who may have been adopted as Labour Party Candidates in various
constituencies was considered, and a general instruction to these comrades
was drawn. In accordance with this instruction, I am directed to ask you to
go forward as a Labour Candidate, subject to the rule of the Party which
governs the relationships between the Party and candidates or elected
representatives.'[16]

The security service agent who had got hold of the letter commented:
'While communists in general and Saklatvala in particular have no faith in
Parliamentary machinery, it is part of their creed to work for the return of
a Labour Party Government as a stepping stone to the overthrow of the
Constitution and the introduction of the Soviet system.'[17]

In December 1924, Saklatvala proudly proclaimed to the House of
Commons: 'I represent a proper, well-organised, well-formed, and rather
too loudly acknowledged political party in this country now. I am not one
of those international Socialists who take offence at having friends in
Moscow, Berlin or Delhi. As a member of the International Communist
Party, I submit that our movement does extend from Moscow to Battersea,
and much beyond that.'[18]

Two years later, he explained, to the same audience of MPs, his reasons
for joining the Communist Party: 'I am the product of the teachings of the
British trade unions. I am a member of the Communist Party because,
rightly or wrongly, it honestly appears to me to be pointing the way through
which the objects laid down by the Labour Party are to be achieved.' He
went on: 'I at once admit that Communists are not infallible, and they make
mistakes. Sometimes they may do things in a clumsy and hasty way, but

these are only human and individual elements.'[19]

He was, though, always a loyal and enthusiastic supporter of the Soviet Union, and if he saw 'mistakes' he never commented on them. In 1923, he had gone with members of the CPGB's central committee to Moscow for crisis talks about the state of the British party.

It was his first visit to the country. He and fellow MP, Walton Newbold, had been invited to Moscow for a private meeting with members of the Communist International – 'more an order than an invitation' as his daughter described it, although she believes that her father was there to advise and discuss, as well as to take party orders, and he stated later that year that he had 'never received a single letter or telegraphic instruction from Moscow'. He took his wife with him. It is likely that the Communist Party wanted the British MP's help to try to gain a closer affiliation with the Labour Party. En route to Moscow he attended an international conference of MPs in Copenhagen, and a Special Branch report stated that he had received £500 from Communist International while in the city.[20]

This was Saklatvala's initiation to communism in Soviet Russia, and his daughter wrote that he was more impressed than her mother, who hated being parted from her children (they were accommodated by their Aunt Annie during their absence) and was horrified at the idea of children being put in a creche while their mothers worked. However, her husband gave her firm instructions not to express her views while they were the guests of Soviet Russia.

He went back four years later for a Congress of the Friends of the Soviet Union. There he delivered a speech on democracy which was closely monitored by the British authorities.[21] He told delegates: 'I sit in the Westminster Parliament making laws for India, and as an Indian I am the despised slave of that parliament.' Referring to his then (1927) banning from India, he complained that, 'under the orders of an autocratic and idiotic minister like Chamberlain (the Foreign Secretary), I am now told not to go back to my own country. That is parliamentary democracy.'

He praised the communist system. 'It is here where cultural development is not aimed at earning dividends, but is aimed at the development of the intellect of the child itself; where social order is not based on social hypocrisy and economic material gauge, but is based upon the free will of the men and women...'[22]

In electoral terms, the Communist Party reached its highest point in Britain in 1922, on the tide of the postwar working-class upsurge. Although the Conservatives won the 1922 General Election, Labour became the second largest party in parliament. Significantly, within the Labour vote there was a marked contrast between support for right-wing and left-wing candidates. In general, the militants with a class approach increased their vote while right-wingers saw their support tumble at the polls. For instance, Arthur Henderson, who later became Foreign Secretary, was defeated.[23] The seven communists and communist sympathisers who stood for parliament scored two wins: J. Walton Newbold, at Motherwell, in Scotland, a directly-elected communist and Saklatvala. Four of the party's candidates took second place, failing to win by 1,018, 744, 115 and 51 votes respectively. Never was the CPGB to return to that highpoint, not least because in the future party members would not be able to stand as 'official' or 'unofficial' Labour candidates – forcing the two parties to compete directly against each other at the polls.

The Communist Party issued a statement saying their two new MPs would 'cooperate with the Labour Party in every struggle against the capitalist parties and will not hesitate, when the Labour Party fails to carry through the struggle, to stand and fight alone for the interests of the working class'.

For the year between 1922 and 1923, when Saklatvala and Newbold were MPs, they both regularly attended meetings of the Communist Party's political bureau and executive committee where they received their instructions. James Klugmann, the party's official historian, commented: 'Here was an important point of principle. The right-wing Labour leaders always resisted the idea that their MPs should be subordinated to the decisions of the Labour Party Conference. The Parliamentary Labour Party was to be a law unto itself.'[24]

In the Commons, after Newbold's defeat in the 1923 and 1924 general elections, Saklatvala sat alone in the middle of the central Labour bench 'like a Daniel among the lions'. During his last years as MP, he was far from friendly towards his neighbours, dismissively referring to them as 'my comrades who aspire to be socialists'.[25] He admonished Labour, telling them 'diffused capitalism' was not socialism, singling out for most scorn the party's nationalisation policy. Even the Post Office run by them, he said, had hardly anything in common with socialism. In Saklatvala's view, communism was the only true socialism because it opposed any individual person owning land, property or industries. He was particularly critical of Labour's 1926 surtax proposals. He said it was no better than the government saying, 'We will square our consciences and call this socialism if you give us two shillings in the pound out of your robbery of the workers'.

He said Labour was just pretending while the capitalists laid their plans to keep the old system going. He denounced their bipartisan approach to the economy because it ensured a 'continuity of policy' no matter which party was in power. The communists, he said, 'represent the section of the working class that does not believe in saying at one time that your employers are your enemies, that individual capitalism is the source of all your evils, and yet that we should sit down with them, make friends and form a joint club so that these evils may disappear from time to time.'[26]

In a 40-minute bravura speech to the House of Commons in 1928, later reproduced by the CPGB as a pamphlet titled *Socialism and 'Labouralism'*, and reprinted as an appendix to this book, Saklatvala eloquently summarised his case against labourist social democracy:

> What is the real problem before the country as between Socialism and Capitalism? It is not merely the question of extending the field to a larger number of shareholders; it is a question of overthrowing the system of private ownership and introducing public ownership. It would become criminal for an individual to own land or houses or places of industry. Such a society would be quite a different society... it is futile and absurd to argue that the whole of the social structure of the nation would quietly remain what it was, and that the relationship of man to man within the State would continue to be what it was... (But) take the example of the Post Office or of the Broadcasting Corporation or the Municipal Tramways; the capitalist state of society has not been altered by merely widening the ownership. The position of the workers within these industries is absolutely the position of workers who are under the dictation of somebody not appointed by themselves. It is the capitalist system.

According to the *Daily News*, the case for Socialism was 'never so ably stated'.[27]

At the same time as Saklatvala's relationship with the Labour Party worsened, his position as a parliamentarian was not without challenge in the Communist Party, some of whose hardliners believed that entering parliament was a waste of time. Saklatvala supported Lenin's position that participation in the bourgeois electoral process was necessary both for the immediate defence of the working class and as one of the stages in the long term revolutionary struggle for political power.

In his pamphlet *Left-wing Communism: An Infantile Disorder*, which attacked the British ultra-left, Lenin wrote:

> Parliamentarianism (may be) politically obsolete... but we must not regard what is obsolete to us as something obsolete to a class, to the masses... [One] must soberly follow the actual state of the class (not only of its communist vanguard), and of all the working people (not only of their advanced elements)... Parliamentarianism... has not yet politically outlived itself, [and] participation in parliamentary elections and in the struggle on the parliamentary rostrum is obligatory on the party of the revolutionary proletariat...[28]

This was the position adopted, with some misgivings, by the British Communists. Thomas Bell's successful motion to the party's founding Unity Convention stated: 'The Communist Party repudiates the reformist view that a social revolution can be achieved by the ordinary methods of parliamentary democracy, but regards parliamentary and electoral action generally as providing a valuable means of propaganda and agitation towards the revolution... In all cases such representatives must be considered as holding a mandate from the party, and not from the particular constituency for which they happen to sit.' CPGB policy on this vexed question was to zig-zag between 'left reformist' flirtation with parliamentary democracy, expressed mainly through their dealings with the Labour Party, and an outright rejection of such 'class collaboration'.

The *Daily Worker* extolled the virtues of having Communist MPs, singling out for particular mention the performance of Saklatvala:

> Single-handed, he was able to raise and develop an agitation around innumerable questions, which other MPs were only anxious to smother.
>
> When the Bill calling the Irish Free State into existence was passed, Saklatvala alone exposed the true slave character of this self-styled 'Free State'. His activities in the opposition to the acceptance of the Irish Free State led to a far wider resistance on the part of Irish workers in Britain than could have otherwise have taken place.
>
> When in 1925, the Army Supplementary Reserve was started for the purpose of organising railway and transport trade unionists as military Blacklegs for service during strikes, Comrade Saklatvala alone led the fight against, and exposed the connivance of Thomas and other trade union leaders with the Government.
>
> Each year when the Army and Navy Estimates came up for consideration it was Saklatvala alone who demonstrated the purpose of the capitalists in maintaining so vast an expenditure upon war service.
>
> In defence of the Soviet Union, in defence of the unemployed and the workers who were, from time to time, on strike, Comrade Saklatvala was the sole steadfast and consistent mouthpiece.
>
> On Indian questions, he not only fought against the blatant imperialism of the Tory Government, but also exposed the hypocrisy of the Labour Opposition. During the few months he was in Parliament after the arrest of the Meerut prisoners his efforts alone and unaided ensured the raising of the widest publicity outside, around which it was possible to organise the highly successful Meerut Defence Committee, now merged in the League Against Imperialism.
>
> The agitation of a Communist Member of Parliament does not end with speeches in the House. That is but the beginning, by means of which an appeal can be made to the widest possible masses for action against capitalism in all its anti-working class manifestations.[29]

There were those in the CP such as Thomas Bell, editor of the party's theoretical monthly, *The Communist*, and one of the twelve CPGB leaders arrested and imprisoned months before the General Strike who were clear about the value of parliamentary work. In his autobiography, *Pioneering Days*, published in 1941, he both pays unstinting tribute to Saklatvala's commitment and effectiveness as a speaker and gives a picture of his contacts with the MP:

To be a communist Member of Parliament is no sinecure. Unlike the other 'democratic' members he is openly held responsible for his behaviour in the House, to the party executive. He cannot get away with any excuse of 'holding his seat in trust for all classes of his constituents'... Many hours have I spent in and about the House – in the smoking room and in the lobbies – carefully discussing with our representatives the political course we wanted pursued in the debates.[30]

However, Andrew Rothstein, who was a member of the Communist Party's central committee at the same time, says that because many of the leaders did not think parliament was particularly important, and they were confident that Saklatvala could be trusted, he was left to get on with it as an MP. This indifference may help to explain why he was not chosen for any leadership position in the party until four years after he first became an MP. He was elected to the central committee, known as the Executive Committee (EC), at the party congress of 1926, which was held at Battersea, joining fellow Indian, Palme Dutt, who had been elected the year before. But, in defence of this tardy recognition of Saklatvala's role, Rothstein claimed: 'from the time he first became an MP... he acted as an EC member'. He served until 1929, 'contributing shrewdly to discussions'. Rothstein is not sure whether or not Saklatvala stood for re-election in 1929, but insisted 'he was never dropped'.[31]

Whether Rothstein was wholly correct about Saklatvala being fully trusted by the Communist Party leadership is open to some doubt. Saklatvala's single-mindedness, where his own views and interests were concerned, did not always endear him to them. They were embarrassed by the conflicts in Saklatvala's personal life, outlined in Chapter Two, especially when these became the subject of public controversy, such as when opponents of the Communist Party were able to ridicule Saklatvala for condemning capitalism while at the same time retaining his salary as a manager for Tata, even after his election as an MP.

However, Saklatvala was never likely to have been one of those who fell victim to party purges in 1925 and 1929, because he was not only in agreement with the 'new line', which opposed 'class collaboration', but actually proposed the hard-line position in the first place. His views towards the Labour Party got tougher by 1925, when its ban on communist membership began to bite, and his disillusionment was compounded by the Labour government's rejection of his advice on India. He said the 'Labourals', as he contemptuously described them, had turned into a Liberal reformist group. Within the Communist Party, he now argued for the adoption of merciless measures to fight what he saw as Labour's class collaborationist politics. In an uncompromising letter to the CPGB's Political Bureau, of 7 October 1925, (reproduced in full as an appendix) he said:

I feel that the extraordinary circumstances prevailing at the moment
call for extraordinary measures to be taken by our party. There is not
much doubt in my mind that without drastic measures to build up our
party we shall be submerged into insignificance in Great Britain.
Parliamentary customs and traditions have still a very great attraction
for the masses. In order to overcome this we must adopt merciless measures
to fight the Labour Party.

Saklatvala's advocacy of the rejection of 'united front' politics, including
his suggestion that the Communists, as the only 'anti-capitalist' party,
should compete with the Labour Party for trade union affiliations, was
initially rejected by the CPGB leadership, but eventually his proposal won
over the majority and ushered in the 'ultra-Left' position, which the party
was to follow before long. Two and a half years after Saklatvala's letter was
written (it was one of the documents seized when the authorities raided the
party's headquarters in 1925), the CPGB leadership adopted the new
'Stalinist' hard-line which, by then, had been pressed on them by the
Comintern.[32]

The CPGB's lurch to the ultra-left was one of the factors behind
Saklatvala's defeat in the Glasgow Shettleston by-election of June 26th 1930
and his pitiful general election showing at Battersea the following year,
when his support slumped to little more than 3,000 votes, putting him in
third place.

The Communist Party's ultra-leftism in this period can be seen both as
a response to the policy of bans and proscriptions adopted by the Labour
Party, and to its own sectarian tendencies. Initially, the CPGB, on the
advice of Lenin, had sought affiliation to the Labour Party, but, as some
commentators have argued, it did not help its case by the crude, combative
way in which it went about applying for this.[33] At that time, it would not
have been impossible for their request to have been granted, since the
Labour Party had other groups such as the ILP, the Cooperative Party and
the British Socialist Party, some of whose members had helped found the
CPGB, affiliated to them and the communists could have become another
'socialist society'. But the CPGB's application seemed to deliberately court
rejection in its blunt statement of its position, an indication that the
leadership was half-hearted about the whole idea. They made it plain that
they did not accept parliament as an instrument for achieving socialism and
championed the Soviet system as the only possible road for the working
class. This allowed Labour's national executive to firmly reject the overture
on the ground that the aims of the communists were self-evidently not in
accord with the 'constitution, principles, and programme' of the Labour
Party. The decision was endorsed by a large majority at the Labour
Conference in 1921. This was the start of an offensive launched by the
Labour leadership against communists in their party, though the campaign

for affiliation went on regardless. At the 1922 Labour Party Conference, the communists lost the bid for affiliation by 3,086,000 votes to 261,000. The chauvinism of some sections of the Labour Party was made apparent when Frank Hodges, secretary of the Miners' Federation of Great Britain, described the CPGB as 'the intellectual slaves of Moscow taking orders from the Asiatic mind'.[34]

Dual membership of the Communist and Labour parties was, however, still allowed, so many Communists concentrated on winning over the Labour Party by penetrating its ranks. As a result of this, claimed CPGB leader J. T. Murphy, in places such as, 'Barrow, Battersea, and other local Labour Parties the Communists have practically got control of the Labour Party organisations.'

Such open infiltration was successful because there was a widespread sentiment in the grassroots labour movement that communists were part of the same struggle. This view was particularly common in the trade unions. A symptom of this was the successful pressure brought to bear by the TUC in 1920 to secure an end to British military intervention against Soviet Russia. Nevertheless, at the October 1924 Labour Party Conference, affiliation was again lost and, most damaging for the communists, a key motion barring them from Labour Party membership was narrowly carried by 1,804,000 to 1,540,000.[35] If the margin was narrow, the effect of the vote was decisive. It made complete the previous ban on Communists standing as Labour candidates by excluding them, for the first time, from party membership.

Saklatvala was a delegate from the St Pancras Labour Party to the annual conference in 1924 and summed up the case for the CPGB. He was minuted as arguing that:

> There were members of the Labour Party who were members of the National Liberal Club and of the Reform Club and if the Communists were to be barred then these men should be barred also... To say that because the Communists held a different opinion from others as to the method or the limit of time within which they would reach their goal they should be kept out of the Labour Party was unjustifiable. They did not apply such a limitation to any other organisation.[36]

The Conference was not swayed by this. Replying on behalf of Labour's national executive, Herbert Morrison (the grandfather of Peter Mandelson, Tony Blair's New Labour spin doctor) was recorded as saying, 'It was not a personal question. There were many members of the Communist Party who were personal friends of his. It was a question of principle – a divergence of method and a divergence of object between the two parties.' The communists, and their left-wing supporters, were effectively marginalised.

Despite this new ruling, it was not until after the collapse of the General Strike two years later that the ban on dual membership was strictly enforced. From then on, anyone who had ambitions to be an MP either did not join the Communist Party or, if they were already a member, left the party pretty quickly. Saklatvala, pursuing principle over personal advantage, stayed put.

Relations between the two parties reached a new low after the 'Campbell affair', which played some part in hastening the defeat of the Labour Government in 1924. This arose from an article written by J. R. Campbell, who was the acting editor of *Workers' Weekly* in the absence of Palme Dutt, who was ill with tuberculosis. Campbell, a war veteran who had been decorated for gallantry, published his famous 'Appeal to Soldiers' on 25 July. It called on the 'workers in uniform' to 'organise passive resistance when war is declared...' The article concluded: 'Turn your weapons on your oppressors!'[37] Campbell was arrested and charged under the Incitement to Mutiny Act.

There was uproar from some Labour backbenchers, angered by this attack on free speech and the CPGB threatened to put Prime Minister Ramsay MacDonald in the witness box and question him about his Commons speech in 1912 when he had defended Tom Mann who had been accused of advising soldiers not to shoot strikers. The court case was dropped, but the Campbell affair was one of the factors which led to the Tories and Liberals uniting to bring down the Labour Government.

In turn, the Labour leadership's battle against the Communists was stepped up, though, given the amount of autonomy enjoyed by local parties, the policy of expelling Communists from Labour's ranks was difficult to enforce. However, in 1926, 13 local Labour Parties, including North Battersea, were disaffiliated for refusing to comply. Labour's London General Secretary, Herbert Morrison, played a leading role in the disaffiliation of the North Battersea party. He helped the party's national leadership set up 'official' Labour parties in place of the disaffiliated ones.

These were denounced by left-wingers as no more than 'pudding clubs'. Saklatvala, in a characteristically forthright manner, said: 'The people who have started rival Labour Parties in Battersea are the ones who are always complaining that the communists are "splitting the movement". Here we have an example of the lengths to which the official clique are prepared to go to in their efforts to show the bosses that the Labour Party means them no harm.'

The Labour leadership was determined to crack down. This was not surprising given the fact the CPGB made no secret of their aim to smash Labour reformism, and that affiliation was only a tactical means to this end. On the CPGB's part, even after 1926, the affiliation fight went on, gaining some support in trade unions and among left-wing constituency Labour parties, but never enough to succeed.

However, even, within the context of the 'new line' opposing class collaboration and the Labour Party's proscription of communists, the CPGB's position continued to be one of critical backing for the Labour Party. They supported Labour candidates, where a Communist was not standing, but sharply exposed the anti-socialist policies of the Labour leadership. To some Communists from outside Britain it was an odd spectacle. On the one hand the CPGB condemned Ramsay MacDonald's increasingly right-wing Labour administration as 'a government of the imperialist bourgeoisie', and on the other, they appeared to be 'a left-wing within the Labour Party' rather than 'a Communist Party really fighting against the government'.[38] The CPGB was open to the charge that it was compromised by its tactic of getting communist candidates like Saklatvala elected to parliament with open or tacit Labour support. The strains within the Communist Party's position are not difficult to explain. Unlike the European Communist parties which challenged the social democratic socialist parties in size, working-class support and trade union allegiance, the British Communist Party was always in danger of small-scale sectarianism on the margins of politics.

The historian E. H. Carr argues:

> The necessity of keeping one foot within the Labour fold, which was the essence of the united front policy in the CPGB, reflected the strong conservative strain in the British Labour movement; a party which stood openly and unreservedly for revolution and refused to cooperate with the constitutional Left was unlikely to count for much in Great Britain, even among the British workers.'[39]

Noreen Branson, a longtime member of the Communist Party in Battersea summed up her party's dilemma:

> Unlike its social democratic counterparts on the Continent, the Labour Party had been formed by the trade unions which still had the decisive voice in the making of its policy and programme. Thus, to the average trade unionist of that period, voting Labour meant voting for your own organisation, for your own side. Communists were beginning to play a leading part in some of these trade unions; yet they could not participate, except indirectly, in the decisions of the party which belonged to them as trade unionists.[40]

Saklatvala himself experienced a particularly acute version of this dilemma. On the one hand, as an anti-imperialist and advocate of the Indian nationalist cause, his role as an MP gave him a platform he would not otherwise have enjoyed. Had he moved to the Labour Party, it seems very probable that he could have continued in this role. Some commentators even say that had Saklatvala torn up his membership of the Communist Party, the least he could have expected was a place in a Labour government, probably as a government minister responsible for India. His private secretary, Reg Bishop, said in 1936: 'For the first year or two after his election as MP for North Battersea there were many who tried to get him to break from the Communist Party. The Under-Secretaryship was held out if only he would be more 'orthodox' in politics.'[41] On the other hand, both on the issue of the General Strike and on its attitude to the colonial empire, membership of the Labour Party must have looked an increasingly unappealing option to a genuinely revolutionary socialist. Saklatvala made this clear in his relationship to the Labour left.

During his two terms in parliament he did work closely with Scottish ILP members. Indeed one of them, David Kirkwood, who represented Dumbarton, was the only Labour MP to stand up in the Commons and defend him after his arrest during the General Strike of 1926. Nevertheless, Saklatvala had observed: 'Some comrades, especially our Scottish left-wing comrades, are quite honest in their intentions. But they are not prepared for a clear breakaway attitude from the front oppositional bench.' He was dismissive: 'The left-wing serves very little use. On the whole it does little more than scratch the surface of the right-wing reactionary attitude.'[42]

One senses that at times Saklatvala, as a lone left-wing MP of Asian heritage, felt that his political instincts were most wholeheartedly endorsed by the degree of opposition his activities and speeches engendered. For instance, in a parliamentary debate he was asked if he was a 'Colonel in the Red Army'. Saklatvala quipped: 'So far I am not... There was an enthusiastic colleague of mine who did become one and who felt very proud of it, but he has found it more convenient since then to retire to the Labour Party.'

MPs instantly demanded: 'Name!' Saklatvala replied: 'Newbold,' in a sarcastic reference to J. Walton Newbold who had defected to Labour.

However, if Saklatvala had the satisfaction of remaining true to his principles, as Chapter Seven makes clear, he also had to face the consequences of this choice in his increasing marginalisation in British politics. It was his position as a committed British Asian communist and Indian nationalist, which made this outcome virtually inevitable.

CHAPTER 6

BLACK POLITICS AND EMPIRE INSURGENTS

Although the concept of a Black British political identity covering peoples of African, African Caribbean, Indian Caribbean, South Asian and Chinese heritage was not part of Saklatvala's vocabulary, he was nevertheless very clear both that racism was an important dimension of colonial oppression and on the need for solidarity among all peoples fighting imperialism. He would no doubt, as a good communist, have asserted the primacy of a class analysis of social relations. But there is an important sense in which he was not just a communist who happened to be of Indian origin, but a person whose political journey never lost touch with his roots, who had been through personal experience of racism at the hands of the British Raj, and who remained attached to his Parsi culture in ways which at times overtly declared his 'difference'. This brought him into conflict with some of his less enlightened British communist comrades. It is for this reason that Saklatvala needs to be put in the historical context of the experience of African, Caribbean and Asian involvement in British politics, not least because amnesia still abounds when it comes to the role and contribution of Black people through the ages.[1]

British society has still to come to terms with the fact that since the Roman occupation, through the Tudor period, and then accelerated by the trans-Atlantic trade in slaves, Black people have been a part of British society long before the mass migration of the post 1945 period.[2] More pertinent to the focus of this biography, it is rarely remembered that there were a number of African and Asian descended participants in the foundation of the radical democratic and labour movements. Saklatvala should be seen as part of this tradition as well as a precursor for what followed.

In the Gordon Riots of 1780, a confused mixture of anti-Catholicism and proletarian rage against wealth and oppression, two Black men, John Glover and Benjamin Bowsey were arrested as part of an assault on Newgate Prison to free prisoners, sentenced to death, which was later commuted to transportation.[3] Olaudah Equiano (1745?-1797) is famed as the author of the anti-slavery classic, *The Interesting Narrative of the Life of*

Olaudah Equiano or Gustavus Vassa the African (1789), but less well known is his involvement with the radical London Corresponding Society, which was inspired by both the French revolution and the writings of Tom Paine (1737-1809), and friendships with its co-founder, Thomas Hardy (1752-1832), with whom Equiano lodged, and with John Thelwall (1764-1834), the Society's militantly republican theoretician whose antislavery writings went beyond humanitarianism to call for solidarity between the revolts of enslaved peoples (particularly in Haiti) and British working people fighting for representation and social justice in a country still dominated by the landed aristocracy.[4] Equiano died in 1797 and many of the radicals with whom he was involved were driven into silence by the repressive state apparatus of the Pitt government. Hardy and Thelwall were both tried for high treason (and could have been hung, drawn and quartered), but were acquitted by their respective juries. By the 1820s, though, there was a new generation of even more militant and generally more proletarian radicals, mostly inspired by the writings and activism of Thomas Spence (1750-1814),[5] who called for the common ownership of land (still the major source of wealth and power) and was a pioneering advocate of the women's and infant's rights. For long after he died, his ideas inspired 'Spenceans', among whom was the Cato Street 'conspirator', the Black Jamaican, William Davidson (1781-1820), who was hanged and beheaded with other Spenceans in 1820, for his part in an attempt to blow up the Tory cabinet.[6] There was William Cuffay (1788-1870), a leader of the Chartists, who was the son of a former Kittian slave and an English woman, Juliana Fox. He was transported to Tasmania for his insurrectionist views.[7] Another Black 19th century radical was Robert Wedderburn (1762-1835), a tailor and preacher, also inspired by Thomas Spence, who like Davidson was born in Jamaica. Wedderburn was sent to prison on the charge of sedition,[8] just as Saklatvala was more than a hundred years later in 1926.

Saklatvala was also part of the beginnings of Asian representation in the British Parliament, arguably the first probably being, as noted in the Preface, David Ochterlony Dyce Sombre (1808-1851).[9] Three other Asian MPs followed Sombre, all of them Parsis,[10] (the longest established Asian community in Britain)[11] and the reaction to them is worthy of note. For instance, when Dadabhai Naoroji (1825-1917) unsuccessfully contested Holborn in the 1886 general election, the Prime Minister, Lord Salisbury commented in tones of aristocratic disdain: 'However great the progress of mankind has been, and however far we have advanced in overcoming prejudice, I doubt if we have yet got to the point of view where a British constituency would elect a black man.'[12] It was not long, though, before the Tories had to eat their words. Naoroji was elected Liberal MP for Central Finsbury in 1892, the year William Gladstone won his last victory. Naoroji's majority of three in 1892 earned him the punning nickname 'Narrow Majority'.[13] However in the general election in 1895 Naoroji lost his seat. Naoroji as a Parsi had trained to be a Zoroastrian priest in his youth, but like Saklatvala he became more radical as he got older. He used his election address of 1895 to describe labour as 'the backbone or foundation of all National wealth and greatness',[14] and during his three years in parliament he had espoused his message of 'India for the Indians'. He became disillusioned with the Liberals over their failure to adopt a more radical position on Indian self-rule and moved further to the left. One of Naoroji's close friends was the socialist pioneer H.M. Hyndman (1842-1921) who got to know him after picking up a copy of Naoroji's pamphlet, *Poverty of India*. In 1904, Naoroji attended the International Socialist Congress in Amsterdam to argue for self-rule for India. He told the Congress: 'The Imperialism of civilisation is the Imperialism of equal rights, equal duties, and equal freedoms. The remedy is in the hands of the British people. They must compel their Government to fulfil the promises that they have made to India. The remedy is to give India self-government.'[15] Returning to the hustings in 1906 under new party colours, Naoroji was heavily defeated when he stood in North Lambeth as a Trades and Labour candidate.[16]

Naoroji was a brilliant academic who became the first Indian professor of mathematics and philosophy at the age of 29.[17] Throughout his time in Britain he was a tireless campaigner for Indian independence, helping to lay the foundations of the Congress Party. He was elected president for three sessions of the Congress – in 1886, 1893 and 1906. He refused the knighthood offered him in Britain and eventually settled in his homeland, becoming the 'Grand Old Man' of India.

I found no record of Saklatvala ever meeting Naoroji, though he was an admirer, and there was a mutual connection through Saklatvala's Battersea colleague, the Pan-Africanist John Archer (1863-1932), whom Naoroji had encouraged to join the Liberal-linked Progressives and get involved in local politics.[18] Naoroji did the same for the panAfricanist Trinidadian barrister Henry Sylvester Williams (1869-1911),[19] whom he introduced to the National Liberal Club. Both Williams and Archer were elected as councillors, the former in Marylebone and latter in Battersea.

Saklatvala's family in India and the Tatas were also acquainted with Britain's third Asian MP, Sir Mancherji Merwanji Bhownagree (1851-1933). Bhownagree was also a Parsi, fair-skinned, Anglicised and wealthy; an outstanding scholar and a graduate of Elphinstone College in Mumbai. He started his career as a journalist and was an active educationalist. The son of a rich merchant, he was an ardent empire loyalist whose politics were described as 'Anglo-Indianism run mad'. Whereas Naoroji concerned himself with India's economic grievances, Bhownagree busied himself with a Gujerati translation of Queen Victoria's *Leaves from the Journal of Our Life in the Highlands*, published in Mumbai in 1877 and dedicated to the Prince of Wales.[20]

He came to England in 1882, aged thirty-one, to study law and was called to the bar at Lincoln's Inn, as was Saklatvala. Though he canvassed for Naoroji in the 1892 General Election, he regarded the 'Grand Old Man', who was twenty-six years his senior, as a dangerous radical. In 1895, Sir Mancherji secured the Tory nomination for a winnable parliamentary seat because he was a useful way for the party to counteract Lord Salisbury's 'Black Man' gaff against Naoroji. He sat as the Conservative MP for the working-class east London seat of Bethnal Green North East from 1895 until 1906, when the Liberal election landslide victory overwhelmed him.

A popular constituency MP, Bhownagree was re-elected for Bethnal Green in 1900 with a considerably increased majority. But his popularity in Tory circles was not mirrored in India. Though he claimed to represent Indian opinion and went back for a visit in 1896, after his election as MP, he was greeted by a hostile press and protest demonstrations. The Congress movement condemned him, derisively nicknaming him 'Bow-and-Agree' and 'Bow-the-Knee'. His only political action on behalf of Indian interests was to join Naoroji and Mahatma Gandhi in a deputation to the Colonial Secretary in 1906 concerning the persecution of South African Indians. Gandhi had worked as a lawyer in South Africa for two decades, not returning to Indian until 1914. His role in South Africa has come in for current critical examination, charged with being exclusively concerned with improving the lot of Indian South Africans and being 'racially prejudiced towards Africans', whom he called by the insulting term 'kaffirs'.[21]

Bhownagree was kept to the sidelines by the Tory leadership which never offered him an important position. They were only prepared to give Indians knighthoods (one of which Bhownagree received) and perhaps a peerage, such as that granted to Satyendra Prasanno, who was created Baron Sinha of Raipur in 1919. In addition, the British Government created some Indian Privy Counsellors and members of the India Council for services rendered. But, when it came to government office, the door was firmly closed.

The outbreak of the First World War brought about a coalition government between Conservatives and Liberals, and, with it, an opportunity for the Tory's token Asian MP to realise his burning ambition for high office. But they snubbed him. Though still smarting from this slight, Bhownagree nevertheless arranged a meeting of 'All Indians Resident In Great Britain' to mark the First World War victory and thank the King for creating the first Indian peer. Bhownagree attempted to keep the event secret, fearing disruption by radicals, but Saklatvala got to hear about it and took his supporters along. They removed Bhownagree from the chair and got a vote passed condemning him for convening such a stupid meeting.[22]

Bhownagree used the 'non-political' public platforms of the Parsi Association and the Indian Social Club to get his revenge. At public functions, Bhownagree made sure that Saklatvala and his wife were placed in obscure corners of the room. Also, though Saklatvala, as an MP, was a leading member of the Indian community, Bhownagree refused to refer to him in his speeches. This did not seem to bother Saklatvala who, while a keen attender at such events, was not one for social status. But some fellow Parsis did take offence. At one dinner in 1923, S. R. Bomanji, a prominent community figure, walked out to protest at what he saw as a deliberate snub to Saklatvala.

Like Naoroji, Bhownagree was defeated in the 1906 General Election and he retired from parliamentary politics. Unlike India's 'Grand Old Man', the former Tory MP settled in England, spending the rest of his life as a pillar of conservative London society.

If the Conservative establishment was prepared to overlook Bhownagree's race, that was far from being Saklatvala's experience. For instance, supporters of his chief opponent in Battersea in the 1924 election, Henry Hogbin, were not above scaremongering with racist appeals to voters. There were the wholly imaginary claims made in the right-wing national press that armed gangs of Irish republicans and 'Continental and Russian' communists were roaming Battersea, committed to disrupting Hogbin's election meetings, with the implication that this was at Saklatvala's behest. There was also the racist jibe that Saklatvala's hold on the support of the white working class could only be explained if he was seen as 'an Indian fakir with a knowledge of black magic'.[23] The local Battersea paper constantly made a point of drawing attention to Saklatvala's 'difference' before he was elected for the first time. It reported: 'Mr Saklatvala does not look like the usual Parliamentary candidate. That is not because of his nationality – he is not as brown as the average Englishman is after the summer fortnight at the seaside. He has a total disregard for appearances, therefore he does not affect the fine gentleman.'[24] Even when Saklatvala invited his rival to share a platform at a public meeting, one of the Liberal candidate's leading campaigners, Councillor A. P. Godfrey, used the meeting to make an overtly racist attack on Saklatvala. He expressed 'an instinctive preference for an Englishman' and, referring to Saklatvala's 'Eastern mentality', declared that he was 'on the wrong side of the Indian Ocean, seeking to exploit people's ignorance and lead them… to revolution.' The local press reported that this provoked a swift rebuke from the audience. Men and women rose to their feet and shouted, 'You are asking for it!' 'Shame!' and

'How about Lady Astor?' (She was a wealthy American who was the first woman to take her seat in the Commons.) Saklatvala calmed his supporters before a shaken Godfrey withdrew his remark.[25] Hogbin refused to distance himself from these obnoxious comments.

Saklatvala then replied with a reasoned analysis of the relationship between poverty in Britain and India. He denounced nationalism and called instead for working-class unity.[26] Nevertheless, while Saklatvala, as a candidate of the Battersea Labour Party and Trades Council, enjoyed broad working-class support, there were some diehard racists in Battersea, including former supporters of socialist candidates who refused to back Saklatvala. Fred Hodges, a retired demolition worker, told the author: 'I supported Labour all my life, but I wouldn't vote for Saklatvala. Why should I vote for an Indian when an Englishman could do the job?'[27] And a Battersea bus conductor was reported as having complained to his passengers: 'We've got a nice crowd 'o politicians here. A black man out for one seat, and a lawbreaking motorist (Viscount Curzon, South Battersea) for another."[28]

Rajani Palme Dutt, Indian colleague of Saklatvala in the CPGB, had his own recollection of the racism faced by Saklatvala. He told the story of how, during a General Election campaign 'I was temporarily staying… in my parents' home… in North Battersea. The Tory candidate came round and, speaking to my mother, who was Swedish with the characteristically very fair Nordic complexion, said: "Of course, you will not want to vote for the black man". Tory habits do not change.'[29]

Even after Saklatvala was elected an MP, the racist abuse continued. In a slander which was manifestly untrue on the evidence of his reported speeches, the Under-Secretary of State for India, Lord Winterton, said of Saklatvala: he has 'a flow of what is commonly known as Babu English which greatly amuses the House'.[30] Even more malicious were the words of Tory Lord Gisborough, reminiscent of how American president Donald Trump in July 2019 denounced four newly-elected radical Black congresswomen – Alexandria Ocasio-Cortez, Ilhan Omar, Ayanna Pressley and Rashib Tlaib – who he said should 'go back and help fix the totally broken and crime-infested places from which they came'.[31] In a speech to the white supremacist British Israel World Federation,[32] Gisborough railed against the 'millions of aliens in this country who were not too proud to take all they could in doles and charity'. Gisborough specifically targeted Saklatvala. He said Britain had 'given him hospitality, allowed him to become a member of parliament and that he should be allowed to run round and bite the hand that fed him was a scandal'. Either he ought to be 'deported or – if that was illegal – shut up in some room where he would be safe.' In his opinion, said Gisborough, with an historically unfortunate but revealing choice of words, 'that would be a lethal chamber.'[33]

Racism also came from some on the left. At its mildest it was the kind of stereotyping comment used by The *Daily Herald* to describe Saklatvala: 'His figure is shorter and slighter than the average Englishman's, but this defect, if it be one, is more than compensated for by the remarkable ease and elasticity of his bearing'.[34] There were those, though, who allegedly wanted to get 'this bloody nigger off our backs'.[35] Around a hundred years later, similar sentiments appear to have been directed towards left-wing Black Labour MPs by party officials, according to the leaked report on the handling of antisemitism, which revealed a determined attempt to undermine the Corbyn leadership.[36]

Saklatvala warned his children about the discrimination they would face in Britain. His daughter Sehri recalled, 'Father always said, "you are foreign people in a foreign land and you will always meet prejudice. You must use education to defeat it".'[37]

In contrast to his two precursors, Saklatvala was feared by the authorities who went to great extremes to limit his influence. This included, as described in Chapter Four, restricting his right to travel abroad, when first he was banned from America in 1925, then India, two years later, after his much acclaimed tour. These episodes were reminiscent of how, a quarter of a century earlier, Saklatvala had been prevented from entering a white man's club in India to speak with a white doctor about anti-plague measures; though afterwards he was allowed to enter by the back entrance. In the case of America, and later India, there was no way in.

None of the treatment Saklatvala received at the hands of the British political establishment or the right-wing press is particularly surprising, but how was the issue of race dealt with by the socialist movement of Saklatvala's time?

Karl Marx had correctly argued that the fortunes of white and Black workers were inextricably bound together because slavery and other forms of racial oppression of Black people were endemic to capitalism,[38] and there has undoubtedly been an important strand of the British labour movement which has always been committed to solidarity with Black political struggles. Ernest Jones (1819-1869), a prominent Chartist leader, as Priyamvada Gopal has documented,[39] made an early political connection with the anti-colonial struggle. Though it was not a part of the movement's programme, Jones used the *People's Paper* to savage Britain's role overseas, saying: 'On its colonies the sun never sets, but the blood never dries.' He urged the British people in 1857 to support the Indian cause.[40] But the international socialist movement frequently fell short of Marx's clarity on the issue and the record of the labour movement in terms of its actual practices on race has not always been exemplary.

At the turn of the century, the influential German Social Democratic Party (SPD) leader Eduard Bernstein (1850-1932) promoted what he described as 'the civilising role of imperialism'. This reactionary position found an echo in the Second Communist International, the organisation which was supposed to represent socialists worldwide.[41] At their 1904 World Congress, Bernstein said: 'We must get away from the utopian notion of simply abandoning the colonies... Socialists too should acknowledge the need for civilised peoples to act somewhat like the guardians of the uncivilised... our economies are based, in large measure, on the extraction from the colonies of products that the native peoples have no idea how to use.' He then quoted approvingly from Ferdinand Lassalle (1825-1864),[42] founder of the Social Democratic Party of Germany, who had stated: 'People who do not develop may be justifiably subjugated by people who have achieved civilization.'[43] The Second International degenerated into an acceptance of the Bernstein position to the extent that Lenin felt compelled to denounce them as 'the International of the White Race'.

Unremitting hostility to imperialism was one of the key differences between the Second and Third Internationals, and it is significant that the Indian scholar M.N. Roy (1887-1954), a founder of both the Indian and Mexican Communist Parties, became a special advisor to the Communist International and contributed to the theses on the National and Colonial Questions passed by the Second World Congress of the Third International in 1920.[44] These theoretically placed the international communist movement firmly behind all those involved in the struggle for national liberation. While Roy's position was more ultra-Left than Lenin's, arguing against communists forming alliances with bourgeois nationalist movements such as the one led by Gandhi in India, Lenin had personally taken charge of drafting the policy and directed the Third International away from this sectarian view. Saklatvala, as already noted, had always taken the view that there had to be dialogue (even if of a critical kind) with other elements of the nationalist movement.

In the end, though, it was Black people themselves who had to organise and put pressure on the international socialist movement for tangible support. Communists from colonised countries got together at a special Congress of the 'Toilers of the East' held in the Russian city of Baku in 1922 and called for a *jihad* (holy war) against the British Empire. The congress was necessary because the political perspectives of these representatives of oppressed peoples were not necessarily shared by those who should have been their class and political allies. For instance, in Germany, African soldiers serving with the French army of occupation on the River Rhine, in the aftermath of the First World War, had to endure racist slander from the main socialist party the SPD rather than an understanding of their plight. Sections of the left in Britain supported the German socialists. E. D. Morel (1873-1924), a prominent Labour MP, wrote a racist pamphlet entitled *The Horror on the Rhine* (1921), in which he used the myth of rampant Black male sexuality to whip up hysteria in the labour movement. A free copy was given to every delegate at the 1920 Trades Union Congress. Morel's attack was eagerly taken up by the ILP paper, *Labour Leader*. (Some years later Morel was to turn his fire on Saklatvala for advocating, as he claimed, the interests of jute workers in Calcutta against those of the jute workers in his Dundee constituency. Saklatvala in fact called for the unity of the Calcutta workers who harvested the jute and the Dundee workers who processed it.[45]) The depths to which the labour movement sank on the issue of what was claimed as *The Horror on the Rhine* was summed up in an article from a surprising quarter, published in the CPGB's weekly newspaper, *The Communist*. It carried a report by German Socialists headlined 'Outcry Against the Black Horror', 'Urgent Appeal to Englishmen'. Its message was all too familiar:

> An awful crime against the white race, against our German women, maidens and children is being perpetuated by the French in using black and coloured troops for the occupation of German territory in an ever increasing number without our being able to prevent it. In the Wild West when a coloured man outrages a white woman, he is lynched without more ado. But what have our German women, girls and children to suffer from the African troops in the occupied districts. What says the world to hundreds of thousands of white people being enslaved by black and coloured savages?
>
> What says the world to the ever-increasing assaults and crimes committed by these wild beasts on German women and children? Do the other white nations of the world know about this?'[46]

Elsewhere in Europe the Dutch communists were widely condemned for being apologists for their country's colonial policy in countries like the Netherlands East Indies, later Indonesia, and, in 1927, the Vietnamese communist Ho Chi Minh strongly criticised the French and British Communist parties for not giving sufficient support to the anti-colonial struggle.[47] He told the Comintern that independence movements like his own had the right to demand much greater backing.

It is apparent, too, that the ILP, the Labour Party and the CPGB drew a distinction between the African colonies and other parts of the British empire. This was based on the patronising view that liberation movements were less developed in Africa and therefore more difficult to support. British communists tended to concentrate their efforts on India, though Egypt and Ireland also received attention. In India there were notable acts of solidarity, such as the work of the Meerut defendants Philip Spratt, Ben Bradley and the journalist Lester Hutchinson, who helped build the fight for self-determination. Even so, the position of the CPGB did not go uncriticised by other communists. In 1928, at the Sixth World Communist Congress, the veteran Japanese Marxist Sen Katayama criticised the CPGB for their 'criminal neglect' of Ireland and India.[48] Later, the Black American activist Harry Haywood, a member of the Comintern's Negro Commission, criticised the CPGB's 'chauvinism.'[49]

At the same Congress, the self-interested opposition of the Communist Party of South Africa's white leadership to the creation of a 'Native Republic' had to be defeated. The South African communists were more concerned about protecting the interests of the privileged white minority, the elite of the labour movement. This was apparent when the South African communists raised no major public objection to the slogan 'Workers of the World Unite for a White South Africa', used by trade unionists in the great mine strike of 1922, which the communists supported. To compound matters, they would not fight for equal pay for equal work, regardless of colour, for fear of provoking a backlash among their white trade union supporters. Furthermore, leading South African communists attempted to liquidate the land question by denying that South Africa 'belonged to the Bantu' in the first place. One of their delegates, Rebecca Bunting, wife of the party's chairman, wanted to know who would guarantee equality for the whites in an independent Native Republic. She claimed that, after all, the Black slogan was 'Drive the whites into the sea'. She was ridiculed by an Ukrainian communist leader, who captured the mood of the Congress when he said:

> Comrade Bunting has raised a serious question, one not to be sneezed at. What is to become of the whites? My answer to that would be that if the white party members do not raise and energetically fight for an independent Native Republic... They may well be driven into the sea!

The Congress duly supported the establishment of a Native South African Republic, but the fact that they were divided on the issue cannot be overlooked.[50]

The issue of racial privilege within the South African labour movement had its parallels in Britain where racial intolerance was part of the consciousness of some sections of organised labour. Black seamen in particular faced pronounced discrimination, yet, far from coming to their aid, the trade union movement made things worse. The National Sailors' and Firemen's Union and the National Union of Ships' Stewards, Cooks, Butchers and Bakers, the two forerunners of the National Union of Seamen, now amalgamated into the Rail Maritime and Transport trade union, were totally against the hiring of Black seamen where white crews were available. Even where they allowed Black seamen into union membership, it was to work as 'donkeymen' below deck on lower wages than white seamen. The Trades Union Congress, as late as 1930, passed a motion, proposed by a delegate from Cardiff, which argued: 'That this Congress views with alarm the continued employment of alien and undesirable coloured labour on British ships to the detriment of British seamen and calls upon the government to use all their powers to provide remedial action.'[51] This was an issue that Saklatvala had taken up as an MP, when in April 1923 he raised in Parliament the situation of 'Asiatic and African shore workers' employed by a government contractor, the Elder Dempster Steamship Company in Liverpool, who had suffered wage cuts and dismissals. He urged the Government to bring in 'fair wages' for 'all classes' of the firm's employees 'in view of the menace to the standard of life of the British seamen and shore workers posed by the employment of such underpaid labour.' He added that the hundreds of men who had been laid off should be given financial help and not be refused it – as if they had gone on strike. He further demanded a government inquiry into 'the conditions under which non-European labour is utilised in this country by shipping firms'.[52]

There is no evidence that, in general, Saklatvala received other than comradely treatment within the Communist Party. However, there was one episode in his relationship with the party that points to its discomfort with issues of cultural difference. This was the occasion when Saklatvala put all five of his children (three sons and two daughters), through the Parsi *navjote* initiation ceremony. This occurred just after his return from India, where his sister pressed on him her unhappiness that the children had not been accepted into the Zoroastrian faith. (There was also the story that if they were not initiated they would have been disinherited by the Tatas from possible participation in a family trust fund. As it happened, an elderly relative gave birth to a nearer male heir and the issue of the trust became irrelevant.)

The *navjote* ceremony gave rise to innuendo in the press about strange goings-on at Caxton Hall, in central London, where it was performed. To Eurocentric commentators, the Parsi initiation rites confirmed the prejudiced view that Saklatvala was a 'fire-worshipper', a pejorative description often used in the West to describe Parsis. It stems from the fact that their place of worship is called the fire temple (Agiary/Dar-i-mihr).[53] Parsi Zoroastrians do recite their prayers in front of a huge silver urn in which sandalwood is burned, but they are no more fire-worshippers than Christians are cross-worshippers.

The *navjote* or 'thread' initiation involved Saklatvala's five children: Dorab, aged 19; Candida (Candy) 17; Beram, 15; Kaikoo, and Sehri, 8. *The Times* reported: 'The ceremony had been delayed longer than usual because Saklatvala only recently became aware that it could be done outside India.' The two girls, Candida and Sehri, were the first to seat themselves on the white dais at the feet of the initiating priests, Mr R. R. Desai and Dr Homi Dastoor. Prayers in Avesta, the ancient Parsi language, were chanted. Then began the ritual of changing clothes. The ceremony included anointing with rosewater; investing with garlands of roses; clothing in a sacred vest, the *sudreh* or 'garment of the good mind'; and knotting round the waist with a *kusti*, the sacred cord. At the end of the ceremony, newly-initiated Zoroastrians or *navjotes* have a red phosphorescent paint applied to their foreheads. Throughout, sandalwood oil, candles, incense and ghee were burned and betel nuts, *batassar* (sugar) and *bura* (a silver cone-shaped vessel containing sweet meats) were used.

'The scene in the hall was a mixed one. Side by side with Parsee women in picturesque dress sat smart English society women, and dapper Indians rubbed shoulders with Communist colleagues of Mr Saklatvala', reported *The Times*.[54] Among the guests, at the initiation ceremony was, ironically, Lord Curzon, Conservative MP for Battersea South and son of an arch-imperialist who had been Viceroy of India; Sir Mancherji Bhownagree, Britain's first Indian Tory MP, was also there.

The Communist Party was greatly embarrassed by it all. In pompous tones, a leading comrade, Albert Inkpin, told the press: 'The proceedings had nothing in common with communist principles.' A statement of censure was issued by the political bureau, which, in patronising language, demonstrated the party's Eurocentric stance: 'The Communist Party of Great Britain recognises that, in capitalist society, many revolutionary workers who are sincere enemies of the capitalism have not yet succeeded in fully shaking off the religious prejudices and traditions in which they were brought up.' It noted that while the party did not require members to be atheists, it 'insists that they shall not actively participate in religious propaganda.' The party even made a specific point of saying that Saklatvala was particularly culpable as an Indian because 'He knows the particularly disastrous effects of religious prejudices and quarrels among the masses of India, and the unscrupulous and successful use made of religion by British Imperialism to perpetuate the enslavement and exploitation of the Indian people.' It was a statement that revealed the party's ignorance. Since Zoroastrianism was not a religion that sought converts, the party could hardly justify the claim that Saklatvala was engaging in religious propaganda; and the strictures about the 'religious prejudices' among the masses in India (no doubt a reference to the Hindu caste system and Hindu-Muslim divisions) was equally wide of the mark since Parsi Zoroastrians were outside the caste system. It was a statement that looked forward to the contemporary rows about Muslim girls and women wearing the *hijab* headscarves, an issue which has divided the secular left, particularly in France. In the same way as the Rushdie affair, the matter has sparked opposition among people only happy to tolerate ethnic or cultural minorities as long as their adherents assimilate – in other words, as long as they cast off the differences that secular society finds threatening. Multi-culturalism in Britain and the rest of Europe effectively means conformity by minorities with the culture and values of the white majority.

Saklatvala did not use the opportunity the Zoroastrian initiation issue gave him to educate the Communist Party, instead he accepted their rebuke. He was reported, by the party's official paper, to be 'in entire agreement... and only wishes to add that the circumstances were outside his control and due entirely to the peculiar position of his people and of a purely domestic character'.[55] In truth, Saklatvala could have told his party comrades that there was a good deal of Zoroastrianism which was compatible with his communist principles, and little which came into conflict with it. Although a monotheistic religion with belief in an afterlife of reward or punishment, Zoroastrians were not otherworldly. They were encouraged to lead industrious, honest and charitable lives, but also to live well and enjoy their time in the world, though without excess. Parsi Zoroastrianism also insisted on equality between the sexes.[56]

If Saklatvala meekly accepted his party's rebuke, strong protest came from his close friend, Arthur Field, a Battersea communist and London correspondent of the *Indian National Herald*, who resigned from the party in protest at the political bureau's statement. In a long and critical article published in India, he contrasted it with the attitude of Battersea Trades Council and Labour Party which, he noted, on religious matters, is neutral 'relegating them to the private affairs of the citizen'. He warned: 'There is an important Catholic and Irish community in Battersea, and it will be painfully affected by this disclosure of the anti-religious basis of Communism.'[57] Indeed *The Catholic Times* promptly made capital from the situation. According to them, the statement was a 'public admission that Communism in England is completely identified with atheism and hostility to religion'.

If the loyal Communist refused to ever chide his party over its stance on religion and culture, Saklatvala's attitude to these important questions can be deduced from a number of his speeches and the words of some of those Black socialists who were more explicit in their criticisms. In a caustic speech in Dublin in spring 1925, he said it was 'a lie' that working-class organisations were 'against religion'. In words that showed Saklatvala had been trained to be a lawyer, he demanded the 'true application of religion', which says 'Thou shalt not steal' and yet 'if we steal under the Imperialist laws of Limited Liability Companies, we are simply enterprising people'.[58] On the issue of unity among Black people Saklatvala was very clear. His connections with John Archer and his presence at the second Pan-Africanist

Congress in London have already been outlined. Saklatvala gave the delegates greetings from the Indian people stating that India was 'very proud to be a part of the coloured world', (the term preferred at that time rather than Black) and that 'coloured people ought to be proud of themselves'.[59]

African-Asian unity was also one of the themes taken up by Saklatvala in an article criticising Mahatma Gandhi in 1930. He said that when Gandhi was in South Africa: 'He never made the slightest attempt socially and politically to unite Negroes and Indians together for the overthrow of the white man's tyranny. ...Whenever some vulgar favour was shown by the British master towards a few rich Indians in South Africa, Gandhi would burst out into a song like the Empire's nightingale... He ignored the fact that South Africa belongs to the Negroes and that the white tyrants were a small minority, and were the worst type of exploiters, gold hunters and diamond diggers.'[60] Again, as Chapter Seven outlines, Saklatvala was also prominent in the international solidarity campaign to save the lives of the nine young Black Americans who had been framed in the notorious Scottsboro rape case of 1931.

The praise accorded Saklatvala by the Trinidadian Pan-Africanist George Padmore draws specific attention to his independence of mind and his record on anti-racist issues. Padmore became a fierce critic of the Communist Party, having resigned in 1933 after the Comintern suddenly dissolved the International Trade Union Committee of Negro Workers, a sort of 'Black Section' of its day. Later he was expelled from the Comintern and ritualistically denounced as a 'petty bourgeois nationalist'. Afterwards he told his nephew he had been sent a series of directives from Moscow ordering him to stop attacking French imperialism, then British imperialism, then American imperialism, till he was left with the Japanese – and, as he acidly observed, they were not the ones with their boot on the Black man's neck. He described Saklatvala as 'a brilliant left-wing Labour MP... a dynamic personality, who denounced British imperialism both in parliament and from public platforms up and down Britain. He was an Indian who had no time for opportunistic trimmers and sycophants. The most independent-minded Communist ever. A Titoist before Tito.'[61] Indeed, one can categorically say that Saklatvala was not just promoting a national independence brand of communism before Tito, but was also a pioneer of African-Asian unity before Bandung.[62]

It can be argued that one of Saklatvala's greatest contributions to the British left was in getting them to take a stronger position against imperialism and colonialism, work he accomplished as chief propagandist for the League Against Imperialism in the 1920s, working as secretary to its leader, Reginald Bridgeman. The CPGB's official historian, James Klugmann

(1912-1977), certainly suggests that Saklatvala pushed the party into a more consistently anti-imperialist position. He paid tribute to the 'fiery anti-imperialist speeches of Saklatvala... denouncing the role of British imperialism in Egypt, India, Palestine' and argued that these speeches did much to 'encourage these early contacts' with the various communist and national liberation movements. Klugmann, looking with hindsight, also begins to sketch the connection between Saklatvala's anti-imperialist work and the future issues of anti-racism, though there is little evidence that the Communist Party at this period gave any focus to this issue. Klugmann wrote:

> It is hard to overestimate the significance of the election by the *English* workers of Battersea of an "Indian immigrant" (as he would be called today) as *their* Communist representative in Parliament.[63] [my italics]

Klugmann does not discuss how far the Communist Party had to be pushed, but the evidence suggests that Saklatvala had to struggle to maintain the support of the party in his anti-imperialist work. George Padmore argues that the Communists internationally were no more than opportunists on these questions, setting up anti-imperialist front organisations when it suited them and just as quickly closing them down when they felt something else was more important. The attitude of the party leadership to the work of the League Against Imperialism illustrates this point.

The League had been initiated by the German communist leader, Willi Munzenberg (1889-1940). While most of the leaders of the British Labour Party refused to have anything to do with it, Munzenberg's political affiliation did not deter the much less sectarian nationalist leaders in the colonial countries from associating with the League, so that Jawaharlal Nehru (1889-1964) of India and Diego Rivera (1886-1957), of Mexico, sat alongside Saklatvala on the executive committee. Some sections of the left in the Labour Party such as George Lansbury (1859-1940), who was briefly its chair, and Fenner Brockway (1888-1988) also kept up links with the League. Brockway ascribed this to Saklatvala's influence inside and outside parliament. He said that it was Saklatvala who managed to get the ILP, most significantly George Lansbury, the future leader of the Labour Party, to attend one of the League's major conferences. The League was the object of fierce attacks in the press, who accused it of being no more than a communist front. Two months after the League's foundation, India's colonial government banned all its literature and the Dutch took stringent action against its representatives in the Netherlands East Indies.

Politicians who knew Saklatvala say that on the issue of anti-colonialism, he did not make a point of emphasising his differences on other matters with Labour MPs and, as a result, his patient, tolerant work won cooperation and sometimes even friendship. Brockway suggests, however, that the

League was never the success it should have been because the Communist Party used it as a convenient front and soon grew tired of the specific issues the League championed. It was this lack of total commitment to the anti-imperialist struggle, at least as defined by those who were the victims of colonialism, that led Black radicals such as George Padmore to break from the Communist Party. This criticism was supported by Fenner Brockway who said:

> One of the disappointing things about the League is that it never did effective work after it was established. [...] The fact of its establishment was an important thing as it had brought together the leaders of the people's movements in the colonial territories with the working class in Europe and particularly with the Communists and their associates in Moscow.
>
> If you look at working-class history at that time, the opportunity which occurred when, in the League, you had the associates of the leaders of a large part of the working-class movement in Europe with the leaders of the nationalist movement in Asia and Africa – the fact it was an extraordinary association – encouraged the view that it might lead to a worldwide movement of significance. It didn't... it had little influence on the course of events.
>
> I would like to know what was happening inside the Communist International at that time. They did not follow up the opportunity of the League to seek close association and cooperation with the nationalist movements.
>
> I think it possible that ideological doubt began to arise within the Communist movement about association with the movements in the colonies which were bourgeois and might be nationalist but not socialist.[64]

In 1929 the Labour Party declared the League a proscribed organisation – one with which no member of the party could be associated. This, and the Communist Party's loss of interest, was the main reason why it eventually withered away, nothing replacing it until the emergence of the Movement for Colonial Freedom after the 1939-45 war.

Correspondence between Ronald Bridgeman, an enlightened thinker on the subject of anti-imperialist activity, and his friend the Communist Party General Secretary Harry Pollitt in 1942 tends to back up Brockway's criticism of the Communist Party's position on this matter. Bridgeman, referring to a draft Communist statement on the colonial question, wrote on 21 May:

> It seems to me important to avoid giving the impression that a Communist statement on the colonial question is influenced by the compulsion of events, that it is primarily governed by the desire to enlist all colonial peoples in the struggle to smash Fascism, rather than by the determination boldly to proclaim in Britain that the immediate need as far as all nations, free and subject, is concerned is the liberation of the colonial peoples from alien domination, in order that they may line themselves with the

progressive forces of the world… I believe it is essential at the present juncture that the right of the colonial peoples to freedom should be plainly announced as a matter of principle by the CPGB before the question of the importance of their participation in the fight against Fascism is defined.'[65]

Pollitt wrote back somewhat equivocally and Bridgeman noted that, in a speech to the CPGB's conference there was 'merely a declaration of solidarity with the Colonial Peoples'. The CPGB's sometimes patronising attitude towards people in Africa and Asia was confronted by Palme Dutt on one of the few times he publicly broke with Pollitt. Palme Dutt supported the Indian communists when they argued for more than mere satellite status in relationship to the CPGB. The row surfaced when the CPGB's programme, *The British Road to Socialism*, was adopted in 1951. Among its proposals was that there should be a form of fraternal association between Britain and the former colonies once socialism had been achieved in this country.

Pollitt's view, supported by the majority on the central committee, was that building up communist parties in the colonies was not high on the agenda. Achieving socialism in Britain should be the first priority. But at the CPGB's Congress in 1957, the minority, led by Palme Dutt, who argued that the formulation was a continuation of the old colonial relationship, prevailed.[66]

Kay Beauchamp, a member of the CPGB's central committee in 1945, remembered a related dispute. This was over whether or not to allow West Africans in Britain to organise their own branch of the Communist Party. Much like those activists who agitated for Labour Party Black Sections in the 1980s, they had to beat the party hierarchy to achieve their aim. But branches for Black people, including those formed by West Indians, were eventually closed down, leading to an exodus of Black members including the Indian Workers Association.[67]

These issues still bedevil the relationships between Black activists and the British left. Recurring problems include the failure of the left to deal adequately with race as a theoretical issue, the tendency to upgrade or downgrade Black issues according to the exigencies of the moment, and the nature of the treatment Black activists receive within predominantly white organisations. On the first issue, Trevor Carter, a Black Trinidadian and former member of the CPGB's central committee before the party split into the Communist Party of Britain and Labourite Democratic Left, attacked the traditional Marxist class before race line. Carter argued that this stance resulted in the white Left theoretically reducing or explaining away racial issues in purely economic terms or, in practice, disregarding them as irrelevant or relegating them to secondary importance.[68] On the second issue there is the example of the way the Socialist Workers Party (SWP) established the Anti-Nazi League, closed it down and then relaunched it after this author and fellow Black activists and their labour movement allies founded the Anti-Racist Alliance (ARA) in 1991. The difference of opinion here was over whether or not Black people themselves should lead the fight against racism, of which fascism is a servant. The SWP preferred a narrow, easier to dominate, anti-nazi initiative and gave only lip-service support to the broad-based ARA. This divisive approach of some influential 'white left' organisations greatly weakened the anti-racist movement in the 1990s. (These issues continue today in white left groups that see them prefer to handpick Black people to stand for office rather than concede to the principles of *Black self-organisation* and *self-determination*.)

Thirdly, Black socialists have too often been forced to conclude that even where white activists have taken up issues, they have kept Black people in the 'second tier' of their organisations. 'Always the sergeants, never the lieutenants and generals'. This was the case with the Movement for Colonial Freedom. One of their Black members remarked: 'It was controlled by white activists, with very few black people in the leadership. Respect is a different thing from being given the opportunity to give leadership. The left is always showing respect – and they make you an outreach worker!... That is at the root of black people's frustration with the organised working-class movement – that lip service, that denial of our potential. They have double standards in their expectations.'[69]

During Saklatvala's time, there were no more than a handful of Black people in the labour movement like himself. For this reason, he did not have to grapple with the question of Black self-organisation in the Labour Party, trade unions or any other such group. We do not know, therefore, what his position on such issues would have been. What is clear, though, is that Saklatvala was much more open to new ideas than his more orthodox colleagues on the left in Britain. And, as we have seen, he was most certainly *for* self-determination.

CHAPTER 7

LAST YEARS

Labour won the General Election in 1929 and Ramsay MacDonald became Prime Minister for the second time. It was not a good year for capitalism. The New York stock exchange in Wall Street crashed and the world economy slumped. But, for the communists in Britain this was little comfort. With Saklatvala's defeat at Battersea they lost their only MP and half of the party's membership had by then deserted them as a result of the disastrous 'Class against Class' policy.

Although the margin of Saklatvala's defeat at the hands of William Sanders, the official Labour candidate, by 13,265 votes to 6,554, was decisive and indicates the loyalty of the majority of working class voters to the Labour Party, whoever the candidate, Saklatvala's vote was undoubtedly damaged by an exceptionally dirty campaign waged against him. He was accused of 'being a rich man posing as a friend of the poor' and 'concealing not only his wealth but a secret mission to promote Indian trade and business at the expense of English workers'. It was claimed that he had built a marble fountain in his garden that cost £250, had personally pocketed part of a donation to his election fund, and been planning to abandon North Battersea and instead contest North St. Pancras.[1] Labour canvassers were also alleged to have told voters that Saklatvala's Bolshevik principles would result in the pulling down of Catholic churches and the robbery of their congregations' personal property. North Battersea was a constituency with a large God-fearing Irish population.[2] The report of the election in the local *South Western Star* does, though, suggest that right up to the final count, the Labour candidate's victory over Saklatvala was not a foregone conclusion, and that Saklatvala still had considerable and vociferous support:

> At times surging above all, came in wave after wave the cries of the angry Communists: 'Sak, Sak, Sak. We want Sak... Mr Sanders was especially noticeable. Flushed with triumph, he seemed almost as much astonished as triumphant. His features glowed with pride, and yet it seemed that if he spoke he could say nothing but, "Wonderful! Stupendous!" [3]

Saklatvala told his supporters that 'One phase of the election may be lost but through all vicissitudes the people's struggle will go forward to victory.' But, on the parliamentary road, try as he might, as he did five more times to get back into elected office, even to his local St. Pancras Borough Council, Saklatvala never again achieved an election victory. Nonetheless he continued to give loyal service to the party. He spoke at meetings all over the country, concentrating on issues such as India, the Soviet Union and students. He was particularly popular at events organised by miners in Wales and Scotland. Dora Cox, widow of the communist Welsh miners' leader, Idris Cox, remembers Saklatvala staying at her home in Cardiff during one such trip. 'He was the perfect gentleman. Sak always made his bed and helped with the washing up. I remember him telling me he always kept a notebook by his bed and wrote down any thoughts that came to him in the night.'[4]

In June 1930, Saklatvala was back campaigning for votes when he contested a by-election in Glasgow's Shettleston constituency, called after the death of Red Clydeside[5] leader and left-wing Independent Labour Party MP, John Wheatley. Saklatvala fought the high-profile by-election as part of the Communist Party's campaign of solidarity during a critical phase of the Indian independence struggle. He used it to raise the issues of colonial oppression at a time when British troops were suppressing mass civil disobedience in India and imprisoning the leaders of its fledgling trade union movement.

The Daily Worker reported that Labour slogans, chalked on pavements, were 'reminiscent of the Tory slogans of five years ago, such as "Send him back to India", "Saklatvala runs on Moscow Gold", "Saklatvala standing for Four Hundred Pounds a Year".' The newspaper commented with unconscious irony: 'Our message of class against class has penetrated every working-class household in Shettleston.'[6] Saklatvala came last, getting only 1,459 votes (5.8%) behind a Scottish nationalist, at the poll on June 26, while Labour, represented by an ex-communist ILP member, John McGovern, only just held off the Tories to retain the seat. Surprisingly, the Glasgow campaign saw Saklatvala bury the hatchet with his old Conservative rival Sir Mancherjee Bhownagree, also a former MP. They exchanged friendly correspondence about a common enemy: the Labour Party. In a letter Saklatvala wrote excusing himself from a function at Zoroastrian House the week after the by-election, he said:

> My politics and standards of fights are otherwise at pole's end from yours, yet there are several factors that often make me think of you. When you first started breaking the Indian superstition that all Liberals are really liberals and all Conservatives were cruel you were considered to be the only 'fool among all wise men'! After 35 years the superstition still lingers. Now in Labour we have worse Impostors even than in Liberals, and in the so-called Left-Wing Independent Labour Party we reached

the maximum of political hypocrisy of present day. My last few years are spent in fighting this error, if injustice and oppression are to be fought. Our old-fashioned countrymen still adhere to this superstition. Gandhi seriously replies to Fenner Brockway, and he and old Panditji [Nehru] waste their time in giving long interviews to Slocomb. What leg-pulling all round! Or is it a case of Birds of the same feather?[7]

Saklatvala tried for election to the London County Council from Battersea in March 1931, but failed. The Municipal Reformers, the local Tories, held on to the two seats. The Communist vote was even less than the winner's majority over Labour, which itself suffered massive abstentions by its traditional voters, probably attributable to disgust at Ramsay MacDonald's defection to the coalition government. One can guess that it did not make much difference to his result that Saklatvala was absent for some of the campaign through illness. The rumour was spread that he had double pneumonia, but he was in fact suffering from flu. If he still had a personal following, it amounted to no more than the 193 additional votes he got than his Communist running-mate, Ellen Usher.

By this time the left, and the communists in particular, had lost their hold on Battersea. This was demonstrated by the general election result seven months later when, on October 27 1931, Saklatvala made a last bid to regain his North Battersea parliamentary seat. He polled only half the number of votes he had received in 1929. The Tory candidate, a naval officer, Arthur Marsden, was returned with a substantial majority. It is said that some constituents felt they had been deserted by Saklatvala when he went off to Glasgow for the by-election. Only his Communist Party supporters remained solid. A party member, Kay Beauchamp, who lived in Battersea and canvassed for Saklatvala that year, remembers him speaking at the Town Hall: 'Every meeting where he was on the platform I made sure to be there. He was a brilliant speaker who mesmerised the audience and himself it seemed.'[8] The extremely anti-Labour election material the Communist Party published did not help his chances. The electorate were warned about 'the rotten policy of the last Labour government for two and a half years'. In the Communist Party's view, 'a vote for the Labour candidates means a vote for a vicious capitalist offensive'.[9]

Much of the election material was centrally written, but it is likely that Saklatvala personally authored the passage in the election address which stated, 'the policy of the Labour Government in the Colonies in India, Burma, China and Africa has been one of naked militarist Imperialism and thousands of workers in these countries have been shot down and hundreds of thousands imprisoned during the Labour rule'. He added: 'This act of terrorism has helped the master class employ colonial labour in modern industries at a penny an hour'.[10] This attack on the Labour Party's failure to challenge imperialism was well founded, but it is unlikely to have been high on the priorities of the majority of working-class voters fed a diet of pro-imperialist propaganda in the popular press.

He stood two further times for election. In March 1934 Saklatvala attempted to get elected to the London County Council from his old North Battersea seat. Ill health again meant he was unable to campaign very actively and his vote suffered. He and his Communist running mate, Bill Johnson, made housing their main issue, calling for slum clearance, a programme of house-building and lower council rents. This was a new departure. Previously, communist campaigning, even at a local level, focused on the need to overthrow capitalism, and often attacked the Labour Party rather than the Tories. But, despite the fact that he had been freed from the need to promote such sectarian propaganda following his party's abandonment of its 'Class Against Class' line, Saklatvala was unsuccessful, polling only a handful more votes than Bill Johnson, an electrician who had joined the Communist Party in 1922 and was the organiser of Battersea Trades Council and Labour Party's Unemployed Association, and even fewer than in the council elections three years before.

Saklatvala made his final attempt to gain elected office when he fought a St Pancras borough council election in November, 1934. The result was his worst ever. Not only did he come 14th out of 18 candidates but, for the first time, he was beaten by a fellow Communist, with Maud Carter getting 237 votes to his 106. He was also beaten by a young Indian called Krishna Menon, who, in the process, began his career as a Labour councillor. Menon, a staunch nationalist, was to go on to become an Indian Government minister after independence.

Saklatvala did find time in the autumn of 1934 to go to his beloved Ireland and attend the famed first session of the Republican Congress, which was a Marxist formation, at Rathmines, a Dublin suburb. It agreed a united front of republican and labour organisations for the breaking of the connection with the British Empire and the establishment of a united Ireland.[11]

He did not contest North Battersea at the 1935 General Election because he wanted to ensure a socialist candidate won and he accepted that the man who had ended his parliamentary career, William Sanders, the Labour candidate, had the best chance. His decision was consistent with the Communist Party's about-turn back to the united front policy which again made it possible for communists to support Labour. The party's change of heart came around 1933, when the threat of fascism loomed large enough for them to seek unity with all other socialist groups against a common threat. Saklatvala was active in promoting the Communist Party-inspired Anti-War Committee, and in July, 1932 he gave a speech at a meeting sponsored by their South West London branch in solidarity with German workers in their fight against fascism.

Even though Saklatvala could no longer have been regarded as a significant political threat, the British government continued to restrict his civil liberties. In particular, Saklatvala would dearly have loved to make a final trip to India, but he was cruelly denied his wish. As we have seen, the British authorities repeatedly refused to lift the exclusion order that barred any visit. He had tried to persuade the Labour administration in 1930 but they too refused his pleas. Indeed, the Labour government's letter of rejection was later used by the Tories as part of their justification for continuing the ban.[12] The same year, he was forced to appeal to his arch enemy, Sir John Simon, who, by then, was foreign secretary:

> I am sure, as a lawyer held in high esteem, you will agree with me, that in spite of the unlimited autocratic powers reserved for all passport offices all over the world, it was never contemplated by the framers of passport regulations anywhere, that a passport law may be used to prevent a person from entering the country of his birth, if such a person had at no time changed his nationality by naturalisation in another foreign country. If a person were obnoxious to his own government, he should be dealt with in some legitimate process of exile...[13]

But Secretary of State for India, Sir Samuel Hoare, was not only determined to keep Saklatvala out of India, but keen that his new passport should exclude him from the USA as well.[14] In 1933 Saklatvala had applied for a US visa, but he was again turned down. According to one of his close advisors, Hoare took this attitude because of the influence Saklatvala's 'anti-British eloquence might have on uninstructed American audiences'. Nonetheless, Hoare was overruled because of fears that 'a refusal to grant the endorsement might invite further correspondence from Mr Saklatvala and even afford him the opportunity for undesirable publicity'.[15]

But it was a Machiavellian manoeuvre because the British authorities knew their friends in the US Government would not grant him a visa anyway. His daughter Sehri says: 'He was a refusenik in this country. The authorities were afraid of the following he had. At one point, when his sister was ill, he said he would go back (to India) and be escorted from the boat by a policeman, speak to his sister for half an hour and be brought back under escort and they wouldn't let him. It was a terrible blow which almost broke his spirit.'[16]

No longer an MP, it is evident, too, that Saklatvala was also marginalised by the party which had been marginalised by the workers. No longer was he on the central committee and there was no leadership role given to him, though he was still in demand as a speaker. As the first national organiser of the Young Communists League, Harry Young, recalled: 'Saklatvala was never in the top brass. The leadership didn't really approve of him because he was a bit of a maverick, always independent.'[17]

It is a tribute to his courage and steadfastness that right up to the moment of his death, Saklatvala did not cease for one moment from devoting his energies to the causes that were central to his life: revolutionary socialism, anti-racism (such as the Scottsboro Boys case, mentioned in the previous chapter), anti-imperialism and the Indian independence struggle.

He continued his work for the Communist Party, enthusiastically engaging in the new 'popular front' activities against fascism. Indeed, though Saklatvala had been one of the earliest proponents of the 'new line' policy of making the Labour Party the target of its most hostile attacks, there is some historical evidence that he was also an early supporter of the policy of left unity. No doubt as a result of what was happening to the left in Battersea, particularly with the adoption of a right-wing official Labour candidate, Saklatvala is reported, while still an MP, to have offered to stand down for John Burns, the veteran left-wing socialist. William Kent, Burns' biographer, claims: 'Saklatvala, a really fine gentleman, well educated and self-sacrificing in the cause of working people, wrote to Burns, offering to retire in his favour if he wished to stand, or to assist him elsewhere, but there was nothing doing.'[18] Some years later, in 1931, according to Kent, 'Burns was invited by Saklatvala to go to one of his Town Hall meetings, and was promised full opportunity to speak as he wished. Burns' response was to say characteristically, 'If Mr Sanders and Mr Saklatvala would resign their candidatures on my behalf, as both of them should, Battersea can be recovered for commonsense and democracy and in that case Labour will have a tried and trusted representative and India a devoted and sincere friend'.[19] Burns was well to the left of Sanders, but his offer was ridiculed by communists who claimed that he was eccentric and past his prime.

Explaining his decision not to stand in Battersea in the 1935 General Elections, Saklatvala wrote: 'The peculiarity and gravity of the present situation make it clear that the best service I can render is by standing down... By so doing I am acting in the interests of working-class Battersea, because thus there will be no splitting of the working-class vote. If the local Labour Party found it permissible, I should readily speak and work on behalf of the Labour candidate.[20] There is no evidence that Saklatvala's offer was taken up and he went instead to campaign for Communist Party candidates, Willie Gallagher (1881-1965), who was standing in the Scottish constituency of West Fyfe, and for Harry Pollitt (1890-1960) in the Welsh constituency of Rhondda East, two mining areas with a tradition of militancy. Gallagher was successful, beating a sitting Labour MP – the only time such a feat was ever achieved by the Communists, but Pollitt lost, polling 13,655 votes (38.2%) to Labour's 22,088 (61.8%).

At the end of the year Saklatvala spoke at the London meeting of the Congress of Peace and Friendship with the USSR, at Friends' Meeting

House in Euston Road. *The Manchester Guardian* quoted him saying it was time England began making loans to Russia.[21] He added that it was essential to world peace that the United States and Soviet Russia join together in the League of Nations. This event offered one of the best examples of the application of the popular-front strategy which had been developed by the Communist Party to fight the rise of fascism.[22] The Party's newly adopted *popular frontism* meant that motley groups of politically disparate people were brought together for Communist-run events, all of them welcome provided they would declare, in some way, their 'friendship' towards the Soviet Union. Critics of the policy within the left argued that this had the effect of demoralising the workers who had previously been told to oppose such people. But Saklatvala was loyal to the last, vigorously supporting Willie Gallagher, one of the most enthusiastic promoters of the new line.

According to *The Manchester Guardian*, the event was a 'non-party' congress with delegates from British 'social, cultural, religious, industrial, co-operative and political bodies', representing more than a million people. The meeting certainly attracted support from a wide cross-section of personalities, including the Black American singer, Paul Robeson, who was to be witch-hunted for his Communist beliefs, Lord Listowel, George Bernard Shaw, F. Seymour Cocks MP, Viscount Hastings, Lord Marley and Vyvyan Adams MP. The Soviet ambassador Ivan Maisky was present for much of the meeting. Robert Boothby, a Tory MP, used the occasion to disassociate himself from Bolshevism but said it would be 'foolish to ignore the note of practical realism which has been struck in the Kremlin ever since Mr Stalin came to power'.

The Foreign Office, in a confidential memorandum sent beforehand to Foreign Secretary Anthony Eden's advisors, described the event as a front for the Comintern. 'We know, from various sources, that the leading spirits behind the proposed congress are connected with a none too desirable organisation. It would be difficult however and perhaps impolitic for Mr Eden to refuse to send the desired message of goodwill'.[23]

Lord Allen of Hurtwood, formerly Clifford Allen, who had been a leading figure in the ILP and Battersea Labour politics, moved a resolution expressing the congress's 'deep appreciation for the Soviet Union's effort to promote world peace, particularly by upholding the Covenant of the League of Nations.' It went on to urge the Government to encourage close trade and other cooperation between Britain and the USSR, stating there should be a widening of friendly contacts between common people of both countries as a solid basis for mutual understanding.[24] The motion was passed unanimously.

In his last years, Saklatvala maintained his uncritical position on the Soviet Union, making his third visit there with his close friend and former parliamentary secretary, Reg Bishop, in the summer of 1934. He spent nearly four months in the USSR. This was, of course, in the year immediately following the ending of Stalin's draconian programme of forced collectivisation of the peasants, when between 1929 and 1933 millions of the country's population lost their lives, particularly in the Ukraine, where they died as a result of a famine brought about by Stalin's policy of centralising, among other things, all food stocks. Of this Saklatvala had nothing to say in his public pronouncements. His son, Beram, did suggest to an earlier biographer that Saklatvala returned to Britain with a number of reservations, but what these were is not known. His daughter, Sehri, records that the copious notes he made on the tour have been lost. In Saklatvala's defence, it is evident that the main focus of his visit was to compare conditions in India with those in the Soviet Union's Central Asian republics, where he spent much of his time. From that perspective, his enthusiasm is rather more understandable. He wrote to the *Daily Worker*:

> I have finished a long and most interesting tour. On the spot I have done things of which I could never have got a real grasp by 'collecting information' at home. New Russia is a wonderful place, but new Soviet Asia even more so. One can never fully realise the tremendous extent of human development made possible by the 'Revolution'... No worker who sees for himself can leave anything but a friend of the Soviet Union ... At large meetings in Tashkent, Fergana, Stalinabad, Ashkabad, Baku, Batoum, Erivan and Tiflis I have been asked to convey resolutions of solidarity and greetings to the British workers, the Indian toilers and the Communist Party of Great Britain.[25]

He travelled to the parts of the USSR, in Central Asia and the Caucasus, including Georgia, Armenia, Azerbaijan, Turkmenistan and Uzbekistan, on the border with Turkey and Iran, where non-Russians lived, and said he was greatly impressed by the advances that had been made.[26] In a letter to a member of the Indian Congress party, he wrote: 'I have visited all the middle Asiatic regions of the USSR and it is here among the Asian Races that one really sees the mighty efforts of Communism for human liberation.'[27] In a letter to Harry Pollitt, he exclaimed: 'Oh, Harry, what my people could do in India if only they were as free as my comrades in those autonomous republics in the USSR.'[28]

Ominously, during the visit he fainted at a big meeting in Moscow's Red Army Theatre. It was a heart attack. Reg Bishop said: 'I remember ... having a long talk with him and trying to persuade him to take things more easily when he came back, but he wouldn't listen.'[29] Bishop wrote: 'If he had spared himself in the last few years, he might have lived longer but he would not have been Sak if he had spared himself.' He had a further heart attack on the ship coming home. His daughter Sehri recalled that when she had pointed out her father when she and her mother had gone to meet the ship, her mother had said, 'That's not Daddy – that's an old man.'[30] Saklatvala, though, kept his good spirits, inviting the entire crew to his home for the day. There was panic in the household because it was not certain enough food could be prepared in time. But, when the forty or so men arrived, they were duly entertained and there was much singing and dancing. The crew invited the Saklatvala family back to their ship for dinner. There they presented Saklatvala with an 18-inch bronze statuette of Lenin which had previously been bolted to a shelf in the ship's Lenin Corner. It is now kept at the Marx Memorial Library in Clerkenwell Green, London.[31]

In addition to his work for the Communist Party, Saklatvala continued to travel all over the country promoting the cause of Indian independence. As mentioned earlier, he was very actively involved in the Meerut conspiracy case. A year before he died he went to the north-east of England to speak at a public meeting in Gateshead. He wrote about the 'Round Table Conference' in 1930, and returned to criticise the Mahatma in an article titled 'Gandhi and the Pacifist Variety of Imperialism' published two years later. One of his final pieces of political journalism was an article called 'The Indian Struggle' published in *India Front*.[32]

His work among Indian students continued unabated. He was helped by a dynamic young man called Niharendu Dutta Mazumdar, who was later to break with Communism in India and become a minister in Dr B.C. Roy's Congress cabinet in Bengal. Mazumdar's student group included other people who later reached prominence like the author M.R. Masani. They were all radical young men from the 'best families' in India.[33] Masani remembers being invited by Saklatvala to address a Communist meeting in 1934. He was reluctant to accept because at the time he was secretary of the Congress Socialist Party, an organisation which the Communists had denounced as 'social fascists'. Saklatvala told him not to worry because he would be chairing the meeting. 'A month later Moscow decided we were comrades,' said Masani. 'Saklatvala knew they were wrong and we were right.'[34] Another student, Himmat Sinha, who had gone to Oxford, recalled that in 1935 Saklatvala attended his university for a debate organised by an Indian students' group. The subject was 'That in the opinion of this house Communism is the last resort of a scoundrel'. Saklatvala was 'the main opposition speaker, and 'with his thundering oration he won an overwhelming majority in his favour'. Sinha added: 'I had the privilege then of being the host of the visiting dignitary who stayed with me in my 'digs'. During the conversation, he astounded us by saying that it was quite easy to learn any European language and deliver a fluent speech in it provided one knew any one of the Indian languages.'[35]

If Saklatvala's optimism concerning the inevitable victory of the nationalists in India was undimmed, there is a note of almost despairing righteous anger in a message he wrote to the weavers of Lancashire and India in *The Daily Worker*. This was over the failure of British trade unionism to either grasp or act on his conviction that the workers' struggle had to cross national boundaries. The article referred to the struggle by British workers against wage cuts: 'What did the Lancashire trade union officials do when Indian textile workers were involved in a deadly struggle against their employers? Did they give a lead to British workers to stand four square behind the Indian workers? No. They did nothing of the sort.' Saklatvala criticised the way the union leaders had 'barefacedly sided with the employers'. He remarked: 'now, as night follows day, cuts in wages of textile workers in India will be followed by cuts in wages in Lancashire.'[36]

Saklatvala had been sick and frail some time before he died, but he kept up his political work to the end. His daughter Sehri said, 'I think there was a good deal of political activity that he didn't discuss with us. Maybe because he wasn't on the up and up anymore… Maybe it was because he knew he was on a losing wicket that we didn't know half of what he was doing. But he was active right up until the last hour of his life.' A letter from an 'ordinary worker' to the *Daily Worker* gives a picture of Saklatvala's undimmed powers as a speaker in the last year of his life. D.C. Jackson wrote:

> No greater testimony could be paid to Comrade Saklatvala than to recall one summer's afternoon on southern Common [at Clapham] – hardly an ideal place for communist propaganda when the military and patriotic tendencies of the locality are considered. Yet Saklatvala drew a crowd of 1,500 people, who listened earnestly and attentively. Ten yards away, Mr Beckett, the renegade socialist who had become one of the Blackshirt 'Stars', was speaking to a small audience. When Saklatvala began, however, they deserted the fascist gentleman and came over to the communist speaker's platform.[37]

Days prior to his death, Saklatvala and his wife worked behind a stall at a Communist Party bazaar at Shoreditch Town Hall, in London. The evening before his fatal heart-attack, he gave a two-hour lecture on 'The Basis of Socialism' to students at the Marx Memorial Library and Workers School in the capital.

On the morning of 16 January 1936, an old friend from India, Mr Yajnik, a journalist and member of the League Against Imperialism, visited Saklatvala at his home and they had a heated discussion about politics over breakfast. Sehri recalls: 'Mother told him (Saklatvala) not to get so excited as she feared it would bring on another of his now frequent heart attacks. When I returned from school in the afternoon, father was seeing Mr Yajnik off at the gate, but they were still arguing and back they came into the house.

Apparently one of the subjects they were discussing was cremation – father was all in favour of it, of course, and at one point said, "Well, when I die I hope the dust-bin men will simply take my body away with the rubbish!"'[38]

Sehri vividly recalled how she learnt the news of her father's death:

> I was to wait for father at the School of Broadcasting because mummy wasn't well and he was going to take me out to dinner with Dr and Mrs Gotla and it was my first adult dinner party going with father and I was feeling rather fearful of it, shy of it. And, after my class at the School of Broadcasting, there was a message saying there was a change of plan, 'Don't wait for your father, go straight home'. I went home joyful, thinking I was relieved from this terrible formal dinner party.
>
> It was snowing and it was a lovely evening. Then I met Dr Gotla. He was also a family friend; he'd been a friend of father's all his life. He was crying and met me at the gate. Somehow I just knew and I went in and my aunt Phyllis opened the door. I don't remember being told, I seemed just to know what had happened.[39]

Saklatvala died, hunched over his desk writing a letter to his son Kaikoo, in the same week as Rudyard Kipling, the poet laureate of British imperialism, passed away. King George V, Emperor of India, died later the same month. An era had come to a close.

Saklatvala's funeral procession was reported to have been more than a mile long and according to the *Daily Worker*:

> The crematorium was filled to overflowing by several hundred people, who had waited for nearly an hour in the slight rain which was falling, in order that they could pay their last tribute to one whom they had known as a great fighter for working-class emancipation and national freedom. Mrs Saklatvala, her three sons and two daughters, followed the motor hearse bearing the coffin from his home to the crematorium. Behind them came a fleet of cars filled with close friends. For several hours before the cortege left St Albans Villas, Highgate, friends and comrades brought wreaths and cut flowers. The room in which Saklatvala lay was filled with floral tributes. 'He was always a lover of flowers', said Mrs Saklatvala as she took us to the room where we saw for the last time 'Sak' as he was always known to thousands. It was hard to realise that we should no more hear his passionate appeal for the oppressed.

The funeral service at Golders Green Crematorium combined Saklatvala's political and religious principles. It was conducted by the three Zoroastrian priests, M. H. Vjifdar, Dr Homi Dastoor and Mr R. R. Desai, who had officiated at the controversial *navjote* initiation ceremony in 1927. The Communist Party leadership, who had publicly rebuked Saklatvala then, had no problem, now he was dead, in attending the sort of Zoroastrian event they had previously condemned as 'religious propaganda'. Harry Pollitt, speaking for the CPGB and Communist International, said: 'It will be hard for us to live up to the work of Comrade Saklatvala, but in paying

him our last tribute we pledge ourselves that the Red Flag which he bore
so nobly aloft shall remain unsullied in our hands.' Saklatvala's wife said:
'He was always working hard. He was working all night some nights. He
never gave up till 2.30am. He worked so hard...[40]

The *Daily Worker* continued:

> The coffin, covered with a purple pall on which lay the red flag was
> placed on a metal platform in front of which stood two Parsee ministers...
> wearing white suits of homespun cloth with round white hats on their
> heads. Close to the edge of the platform was a large silver cup in which
> a fire of sandalwood chips burned and was fed by the ministers. Incense
> and spices were added from time to time. The service, in the sacred
> language of the Parsees, was intoned by the ministers.[41]

Once the Zoroastrian prayers for the dead were over, Saklatvala's widow
and children each added a symbolic chip of sandalwood to the flames.
Finally, the Communist Internationale was sung as his body passed to be
cremated. Letters from Saklatvala to his wife and her cherished wedding
shoes were burnt with him. His ashes were buried at Brookwood Cemetery, Surrey, where the British Parsi community owns a large plot of land,
next to his parents and J. N. Tata, whose last resting place was also England.
Beram, Saklatvala's son, composed the words on the tablet of stone
marking his last resting place. 'Nothing but death could end his courage
and determination in the cause of humanity. Nothing but such determination could conquer death... His work lives on.'

Condolences came in from all over the world. Among those who for-
warded messages to Saklatvala's family were Jawaharlal Nehru who tel-
egraphed from Austria where he was in hospital. Labour leaders Clement
Attlee, George Lansbury and Ben Tillett, as well as the Soviet Ambassador to
London, Ivan Maisky, also sent tributes. Reporting his death, the *New York
Times* commented that Saklatvala, 'created an impression of being a remark-
ably mild man in vast contrast to the extreme character of his views'.[42]

There is no doubting, on the evidence of the eulogies that followed his
death, the contemporary respect in which Saklatvala was held, not only by
his fellow communists, but also among the wider labour movement, and
particularly among Indian nationalists and anti-imperialists. Clement
Attlee, who later became Labour's most radical prime minister, said: 'Mr
Saklatvala was a devoted worker for the causes in which he believed. He was
always a very pleasant man with whom to have dealings.' India's first prime
minister, Jawaharlal Nehru, in a message after Saklatvala's death, said: 'I
wish to pay my tribute to the memory of Shapurji Saklatvala, who throughout his life was a brave and intrepid soldier of freedom.'[43]

After Saklatvala's passing, his children's lives followed various paths.
His eldest son, Dorab, became a doctor in Birmingham. He was the

Saklatvala who completely broke with his father and became a staunch Conservative before he died. Candida, the eldest daughter, worked as a barrister and took a degree in psychology at the University of Reading. She died of cancer. Beram, the second son, joined Tatas after his father's death, and became managing director of the London branch. He was a poet and author who toyed with the idea of writing a book about his father, but never did. Instead he co-authored the official volume on Tatas' founder, Jamsetji, published in India the same year as Panchanan Saha's short biography of Saklatvala. Beram was a socialist, though not as radical as his father. One of his last books, using his maternal grandfather's name, Henry Marsh, was about 'slavery and race', but in the main Beram preferred to work on Roman and Greek history. He died of pneumonia at his Peckham, South London home in 1976, aged 65. He had a son, Paul. Saklatvala's third son, Kaikhoshro, served with the British Air Transport Auxiliary organisation in World War II as a pilot (Second Officer).[44] He flew most frontline aircraft, including Mosquitos, Spitfires and Lancasters. After the war he became an engineer for Kodak. Kaikoo, as he was known, also died before his mother. Sally Saklatvala lived to be 88, dying in 1977, 41 years after her husband. Sehri Jeevanbai, the youngest daughter, had a career on the stage before going to work for India House from 1947, the year of the independence for which her father had fought. She was also on the staff of the former Greater London Council until the mid-1980s, when she retired. Before her death in 2016, aged 97, she lived in Salford, Greater Manchester, and then Brent in northwest London. In a similar political trajectory to her father's, in the late 1990s she left the 'new' Labour Party of Tony Blair in disgust and joined Arthur Scargill's Socialist Labour Party.

In the longer view of history, how is Saklatvala's contribution to be weighed?

It is evident, for instance, that even among the comrades, he was regarded as having limitations. Of course, Saklatvala's privileged family background would not have helped his communist career in the days when the 'cult of the industrial worker' held sway in the British Communist Party. This meant that people such as Harry Pollitt, a boiler maker, who were very definitely from the proletariat, were favoured over others who were seen as middle-class intellectuals. Robin Page Arnot, a former CPGB central committee contemporary of Saklatvala's, admitted the leadership had 'somewhat underrated him'.[45] But it was not just his continuing connection with the Tata family, his religious commitments or his famed independence of mind that disturbed the comrades, but the whisper that his understanding of Marxist-Leninist theory was 'not adequate'. They appreciated his gifts as a speaker and his devotion to the cause, but never

seriously considered him for any leadership position. This is a view which
was endorsed by the Marxist historian, John Saville, who wrote:

> He was not very sophisticated theoretically but he was extremely quick-
> witted and very practically orientated... The central core of Saklatvala's
> thinking was undoubtedly his insistence upon the freedom of the Indian
> people. It was that which he started with in political life as a Liberal
> and it was that with which he ended his life as a Communist.[46]

It is certainly true that a survey of Saklatvala's speeches and writings
suggests that his gifts were more polemical than theoretical – and there is
no doubting his ability in the former. As a contemporary journalist
reported: '...he is so literally logical... His powers of speech are remarkable, and he seems to be thoroughly acquainted with every aspect of the
leading social and political questions.' It is also plain that the basis of
Saklatvala's convictions were more ethical than intellectual. There is little
sense of the kind of 'scientific socialist' dialectic which encouraged some
of the comrades to have an almost religious faith in the inevitability of
capitalism's collapse and the triumph of socialism. Equally, it is unlikely
that Saklatvala would have felt much sympathy for contemporary academic
Marxist discourse and its remoteness from political practice. He was never
to be a party apparatchik like Harry Pollitt, Willie Gallagher or Rajani Palme
Dutt because it was not a theoretical ideology that formed him, but a
passionate fire against injustice that drove him to his own political conclu-
sions. He once told a journalist: 'I am an extremist. An extremist from
conviction, not from any proselytising influence nor as the result of any
propaganda.'[47]

Perhaps more central to Saklatvala's increasing marginalisation in British political life were the contradictions he faced as a revolutionary Indian
nationalist within a political culture where even the Communist Party
wavered in its commitments to making the rights of subject peoples to self-
determination a priority within its political programme. The contradiction
is made clear by juxtaposing two comments about his life. Long afterwards,
the political journalist, Iqbal Singh (who, as a student had heard Saklatvala
speak) said: 'I think he was operating in the wrong country. He became an
object of curiosity but he could not get near the levers of power.'[48] At the
time, Saklatvala's local paper commented sourly: 'North Battersea does not
want to elect a member for the Empire, it wants its own Parliamentary
representative...'[49] This was, though, a view that overlooked the fact that
the inhabitants of the empire were no less British subjects than the
electorate of Battersea.

He was a precursor, in many ways, of the future generations of migrants
to Britain from India, Pakistan, Bangladesh, Africa and the Caribbean who
have tried to forge for themselves a role in shaping their own destiny in

Britain while at the same time remaining concerned with the fate of their country of origin. Like many of them, one suspects that Saklatvala was never wholly reconciled to the fact that he would never return to his homeland. As someone who was ethically committed to the self-determination of his own subject country and of all subject countries – almost without exception, as he once described it, 'the coloured' world – he looked to ways of advancing those views within the British political context. As this book has described, he moved from the Liberals to the ILP, only finding in the Communist Party a commitment to anti-imperialism which began to match his own. There is much in Saklatvala's life that indicates that he constantly struggled against marginalisation – the choice he made to work in the broadly-based ILP rather than in the Marxist SDF, and his position with regard to Congress in India. But the contradictions of his position drove him towards the margins. Thus, though he was one of the biggest casualties of their ultra-left turn in 1928 – the 'new line' he helped to bring about – he remained loyal to the Communist Party until he died. For Saklatvala it was inconceivable that he should go the way of his former communist comrade in parliament, J. Walton Newbold, by travelling rightwards back into the Labour Party. For him, because of the centrality of Indian nationalism and anti-imperialism to his very being, there was no way he could return to a Labour Party that in office continued the imperialist policies of Conservative administrations, even though membership of the Labour Party might have offered a brighter political future. He saw through the Labour Party on the fundamental issues of capitalism and imperialism, and had no illusions about it ever changing, a view vindicated by the direction of today's party for most of the past fifty years, with the brief exception of Jeremy Corbyn's leadership, opposed as he was by the vast majority of Labour MPs and party officials, and widely supported only among a membership enthused by his election. In Saklatvala's day, while the Labour Party policy purported to be for Indian self-determination, Clement Attlee, one of their leading left-wing MPs, was only too happy to sit on the all-British 'Simon' Commission looking into 'reforms'. A Battersea journalist offered this cynical explanation: 'Mr Saklatvala apparently fails to realise that the English are practical rather than logical. They are devoid of that fantastic desire, characteristic of the East, to press a theory to its logical conclusion.[50]

The racism of this assessment, rooted in its orientalist stereotype, misses the point in a revealing way. For Saklatvala, as an Indian, even though a relatively privileged one, the issue of self-determination and the respect bound up with it was necessarily an absolute one. Indians were either free or not free, and on that question the British political mainstream, including in practice the Labour Party, was on the other side. Indeed, as an Indian in exile in Britain, for a time functioning at the very heart of British political institutions, the equation was particularly acute. Unlike the nationalists in India who had the solidarity of numbers and for whom the British were essentially an alien enemy, very clearly on the other side of the barricades, for Saklatvala, as a member of a tiny Indian minority in Britain, his relationships with the British were inevitably far more diffuse, including as they did his marriage and many of his closest comrades as well those whose views made them his political enemies. In such a situation, it is not surprising that Saklatvala was completely unwavering in his attachments and as a result was perceived as 'extreme'. Even within the Communist Party, as this book has observed, where on the national and colonial questions, Saklatvala was perhaps inevitably ahead of his white contemporaries, there was an element of difference which resulted in his being sidelined. In the context of the role of Black people within the British left, these are still issues which have to be resolved.

Where would he be politically today? Such speculation, across the years and the differences of context, is perhaps idle, but at the time of this book's first publication some contemporaries, like Andrew Rothstein, were prepared to venture a guess. 'I'm no soothsayer, but he'd probably have been in the Communist Party of Britain'. (This is the pro-Soviet CPGB successor that Rothstein and the daily *Morning Star* newspaper support.[51]) Saklatvala's daughter disagreed. 'I think he wouldn't have waited until now to start asking questions. He would have queried 1956 (the Warsaw Pact invasion of Hungary) and 1968 (the Soviet invasion of Czechoslovakia).'[52]

What would his view have been of India, the beloved country whose independence he never lived to see? Sehri's view was that 'He would have said, "I told you so." It's no better having capitalism run by brown people than by white ones. He was for a Communist India.'

Saklatvala was honoured by the international Communist movement with a brigade in the Spanish Civil War named after him. During the Greater London Council-attempted revival of municipal socialism in the 1980s, Lambeth Council, prompted by its 'Black Sections' councillors, including leader Linda Bellos, attempted to give his name to a park in the south London borough. But the authority backed off after adverse publicity in the national press. The Communist Party of Great Britain (Marxist-Leninist) have their Saklatvala Hall in Southall, west London, which is used for public meetings and events.

Saklatvala deserves more than a historical plaque, which he does not yet have, because there is so much that he stood for that warrants a more living kind of tribute. Though the collapse of the communist political project in Europe, and its failure to deliver the full human liberation he believed was its aim, make some of Saklatvala's pronouncements sound naive and self-deceiving today, the goal of the 'real and truly free man, the real and truly emancipated woman and the truly cared for children', which he believed the Soviet Union was enabling, are still political objectives to be cherished. He would have been disgusted but probably not surprised by the necessity of food banks for the poor, the racist treatment of the inhabitants of Grenfell, migrants and of the 'Windrush generation', or the fact the Covid-19 pandemic exposed deep inequalities of race, income and living conditions in its mortality rates. He would undoubtedly have been on the streets with Black Lives Matter. In his internationalism, his unceasing commitment to the struggles of those who were oppressed by the forces of global capitalism must win our respect. Much of what he fought for remains unwon, and after the upheavals in Eastern Europe, the fall of the Soviet Union and its Communist satellites, there has been a general tendency to relegate the social vision of Marxism to the museum of history. But right-wing commentators are more cautious. The *Spectator* observed '...in these days of West European triumphalism... the proclamation of the death of Marxism is premature. Eastern Europe is not the world... Only the incurably Eurocentric could maintain that Marxism is dead.'[53]

After Saklatvala's death, a comrade, J. H. Kilmarnock wrote the following verses:

He is gone from our midst,
The stalwart and brave;
A foe to the tyrant, a friend to the slave.
We hearken in vain for the voice that is stilled.
In our hearts there's a void that can never be filled.
Keen, tireless and brave was the life he led;
We mourn over the loss of the comrade that's dead.
At the horns of the plough we may pause and look back.
To scan o'er the furrow and follow our 'Sak'.

But perhaps Saklatvala's own words, when he urged the House of Commons, in his first speech 'to burst out of these time-worn prejudices and boldly take a new place', serve as a more fitting epitaph.

In a speech the author gave in Glasgow about Saklatvala, organised by the city's Anti-Racist Alliance in October 2005, I said his not long previously released MI5 file showed that he had been under surveillance from 1910 long before he joined the Communist Party in 1921.

Saklatvala had been drawn to the Communist Party because of its unequivocal stand against imperialism. But his key contribution was to understand the class dimension of black oppression and the black dimension of class oppression. In his Commons speeches, he demonstrated how exploitation of the black world damaged Black and white workers alike.

Saklatvala bridged the class and cultural barriers with his powerful commitment to the revolutionary cause.

Still, today the left are sometimes just as guilty as they were in Saklatvala's time of failing to understand that the cultural and religious differences they sometimes dismiss as 'identity politics' or 'culture wars', are not counterposed to socialist politics. The Black British scholar, Dalia Gebrial, spoke for exasperated youth in a Novara Media online broadcast in the summer of 2020, when she said:

> The whole point is, when we [Labour's left] galvanised our power from the street and from... dispossessed communities we did much better. Whereas, when you look at the concessions around the issues like militarism, like policing, like immigration enforcement, these are not 'cultural war' issues these are 'class war' issues. Immigration policy, policing policy, mass incarceration, these are ways of forming dispossessed working class people in a racialised way... The concession of all of these issues broke apart the social coalition that nearly got Corbynism in government in 2017.

The author contends that if Saklatvala was still alive, his critique of how the once in a generation radical left leadership of the Labour Party failed would be similar. Tariq Ali told a YouTube meeting about Free Speech in the Labour Party on 28 July 2020:

> The left has lost, it has been defeated. It is not going to come anywhere near to getting a leader as left-wing as Corbyn for the next half century, that is if the United Kingdom exists by then... The right are not going to make the same mistakes again, which enabled the left to come in and score these victories in a situation where they [the left] had virtually no support within the Parliamentary Labour Party and were unable to create an organisation which did more than electoral campaigning.[54]

Speaking at the Glasgow Anti-Racist Alliance meeting on behalf of the Communist Party, its international secretary John Foster struck a more optimistic note when he commented: 'Today, the Communist Party is proud that Saklatvala was one of its first MPs and that his memory continues to inspire.' Palme Dutt was even more emphatic in his praise of his comrade after he died, describing Saklatvala as: 'A heroic figure of international Communism and of the fight for Indian national liberation and of the British working-class movement.' As such tributes made plain, Saklatvala's role as anti-imperialist 'MP for India' is not to be forgotten.

ENDNOTES

Preface

1. Alex Wessely blog, 6 October 2017, Leigh Day solicitors https://www.leighday.co.uk/Blog/October-2017/Kenyan-colonial-abuses-apology-five-years-on
2. The Windrush Scandal explained, Joint Council for the Welfare of immigrants, online https://www.jcwi.org.uk/windrush-scandal-explained. And see Amelia Gentleman, *The Windrush Betrayal: Exposing the Hostile Environment* (London: Guardian Faber Publishing, 2019).
3. See S.G. Checkland, *The Gladstones: A Family Biography 1764-1851* (Cambridge: Cambridge University Press, 1971) S.D. Smith, *Slavery, Family and Gentry Capitalism in the British Atlantic: the World of the Lascelles, 1648-1834* (Cambridge: Cambridge University Press, 2006); Katie Donington, *The Bonds of Family: Slavery, commerce and culture in the British Atlantic World* (Manchester: Manchester University Press, 2020).
4. See David Olusoga, *Black and British: A Forgotten History* (London: MacMillan, 2017) and television programmes such as *The World's War*, *A House through Time* and *Britain's Forgotten Slave Owners*.
5. See www.colonialcountryside.wordpress.com and www.nationaltrust.org.uk/features/colonial-countryside-project
6. See www.economist.com/britain/2020/02/08/british-universities-are-examining-how-they-benifited-from-slavery. For the Caribbean and African American case see respectively, Hilary McD. Beckles, *Britain's Black Debt* (Jamaica: University of the West Indies Press, 2013) and Ana Lucia Araujo, *Reparations for Slavery and the Slave Trade* (London: Bloomsbury, 2017).
7. See for instance www.bera.ac.uk/blog/blacklivesmatter-in-education.
8. See https://rmfoxford.wordpress.com/
9. See Tom Heyden, "The 10 greatest controversies of Winston Churchill's career", BBC online News Magazine, 26 January 2015.
10. 12 May 1919, War Office Memorandum, America's National Churchill Museum.
11. See for instance www.express.co.uk/news/uk/1295858/Boris-Johnson-Churchill-statue-black-lives-matter-latest-news.
12. See Priyamvada Gopal, *Insurgent Empire: Anticolonial Resistance and British Dissent* (London: Verso, 2019), pp. 419-424.
13. A Media Reform Coalition academic report by scholars Dr Justin Schlosberg and Laura Laker, deals with the biased way the news media covered Marc Wadsworth's case: https://www.mediareform.org.uk/blog/new-mrc-research-finds-inaccuracies-and-distortions-

in-media-coverage-of-antisemitism-and-the-labour-party. On British treatment of colonial Palestine see Zeina B. Ghandour, *A Discourse on Domination in Mandate Palestine: Imperialism, Property and Insurgency* (London: Routledge, 2009), and Rashid Khalidi, *The Hundred Years War on Palestine* (London: Profile Books, 2020), pp. 17-54.

14. On role of ethnic cleansing in the foundation of the state of Israel see the work of the Israeli historian Ilan Pappe, *The Ethnic Cleansing of Palestine* (London: Oneworld Publications, 2006).

15. On the Israeli occupation of Palestinian lands and virtual imprisonment of Palestinians in the occupied territories and Gaza see Ilan Pappe, *The Biggest Prison on Earth: A History of the Occupied Territories* (London: Oneworld Publications, 2017)

16. For coolly documented study of the media treatment of the antisemitism issue, see Greg Philo, Mike Berry et al., *Bad News for Labour: Antisemitism, The Party & Public Belief* (London: Pluto Press, 2019).

17. On YouTube, 28 July 2020, https://www.youtube.com/watch?v=MSjlMHNkEWg&t=3632s

18. Ibid.

Chapter One

1. As can be seen on the film footage of Saklatvala contained in the Channel Four documentary, *Comrade Sak*, 6 April 1990.

2. *South Western Star*, February 24, 1922.

3. Online article *The Making of an Indian MP*, based on a March 1936 obituary of Shapurji Saklatvala, on the Indian History Collective website https://indianhistorycollective.com/an-indian-mp-in-the-british-house-of-commons/

4. *The Evening News*, 29 August 1925. (National Minority Movement Meeting, Battersea Town Hall).

5. *Daily Worker*, 18 January 1936.

6. Thomas Bell, *Pioneering Days* (London: Lawrence and Wishart, 1941), p. 266.

7. Herbert Bryan, 'Saklatvala, An Appreciation', *Daily Herald*, 24 November 1922 – typed copy in Saklatvala Papers, MSS.EUR D 1173/4.

8. Priyamvada Gopal, *Insurgent Empire: Anticolonial Resistance and British Dissent* (2019), p. 236.

9. *The Times*, 28 February, 1923.

10. *The Manchester Guardian*, 22 March 1928.

11. *The Times*, 13 February 1925.

12. Hansard, 23 November 1922.
13. A private all-male dining club for Oxford University students, noted for its wealthy members, including Conservative prime ministers David Cameron and Boris Johnson, who indulged in grand banquets, bizarre rituals and bad behaviour.
14. Hansard, 15 January 2020, vol. 669, cols. 1057-1060.
15. Hansard, 30 January, 2020, vol. 650, cols. 993-997.
16. Ibid.
17. Election Address, 1923.
18. *Sunday Worker*, May 1925.
19. Karl Marx, *Capital* Vol. 1, Penguin Classics Edition (London: Penguin, 1976, 1990, p. 414.
20. *The Guardian*, 11 January 1997.
21. Ibid.
22. See Michael Fisher, *The Inordinately Strange Life of Dyce Sombre: Victorian Anglo Indian MP and Chancery 'Lunatic'* (London: C. Hurst and Co, 2010) and British Parliament website https://www.parliament.uk/about/art-in-parliament/online-exhibitions/ parliamentarians/pioneers/page-1/.
23. House of Commons Debate, 17 June, 1927, 1388ff.
24. British Library, India Office Records, Indian Political Intelligence files, L/PJ/12/226: Extract from Scotland Yard Report, 19 November 1924.
25. Gopal, op cit., p. 217
26. Herbert Bryan, op cit. Quoted in Gopal, p. 217
27. Gopal, op. cit., p. 216.

Chapter Two

1. Harry Wicks, *Battersea and Wandsworth Labour and Social History Newsletter*, Issue 151.
2. The Parsis are a community in India, numbering less than a hundred thousand people, who have their own religious and cultural heritage. The Parsis arrived in India from Persia, now known as Iran, more than a thousand years ago to escape oppression. They speak Gujarati. Their own language Avesta has only been preserved in a religious context. Many feel an affinity with their original homeland, indeed Saklatvala's brother Phiroz was Honorary Persian Consul in New York before his death in 1934.
3. Jamsetji Saklatvala, a cousin of Shapurji, writing about the family in 1932, extract from Jamsetji's private papers by kind permission of Yasmin Saklatvala. The reference to sailcloth in the account of

the family's origins comes from Shapurji's grandson, Christopher Saklatvala, in conversation with the author, 19 June 1990.

4. Tata Enterprises official brochure, circa 1998. For a biography of Jamsetji Tata see B. Saklatvala and K. Khosla *Jamsetji Tata* (Bombay: Government of India Press, 1970).

5. See 'Tata in Britain', *The Manufacturer*, 3 Feb 2014, online. Current holdings include Jaguar, Land Rover, Tetley Teas, the Taj hotels chain and what remains of the British steel industry.

6. Jamsetji Saklatvala, private papers op. cit.

7. See Sehri Saklatvala, *The Fifth Commandment* (Manchester: Miranda Press, 1991), p. 4.

8. The Svadeshi Movement "inspired national-minded Indians to buy only Indian made goods", Tata Enterprises brochure, 1990.

9. *South Western Star*, 24 February 1922.

10. Hansard, November 25 1927.

11. Ibid.

12. See Sehri Saklatvala, *The Fifth Commandment*, p. 43.

13. Author's correspondence with Chris Saklatvala, July 11 1990.

14. *The Fifth Commandment*, p. 43.

15. Tansley Parish website http://www.tansleyparish.com/TansleyVillage/byegone3.html

16. *The Fifth Commandment*, p. 45.

17. See Tansley Parish website, and June Lait, *A brief history of Matlock*, essay, Matlock Civic Association and Matlock Town Council, 2010, pp 1-2

18. *The Fifth Commandment*, p. 46.

19. *The Fifth Commandment*, ibid.

20. Author's interview with Sehri Saklatvala, 25 February 1990.

21. Author's interview with Sehri Saklatvala, 25 February 1990.

22. Post card to Hannah Harding, née Marsh, Oldham, 1934.

23. Author's interview with Sehri Saklatvala, 2 March 1990.

24. Letter from Alice Jones to Sehri Saklatvala, 19 January 1936.

25. *The Fifth Commandment*, p. 309.

26. Author's correspondence with Chris Saklatvala, July 11 1990.

27. Memorandum to Arthur Henderson, November 1929, Public Record Office /FO372/2561.

28. Author's interview with Sehri Saklatvala, 2 March 1990.

29. R. Palme Dutt, Foreword to Panchanan Saha, *Shapurji Saklatvala: A Short Biography*, New Delhi, People's Publishing House, 1970, p. VIII

30. J.R. Clynes, *Memoirs 1869-1924* (London: Hutchinsons, 1937).

31. York House is now occupied by Richmond Council.

32. Memorandum to Arthur Henderson, November 1929, Public Record

Office /FO372/2561.

33. Ibid.

34. Author's interview with Sehri Saklatvala, 2 March 1990.

35. *The British Weekly*, 11 December 1924.

37. *The Daily Graphic*, 18 September 1925.

38. The £500 was paid to him by London financier, Richard Tilden-Smith, a British business associate of the Tatas. The money was the subject of a successful action brought by Saklatvala against Tilden-Smith for non-payment in July 1928.

39. Memorandum to Arthur Henderson, November 1929, Public Record Office/FO372/2561.

40. The Twickenham electoral register lists Saklatvala at 51 Lebanon Park between 1914 and 1921.

41. *Labour Leader*, 26 April, 1917.

Chapter Three

1. *The Times*, 15 October, 1924.

2. Sean Creighton, *Not For Me, Not For You, But For Us*, pamphlet, Battersea Labour Party Booksales, 1988.

3. Ibid.

4. *The British Weekly*, 11 December 1924.

5. Ramsey Sherwood, *Historic Battersea* (London: G. Rangecroft and Co., 1913).

6. Michael Ward, *Red Flag Over the Workhouse*, Battersea and Wandsworth Labour and Social History Group, pamphlet, 1983.

7. *The British Weekly*, 11 December 1924.

8. Michael Ward, op. cit.

9. *The Daily Telegraph*, 28 November 1923.

10. Charlotte Despard 1844-1939): Anglo-Irish suffragette, Irish nationalist, novelist; sister of Field Marshal John French, Lord Lieutenant of Ireland; radicalised by her experience of conditions in London slums she visited; moved to Ireland in 1910; member of the Independent Labour Party; became a member of the Communist Party of Ireland in the 1930s.

11. Michael Ward, op. cit.

12. Ibid.

13. *South Western Star, c. 1902.*

14. Harry Wicks, *Battersea and Wandsworth Labour and Social History Newsletter*, Issue No. 8, 1979.

15. Burns, a pacifist, resigned from the government at the outbreak of the First World War in 1914.

16. Sean Creighton, op. cit.
17. Roy Webb, 'John Archer, Battersea's Black Activist – 1863-1932', article in *The South London Record*, No. 2, pub. South London History Workshop, 1987. Archer lived, between 1878 and 1915, at 55 Brymaer Road, and then from 1915, at 214 Battersea Park Road. In his later years, he closed his photographic business and devoted all his time to politics. He died in 1932, aged 68. At his funeral, Battersea Borough Council's Labour leader F.C.R. Douglas said: 'He was a very ardent worker for the coloured races, and particularly for the Negro races.' He added: 'There was no venom in his attacks on those opposed to him. There was always a streak of humour in whatever he said and when he hit hardest there was no barb left behind to rankle.' Councillor A. P. Godfrey said: 'Among his attributes were doggedness, sincerity and determination.' A school in Wandsworth was given his name and, in 1982, the headquarters of the South London Catholic Caribbean Chaplaincy in Nightingale Lane at Balham was also named after him.
18. *The Daily Chronicle*, 5 November 1913.
19. *Daily Express*, 5 November 1913.
20. Webb, op. cit.
21. Ibid.
22. The Security Service: Personal (PF Series) COMMUNISTS AND SUSPECTED COMMUNISTS, INCLUDING RUSSIAN AND COMMUNIST SYMPATHISERS. A.P. Godfrey letter to Sir Waldron Smithers MP, 16 December 1924.
23. Ibid.
24. The Security Service: Personal (PF Series) COMMUNISTS AND SUSPECTED COMMUNISTS, INCLUDING RUSSIAN AND COMMUNIST SYMPATHISERS. A.P. Godfrey letter to Sir Waldron Smithers MP, 16 December 1924.
25. *The South Western Star*, 22 July 1932.
26. Creighton, op. cit., p. 18.
27. Harry Wicks, *Battersea and Wandsworth Labour and Social History Newsletter*, Issue No. 8, 1979.
28. *The British Weekly*, 11 December 1924.
29. See Minutes of the Executive Committee, Labour Party, 7 December 1921, National Museum of Labour History.
30. Tom Bell, *Pioneering Days* (1941).
31. *The Communist*, 25 November, 1922.
32. Author's interviews, 2 February, 1990.
33. Minnie Bowles, then M.E. Adams, in correspondence with Christopher Mitchell, 14 March, 1989.
34. Harry Wicks, *Battersea and Wandsworth Labour and Social History Newsletter*,

Issue No. 8, 1979.

35. *South Western Star*, 24 January 1936.

36. The Security Service: Personal (PF Series) COMMUNISTS AND SUSPECTED COMMUNISTS, INCLUDING RUSSIAN AND COMMUNIST SYMPATHISERS. A.P. Godfrey letter to Sir Waldron Smithers MP, 16 December 1924.

37. Minnie Bowles, op. cit.

38. *South Western Star*, 1 February 1929.

39. James Klugmann, *History of the Communist Party of Great Britain, Volume 1, Formation and early years 1919-1924* (London: Lawrence and Wishart, 1980), p. 318.

40. *Daily Graphic*, 13, August, 1925.

41. W. J. Brown, General Secretary of CSCA, *Labour Party Annual Report 1928*, p.207.

42. *Sunday Worker*, 11 July 1926.

43. *South Western Star*, 7 May 1926.

44. *The Times*, 3 May 1926.

45. *The Times*, Ibid.

46. *The Young Striker* (newspaper of the Young Communist League), 6 May 1926.

47. The Security Service: Personal (PF Series) COMMUNISTS AND SUSPECTED COMMUNISTS, INCLUDING RUSSIAN AND COMMUNIST SYMPATHISERS. National Archives, Kew - Security Service, 21 July 1921 - 12 January 1932, KV 2/614. Subjects Communism and Shapurji Dorabji SAKLATVALA: Indian/British.

48. *South Western Star,* 7 May 1926.

49. *The Times*, 7 May 1926.

50. The Security Service, Ibid, Official report of the court case, 2.38.

51. Ibid.

52. The Security Service: Personal (PF Series) COMMUNISTS AND SUSPECTED COMMUNISTS, INCLUDING RUSSIAN AND COMMUNIST SYMPATHISERS. National Archives, Kew - Security Service, 21 July 1921 - 12 January 1932, KV 2/614. Subjects Communism and Shapurji Dorabji SAKLATVALA: Indian/British.

53. *The Times*, 7 May, 1926.

54. *Workers' Weekly*, quoted in The Fifth Commandment, p. 313.

55. Rupert Allason, *The Branch, A History of the Metropolitan Police Special Branch 1883-1983* (London: Secker & Warburg, 1983), pp. 78ff.

56. Intelligence report on a search of Saklatvala's home, 18 October 1920. National Archives of India – Home: Political. January 1921. PIB 306-7.

57. Memorandum to Arthur Henderson, PRO/FO 372/2561, 1929.

58. American Civil Liberties Union, *The State Department's Ban on*

Saklatvala: The Facts in a Case of International Significance, Pamphlet, New York, November, 1925.

59. *The Sunday Worker*, 20 September 1925.
60. American Civil Liberties Union, op. cit.
61. Jacob Zumoff, New Jersey City University, USA, "'Is America afraid of the truth?' The aborted North American trip of Shapurji Saklatvala MP", *The Indian Economic and Social History Review* volume 53, 3 (2016) pp 1–43.
62. Sean Creighton, *John Archer, Battersea's Black Progressive Labour Activist 1863-1932*, p.37.
63. *The Sunday Worker*, 4 December 1927.
64. *South Western Star*, 24 February 1922.
65. *Clapham Observer*, 23 May 1924.
66. Hansard, April 1929
67. *Daily Herald*, 8 October 1927.

Chapter Four

1. Tributes to his wife Sehri, January 1936, private collection.
2. Marking the 100th anniversary of the Amritsar massacre, Dominic Asquith, Britain's high commissioner to India laid a wreath on Saturday 13 April 2019 in commemoration. But there was no apology from prime minister Theresa May's government, as demanded by Sikh campaigners. Known in India as the Jallianwalla Bagh massacre, it was one of the worst atrocities of Britain's colonial rule. On 13 April 1919, British troops fired on hundreds of unarmed Sikh men, women and children in the northern town of Amritsar. Colonial records put the death toll at 379, but Indian figures say the number was closer to 1,000. A century later, Britain had still made no official apology, and Asquith also failed to do so at the Jallianwala Bagh walled garden, where bullet marks are still visible. "You might want to rewrite history, but you can't," he said. "What you can do, as the Queen said, is to learn the lessons of history. We will never forget what happened here." In the memorial's guest book Asquith, a descendant of Herbert Asquith, prime minister from 1908-16, called the events "shameful", reported *The Guardian* on 14 April 2019. "We deeply regret what happened and the suffering caused," he wrote, echoing comments by the prime minister May in parliament when she also stopped short of apologising. About 10,000 unarmed men, women and children had gathered in Amritsar's public garden to celebrate a spring festival that day. Many were angry about the arrest of two of their leaders whose detentions had already sparked violent protests.

Brigadier General Reginald Edward Harry Dyer arrived with dozens of troops, sealed off the exit and, without warning ordered the soldiers to open fire. Many local people tried to escape by scaling the high walls surrounding the garden. Others jumped into a deep, open well at the site as the troops fired. "Heaps of dead bodies lay there, some on their backs and some with their faces upturned. A number of them were poor innocent children," one witness later recalled. Dyer said the firing had been ordered "to punish the Indians for disobedience". Winston Churchill, then secretary of state for war, later called the decision "monstrous". During a visit in 2013, the then British prime minister, David Cameron, described what happened as "deeply shameful", but he too stopped short of an apology. In 1997, the British Queen laid a wreath at the site, but her gaffe-prone husband Prince Philip stole the headlines by reportedly saying that the Indian estimates for the death count were "vastly exaggerated". May told the House of Commons that the massacre was "a shameful scar on British Indian history". "We deeply regret what happened and the suffering caused." Amarinder Singh, chief minister of Punjab state, said May's words were not enough. He said "an unequivocal official apology" is needed for the "monumental barbarity". Indian newspapers also repeated calls for an apology. "Even in the centenary year of the massacre, Britain has refused to… take that important step," said the *Hindustan Times*, 13 April 2020.

3. Rozina Visram, *Ayahs, Lascars and Princes, The Story of Indians In Britain 1700-1947* (London: Pluto Press, 1986), p.155.
4. *The Fifth Commandment*, pp. 84-85.
5. Indian Agitators Abroad, compiled in the Criminal Intelligence Office, 1911, quoted in *Ayahs, Lascars and Princes*.
6. Gopal, *Insurgent Empire*, p. 217
7. PRO/FO371/12354, 1927
8. Hansard, 25 November 1927.
9. *South Western Star*, 17 March 1922.
10. Ibid.
11. Saklatvala's message to Madras Congress, quoted in Saha, op. cit., p. 93.
12. 'India in the Labour World', article in *Labour Monthly*, 1921.
13. Ibid.
14. Ibid.
15. *South Western Star*, 17 March 1922.
16. Letter from J.W. Hose (a senior civil servant in the India Office) to J. Crerar (Secretary to the Government in Bombay), 16 May 1923.
17. James Klugmann, *History of the Communist Party of Great Britain, Vol.*

2: The General Strike 1925-1926 (London: Lawrence & Wishart, 1980).

18. Francis Devine, Correspondence, *'Shapurji Saklatvala and Irish Labour, 1920-36'*, in the Irish history publication, *Saothar*, Vol. 31, 2006, p. 19. Ibid., p. 21.

20. Ibid.

21. *Irish Times* 23 February, 1932.

22. Francis Devine, Correspondence, *Shapurji Saklatvala and Irish Labour, 1920-36*, *Saothar*, Vol. 31, 2006, p. 23.

23. Ibid., p. 23.

24. Ibid. p. 23.

25. Ibid. p. 22.

26. The Anglo-Irish Treaty of 1921 (commonly known as 'the Treaty') ended the War of Independence and established the Irish Free State as a self-governing dominion with the British Empire. It contained provisions which enabled the six counties of Northern Ireland to opt out of the Irish Free State. The Irish Civil war broke out in the aftermath of the signing of the Treaty. During the negotiation of the Treaty, Irish republican leader Michael Collins met Saklatvala, and other Indian nationalists, in London. (Collins was Chairman of the Provisional Government of the Irish Free State from January 1922 until his assassination in August of the same year.) Plans were made to send an Irish nationalist to India with a British-based Indian activist on a fact-finding mission, much as the Labour Party Black Sections did years later in the 1980s after meeting a Sinn Fein delegation, headed by its leader Gerry Adams, in the British capital. Because of the Civil war, the Collins-proposed trip did not happen. See correspondence in the Art O'Brien papers relating to the 'Indian case', MS 8461/4 and MS 8446/31.

27. Hansard Parliamentary Debates, vol. 159, 27 November 1922, cols 359-63.

28. Kate O'Malley, *Ireland, India and Empire: Indo-Irish radical connections 1919-64* (Manchester: Manchester University Press, 2008), pp. 26-27.

29. O' Malley, op. cit., p. 28.

30. Hansard Parliamentary Debates, vol. 161, 12 March 1923, cols 1044.]

31. O'Malley, p. 29.

32. O'Malley, p. 30.

33. Euan O'Halpin, *Defending Ireland* (Oxford: Oxford University Press, 2000), p. 22.

34. O'Malley, p. 42.

35. Ibid.

36. Ibid.

37. See Brinsley Samaroo, 'East Indian-West Indian: The Public Careeer

of Adrian Cola Rienzi', *UWI Home Today*, 2017, Online, p. 1

38. Arthur Calder-Marshall, *Glory Dead* (London: Michael Joseph, 1939), p. 230.

39. For this period see Kelvin Singh, 'East Indians and the Larger Society', *Calcutta to Caroni: The East Indians of Trinidad, ed. John La Guerre*, (London: Longman Caribbean, 1974), pp. 39-68.

40. See Kate O'Malley, *Ireland, India and Empire: Indo-Irish radical connections 1919-64* (2008), p. 42, who records that the correspondence between Saklatvala and Rienzi was regularly intercepted by the Indian Political Intelligence branch of the secret service.

41. Arthur Calder-Marshall, *Glory Dead* (1939), p. 230.

42. See Leslie James, *George Padmore and Decolonization from Below* (London: Palgrave, 2015) who references IASB Special Branch Reports MEPO/ 38/91, p. 314.

43. For this episode in Trinidad's politics see *Butler Versus the King: riots and sedition in 1937,* ed. W. Richard Jacobs (Trinidad: Key Caribbean Publiations, 1976).

44. See Brinsley Samaroo, 'East Indian-West Indian'.

45. Supply Committee, Hansard, Vol. 186 9 July 1925, pp 705-19.

46. Hansard, Vol. 191, 1926, p. 84.

47. Palme Dutt, Foreword to Saha, op. cit., p. IX.

48. *Daily Herald*, 30 December 1926.

49. *Daily Worker*, 21 February 1926.

50. Sashi Joshi, *Comrade Sak*, C4, April 6 1990.

51. PRO/CAB24/180, 1926.

52. The Meerut Conspiracy Case was a controversial court trial started in British India in March 1929 and decided in 1933. Several trade unionists, including three Englishmen were arrested for organizing an Indian railway strike. The British Government convicted 33 leftist trade union leaders under a false lawsuit. The trial immediately caught attention in England, where it inspired the 1932 play Meerut by Manchester street theatre group the 'Red Megaphones', highlighting the detrimental effects of colonisation and industrialisation.

53. India Office Library, MSS Eur. C. 152/3 Vol II, 3 February 1927.

54. India Office Library, MSS Eur. C. 152/8 Vol.II, 3 March 1927.

55. On 17 March 1924, M.N. Roy, S.A. Dange, Muzaffar Ahmed, Nalini Gupta, Shaukat Usmani, Singaravelu Chettiar, Ghulam Hussain and others were charged that they as Communists were seeking "to deprive the King Emperor of his sovereignty of British India, by complete separation of India from imperialistic Britain by a violent revolution.", in what was called the Cawnpore (now spelt Kanpur) Bolshevik Conspiracy case. The case attracted interest of the people towards Comintern plan to bring about violent revolution in India.

"Pages of newspapers daily splashed sensational communist plans and people for the first time learned such a large scale about communism and its doctrines and the aims of the Communist International in India." Singaravelu Chettiar was released on account of illness. M.N. Roy was out of the country and therefore could not be arrested. Ghulam Hussain confessed that he had received money from the Russians in Kabul and was pardoned. Muzaffar Ahmed, Shaukat Usmani and Dange were sentenced for four years of imprisonment. This case was responsible for actively introducing communism to the Indian masses. After Kanpur, Britain had triumphantly declared that the case had "finished off the communists". But the industrial town of Kanpur, in December 1925, witnessed a conference of different communist groups, under the chairmanship of Singaravelu Chettiar. Dange, Muzaffar Ahmed, Nalini Gupta, Shaukat Usmani were among the key organizers of the meeting. The meeting adopted a resolution for the formation of the Communist Party of India with its headquarters in Bombay (new spelling: Mumbai). The British Government's extreme hostility towards the bolsheviks, made them to decide not to openly function as a communist party; instead, they chose a more open and non-federated platform, under the name the Workers and Peasants Parties.

56. K. Troyanovsky, *Vostok i Revolyutsiya*, 1918, p. 29.
57. Lenin, *Theses submitted to the Third Congress of the Comintern*, 1921.
58. E.H. Carr, *History of Soviet Russia, Socialism In One Country*, Vol. 3, (London: MacMillan, 1963), p. 674-5.
59. Bombay Citizens, 24 January, 1927, quoted in Saha, op. cit., p. 90.
60. *The Labour Monthly*, July, 1930.
61. *Amrita Bazar Patrika*, 22 January 1927, quoted in Saha, op. cit. p.
62. *Forward*, April, 1927.
63. *Amrita Bazar Patrika*, 11 February 1927, quoted in Saha, op. cit. p. 64. *Amrita Bazar Patrika*, 11 February 1927, quoted in Saha, op. cit. p. 39.
65. Joshi, *Comrade Sak*, Channel 4. Supporting Joshi's argument, the Chief Minister of West Bengal argues that Communism has flourished in his state precisely because it is based on the consent of an electorate which has voted the Communists into office, unlike in Eastern Europe.
66. C.L.R. James, from an article first published in 1958 and reprinted in *At the Rendezvous of Victory* (London: Allison and Busby, 1984).
67. Saklatvala-Gandhi Correspondence, Saha, op. cit., p. 75.
68. 'Who is this Gandhi?', *Labour Monthly*, July, 1930.
69. M. K. Gandhi to the Under-secretary of State for India, 14 August 1914, IOR: MSS EUR F 170. See also M.K. Gandhi, *An Autobiography or The Story of My Experiment with Truth* (London: Penguin Books, 1982), pp. 316-18.

70. 'Who is this Gandhi?', *Labour Monthly*, July, 1930.
71. India Office Library, MSS Eur. C. 152/3 Vol II, 22 September 1927.
72. Letter, 1 November, 1925, PRO/FO372/2561.
73. Letter, 15 November, 1929, Ibid.
74. Ibid. 5. Hansard, 9 December, 1929.
76. Ibid.
77. Hansard, 22 November 1927, also all above.
78. Report of the 27th Annual Conference of the Labour Party, pp. 255-59, 1927.
79. *Daily Worker*, January 1933
80. *Sunday Worker*, July 28, 1928.
81. M. R. Masani, *The Communist Party of India. A Short History* (London: Derek Verschoyle, 1954).
82. He was born in 1896 at Cambridge. His father Upendra Dutt, was a surgeon, and his mother Anna Palme, a writer. Anna's family connections made her son a first cousin of Olaf Palme, the Socialist Swedish Prime Minister. Palme Dutt studied at Balliol College, Oxford, after winning a scholarship. His brother Clemens was also at the university and involved in left-wing politics. Rajani got into trouble with the authorities for refusing to be conscripted into the army. He was expelled from Oxford in 1917 but later allowed back to take his examinations, passing with First Class Honours in Classics. His foray into electoral politics was confined to unsuccessful attempts to get elected to parliament as the Communist candidate in Birmingham, Sparkbrook, in 1945, and Woolwich East, five years later. Palme Dutt married the Estonian writer Salme Murrick in 1924. She died in 1964 and there were no children. During his life, Palme Dutt wrote 16 books (including the classic *India Today*), as well as hundreds of articles and pamphlets. He died in London on 20 December 1974

Chapter Five

1. Report of the Communist Unity Convention, London, 1920, quoted in Mike Squires, *Saklatvala: A Political Biography* (London: Lawrence and Wishart, 1990), p. 27.
2. Report of the 29th Annual Conference of the Independent Labour Party, March 192, National Museum of Labour History.
3. *Daily Worker*, 18 January, 1936.
4. PRO/CAB, Report on Revolutionary Groups, 30 March, 1920.
5. *Labour Leader*, 10 June, 1921.
6. Interview with Setha Kumur, December 1987, for *Comrade Sak*, Channel 4.

7. Letter to Mrs Sehri Saklatvala, 18 January 1936.
8. Ibid.
9. *Daily Worker*, 24 October 1931
10. Saha, op. cit., p. 41.
11. *The Times*, 18 June 1927.
12. P. S. Gupta in 'British Labour and the Indian Left 1919-39' in *Socialism in India*, edited by B. R. Nanda (Delhi, 1972).
13. Report on Revolutionary Organisations, PRO\CAB\24\12, November 1919.
14. *South Western Star*, 10 April, 1921.
15. *The Times*, 22 September 1921.
16. The Security Service: Personal (PF Series) COMMUNISTS AND SUSPECTED COMMUNISTS, INCLUDING RUSSIAN AND COMMUNIST SYMPATHISERS. National Archives, Kew - Security Service, 21 July 1921 - 12 January 1932, KV 2/614. Subjects Communism and Shapurji Dorabji SAKLATVALA: Indian/British, Communist Policy Towards Parliament.
17. ibid
18. Hansard, Vol 194: 21 April, 1926, p. 1337.
19. James Klugmann, *History of the Communist Party*, Vol. 1, 1919-1924 (London: Lawrence and Wishart, 1980).
20. The Security Service: Personal (PF Series) COMMUNISTS AND SUSPECTED COMMUNISTS, INCLUDING RUSSIAN AND COMMUNIST SYMPATHISERS. National Archives, Kew - Security Service, 21 July 1921 - 12 January 1932, KV 2/614. Subjects Communism and Shapurji Dorabji SAKLATVALA: Indian/British, Communist Policy Towards Parliament.
21. Ibid.
22. *Daily News*, 22 March 1928.
23. House of Commons, 17 December 1925.
24. James Klugmann, op. cit.
25. *Daily News*, 22 March 1928.
26. Hansard, Vol 2/7, House of Commons, 17 December 1925.
27. *Daily News*, 22 March 1928.
28. V.I. Lenin, *Left-wing Communism: An Infantile Disorder* (Moscow, nd.)
29. *Daily Worker*.
30. Thomas Bell, *Pioneering Days* (London: Lawrence and Wishart, 1941), p. 266.
31. Correspondence with author, 2 February, 1990.
32. The Communist International (CI), made up of Communist parties throughout the world and based in Moscow, was known as the Comintern. For instance, the CPGB was the British section of the CI.

33. Hugo Dewar, *Communist Politics in Britain: The CPGB from its Origins to the Second World War* (London: Pluto Press, 1976).
34. L. J. Macfarlane, *The British Communist Party. Its Origins and Development Until 1929* (London: MacGibbon and Kee, 1966).
35. Report of the 24th Annual Conference of the Labour Party, 1924, pp. 109, 131.
36. Ibid.
37. *Workers' Weekly*, 25 July 1924
38. ibid.
39. E.H. Carr, *History of Soviet Russia, Socialism In One Country.*
40. Noreen Branson, *History of the Communist Party of Great Britain* (London: Lawrence and Wishart, 1985).
41. *Daily Worker*, 19 January 1936.
42. CPGB Congress Report, 1925.

Chapter Six

1. Politicians and social commentators have long been haggling over whether or not there is a general term like 'Black' to describe people of African and Asian descent. A satisfactorily all-embracing name has not emerged. There is a move away from 'Black' to 'African' or 'Asian'. Saklatvala might have welcomed this because it locates individuals according to their national rather than racial identity and is therefore less exclusive. A politically more corrupted description, gaining ground today, is the term 'Black and Asian'. It must be said that, as a dedicated Communist, Saklatvala would not have wanted to dwell on descriptions which differentiated between people apart from on the grounds of them being for or against the working class. Influential groups in our communities, including the Labour Party Black Section, say Black is a political term widely accepted on the basis of self-definition. So, in a contem-porary sense, Saklatvala lined up with all those people of colour who today describe themselves as Black.
2. See as a general surveys, Edward Scobie's pioneering *Black Britannia: A History of* Blacks in Britain (Chicago: Johnson Publishing, 1972); Peter Fryer's respected work *Staying Power: The History of Black People in Britain* (London: Pluto Press, 1984); Rozina Visram's *Ayahs, Lascars and Princes: Indians in Britain, 1700-1947* (London: Pluto Press, 1986); Gerzina Gretchen's *Black England.Life Before Emancipation* (London: John Murray, 1995); Miranda Kauffman, *Black Tudors: The Untold Story* (London: Oneworld Publications, 2017).
3. See www.nationalarchives.gov.uk/pathways/blackhistory/rights/gordon.htm.

4. For Olaudah Equiano see Vincent Carretta, *Equiano The African* (Athens: University of Georgia Press, 2005); for John Thelwall and the London Corresponding Society see Mary Thale, *Selections from the Papers of the London Corresponding Society 1792-1799* (Cambridge: Cambridge University Press,1983); Michael Scrivener, *Seditious Allegories: John Thelwall and Jacobin Writings* (Pennsylvania: Penn State UP, 2001) and Gregory Claeys, ed.,*The Politics of English Jacobinism: The Writings of John Thelwall* (Pennsylvania: Penn State UP, 1995).
5. See Alastair Bonnett & Keith Armstrong, eds., *Thomas Spence: The Poor Man's Revolutionary* (London: Breviary Stuff, 2014); and Malcolm Chase, *The People's Farm: English Radical Agrarianism 1775-1840* (London: Breviary Stuff, 2010). Spence's emphasis on the political and economic importance of land has been renewed in our own time by Guy Shrubsole's *Who Owns England? How We Lost Our Land and How We Take it Back* (London: William Collins, 2019)
6. See John Stanhope, *The Cato Street Conspiracy* (London: Jonathan Cape, 1962) and David Johnson: *Regency Revolution: the Case of Arthur Thistlewood* (London: Compton Russell, 1975).
7. See Malcolm Chase, *Chartism: A New History* (Manchester: Manchester University Press, 2007) and Martin Hoyles, *William Cuffay: The Life and Times of a Chartist Leader* (London: Hansib, 2013).
8. See Iain McCalman, *Radical Underworld: Prophets, Revolutionaries and Pornographers* (Oxford: Oxford University Press, 1988) and Iain McCalman ed., *The Horrors of Slavery and Other Writings of Robert Wedderburn* (Princeton: Marcus Weiner, 2017).
9. See Michael Fisher, *The Inordinately Strange Life of Dyce Sombre: Victorian Anglo Indian MP and Chancery 'Lunatic'* (2010) and Parliament website https://www.parliament.uk/about/art-in-parliament/online-exhibitions/parliamentarians/pioneers/page-1/].
10. The first Indian to seek election to parliament so as to put forward the 'native view' was Lalmohun Ghose who unsuccessfully contested Deptford as a Liberal in 1885. (British Parliamentary Election Results 1885-1918, Second Edition. Compiled and edited by F. W. S. Craig, pub. Parliamentary Research Services, 1989.) In a contest which attracted a big turnout of 79.9%, the Tory William Evelyn beat Ghose by 367 votes. Ghose, like Naoroji at Central Finsbury the same year, fell victim to the huge swing against Gladstone and Home Rule. A prominent member of the British India Association, Ghose had come to England in 1879 to study law at the Middle Temple. Election result (Deptford) – Total Electorate: 9,371. Turnout: 79.9%. 1. W. J. Evelyn (Conservative) 3,927. 2. L. Ghose (Liberal) 3,560.
11. See *New Society*, 22 January, 1988, 'Parsis, The Jews of India'.

12. As quoted by R. P. Masani, *Dabadhai Naoroji: The Grand Old Man of India* (London: George Allen Unwin, 1939).

13. Peter Fryer, *Staying Power, The History of Black People in Britain* (London: Pluto Press, 1985).

14. Address to his Fellow Electors in Central Finsbury, July 1895.

15. Zerbanoo Gifford, *Dadabhai Naoroji, Britain's First Asian M.P.* (London: Mantra, 1992).

16. This was not the end of Indians as Liberal parliamentary candidates. The party put forward Manmath Mallik for St George's, Hanover Square, in 1906 and Uxbridge in 1910. Both times he failed to get elected.

17. Fryer, op. cit.

18. Omar Ralph, *Naoroji, The First Asian MP* (London: Hansib, 1995), p. 146-7.

19. See J.R. Hooker, *Henry Sylvester Williams: Imperial Pan-Africanist* (London: Rex Collins, 1975).

20. Zareer Masani, Article in *The Asian*, vol. 3, 1980. See also, John R. Hinnells and Omar Ralph, *Bhownagree, Parliamentary Centenary of Britain's First Asian Conservative MP*, pamphlet (London: Hansib, 1995).

21. Gandhi's biographer and grandson Rajmohan Gandhi says his grandfather was undoubtedly "at times ignorant and prejudiced about South African blacks" ["Was Mahatma Gandhi a racist?" BBC online 17 September 2015 http://www.bbc.co.uk/news/world-asia-india-34265882]. South African Indian authors of the controversial book *The South African Gandhi: Stretcher-Bearer of Empire*, Stanford University Press, 2015, go further. Academics Ashwin Desai and Goolam Vahed, spent seven years researching Gandhi and discovered he once wrote to the British authorities in Natal that there was a "general belief in the Colony that the Indians are a little better, if at all, than the savages or the Natives of Africa".

22. *Indian National Herald*, 4 September 1927.

23. *The Daily Graphic*, 20 October, 1924.

24. *South Western Star*, 24 February 1922.

25. *Daily Telegraph*, 4 December 1923.

26. Ibid.

27. Interview with author, 2 February 1990.

28. *Daily Graphic*, 7 December 1923.

29. Palme Dutt, Foreword to Saha, op cit., p. VIII.

30. National Archives of India, Home – Political (Secret) File 154 of 1923.

31. See *The New York Times*, 'Trump Tells CCongreswomen to 'Go Back' to the Countries they Came From', 14 June 2019, online.

32. The British-Israeli World Federation was (and still is) a bizarre, generally extreme right wing, international organisation, white

supremacist in Saklatvala's time, that believes that white Europeans are the direct descendants of the Ten Lost Tribes of Israel. They combined Christian anti-semitism with a support for Zionism as fulfilling millenarian Biblical prophecy, a belief that is almost certainly behind Trump's support of Greater Israel. See *The Washington Post*, 'Christian Zionist philo-Semitism is driving Trump's Israel Policy', January 28, 2020 (online).

33. *The Times* 13 October 1925.
34. *Daily Herald*, 19 April 1923.
35. Arthur Field to Beram Saklatvala, 7 March 1937, in Saklatvala Papers, MSS.EUR D 1173/4.
36. See http://inews.co.uk/opinion/leaked-labour-report-reveals-shocking-racism-sexism-black-mps-419619.
37. Sehri Saklatvala, Interview with author, 25 February 1990.
38. Quoted in 'Marx and Black Liberation', paper by Ken Biggs, 6 June, 1988.
39. See Gopal, *Insurgent Empire*, pp. 59-69
40. Quoted in *London Labour and Colonial Freedom – Two Centuries of Struggle*, CPGB Publication.
41. Its successor, which still survives to represent Social Democratic parties, has been renamed the Socialist International.
42. Lassalle was a prominent early member of the SPD. He was friendly with Marx and Engels, but had some major disagreements with them.
43. Debate on Colonial Policy at the 1904 Congress of the Second International from V.I. Lenin, *Struggle for a Revolutionary International, documents 1907-1916*, edited by John Riddell (New York: Nomad Press, 1984).
44. Manabendra Nath Roy's influence on international questions was demonstrated by the fact he helped found the Mexican Communist Party. See *Theses Resolutions and Manifestos of the First Four Congresses of the Third International* (London: Pluto Press, 1983).
45. Letter from S. Saklatvala to E.D. Morel, 24 January, 1923. Quoted in Squires, op. cit., p. 165.
46. *The Communist*, April 8 1922.
47. A major debate on anti-imperialism took place at the CPGB's 1925 Congress in Glasgow and policy was passed which put the party at the disposal of colonised peoples in their fight for self determination.
48. As quoted in *Black Bolshevik*, by Harry Haywood (Chicago: Liberator Press, 1978.
49. Haywood, op. cit.
50. It was not until 1930 that support was won for Black self-determination in America through the so called Black Belt policy. The Finn Otto

Kuusinen, who chaired the Comintern's Negro Commission, played a key role in this. In the context of later Labour Party attitudes towards the declaration of white settler UDI in Rhodesia/Zimbabwe in 1965, my editor has mentioned to me that when he was a student taking part in a demonstration/lobby of parliament over the pitiful response of the Harold Wilson Labour government, his Labour MP, Jack McCann, told him that he thought Labour had to support the position of white trade unionists in that country.

51. TUC proceedings, 1930, p. 413.
52. Hansard, April 1927.
53. Kholeste P. Mistree, *Zoroastrianism. An Ethnic Perspective* (Bombay: Good Impressions, 1982).
54. *The Times*, 23 July 1927
55. For the CPGB statement and Saklatvala's response, see *Workers Life*, 5 August 1927.
56. See Mistree, op. cit.; and 'Parsis, Jews of India', op. cit.
57. *Indian National Herald*, 4 September 1927.
58. Francis Devine, Correspondence, 'Shapurji Saklatvala and Irish Labour, 1920-36', *Saothar*, Vol. 31, 2006, p. 22.
59. *The Labour Monthly*, July 1930.
60. *The Labour Monthly*, July 1930.
61. George Padmore, *Pan-Africanism or Communism* (London: Dennis Dobson, 1956).
62. Bandung in Indonesia is where, in 1955, representatives of Asian and African countries gathered for a big anti-imperialist conference. The Non-Aligned Movement resulted from this.
63. James Klugmann, *History of the Communist Party of Great Britain, Vol. 2, The General Strike, 1925-1926* (London: Lawrence and Wishart, 1976).
64. *Comrade Sak*, Channel Four, April 1990.
65. Private papers, quoted in John Saville, *Dictionary of Labour Biographies*, Vol 7 (London: MacMillan Press, 1984), p. 37.
66. CPGB Conference 1957.
67. Interview with the author.
68. Trevor Carter, *Shattering Illusions, West Indians In British Politics* (London: Lawrence and Wishart, 1986).
69. Quoted ibid. The Movement for Colonial Freedom was also eventually replaced by Liberation, founded by the late Lord Brockway, and run by Communists the late Tony Gilbert and Kay Beauchamp.

Chapter Seven

1. Arthur Field, *Indian National Herald*, 15 February 1929.
2. Ibid.
3. *South Western Star*,
4. Interview with author, January 30 1990.
5. Red Clydeside refers to the political radicalism in Glasgow, Scotland, and areas around the city, on the banks of the River Clyde, such as Clydebank, Greenock, Dumbarton and Paisley, from the 1910s until the early 1930s. It is a significant era in the history of the British labour movement. Charismatic individuals emerged, including Independent Labour Party left-wing MPs John Wheatley, James Maxton, Manny Shinwell and communist Willie Gallagher. Organised movements, including left-wing suffragettes, and trade unions, were the backbone of Red Clydeside, which had its roots in working-class opposition to Britain's participation in World War I, although the area had a long history of political radicalism. There were strikes by workers over poor wages and conditions and the Glasgow Rent Strike of 1915, a popular protest against greedy landlords raising rents on often sub-standard housing whilst many breadwinners were on the Western Front dying for their country.
6. *Daily Worker*, June 1930.
7. Letter of June 1930, Bhownagree Archive, Zoroastrian House, London.
8. Interview with the author.
9. Election address 1931.
10. Ibid.
11. Kate O'Malley, *Saothar*, Vol. 29, p. 51.
12. Letter of 2 October 1930.
13. Letter to Sir John Simon, 11 August 1933.
14. PRO/FO372/2384.
15. Ibid.
16. *Comrade Sak*, Channel Four, April 1990.
17. Interview with the author, January 1990.
18. William Kent, *John Burns. Labour's Lost Leader* (London: Williams and Norgate, 1950).
19. Kent, op. cit.
20. *Daily Worker*, 4 November 1935.
21. *The Manchester Guardian*, 9 December 1935.
22. Hugo Dewar, *Communist Politics In Britain: The CPGB From Its Origins To The Second World War* (London: Pluto Press, 1976).
23. PRO/FO371/19471.
24. *The Manchester Guardian*, December 1935.
25. *The Daily Worker*, 26 July 1934.

26. Ibid.
27. Palme Dutt compared the socio-economic achievements of the Soviet Union's central Asian republics with India under the British. 'In 1914, there were 13 doctors in Tajikistan; in 1939, there were 440. In 1914, there were 100 hospital beds for the whole population; in 1939, there were 3,675. In India in 1930 there was 94 per cent illiteracy; in 1931, it was 92 per cent. In Tajikistan before the revolution only one half of one per cent of the population could read and write; by 1933 60 per cent could do so'. *India Today* (London: Victor Gollancz, 1940).
28. *Daily Worker*, 18 January 1936: Pollitt's tribute.
29. Reg Bishop, Letter, 17 January 1936.
30. *The Fifth Commandment*, p. 471.
31. Bulletin of the Marx Memorial Library, October 1983.
32. *India Front 2*, No. 9.
33. M. R. Masani, *op. cit.*
34. Ibid.
35. *The Daily Worker*, 18 January 1936.
36. *The Daily Worker*, 28 August 1934.
37. *The Fifth Commandment*, p. 479.
38. Interview with the author, 2 March 1990.
39. Ibid.
40. *The Daily Worker*, 20 January 1936.
41. Ibid.
42. *New York Times*, 17 January 1936.
43. See Appendix
44. http://www.rafcommands.com/forum/showthread.php?14801-Indian-Ceylon-(Sri-Lanka)-Pilots-in-ATA-(from-Brief-Glory)
45. Interview with author, January 1990.
46. Comrade Sak, Channel 4.
47. *South Western Star*, 24 February 1922.
48. *Comrade Sak*, Channel Four.
49. *South Western Star*, 17 March 1922.
50. Ibid.
51. Interview with the author, 1990.
52. Interview with the author, 1990.
53. *The Spectator*, 3 March 1990.
54. Novara, Michael Walker broadcast, 29 July 2020, https://youtu.be/EBXHHI7v798
55. On YouTube, 28 July 2020, https://www.youtube.com/watch?v=MSjlMHNkEWg&t=3632s

1. Shapurji Saklatvala and his bride, Sally Marsh

2. The Saklatvalas and their young family, with Sally in a sari

3. Saklatvala reads to two of his sons

4. St. Xavier's College, Mumbai, built in Indo-Gothic style and now a heritage site.

5. Saklatavala's children during the Zoroastrian Navjote ceremony of 1927

6. Postcards sent by Saklatvala to his religious sister-in-law, Hannah

7. 51, Lebanon Park, Twickenham, on the right

8. York House, currently Richmond Town Hall

9. Clapham Junction in 1920

TOWN HALL & SHAKESPEARE THEATRE, CLAPHAM JUNCTION

10. Battersea Town Hall in the 1920s

11. Workers' houses in Battersea, in 1920

General Election, 1922.

NORTH BATTERSEA DIVISION.

Vote for SAKLATVALA

The LABOUR Candidate.

Printed by H. J. ROWLING (T.U.), 48 York Road, Battersea, S.W. 11; and
Published by LOUIS COLTMAN, 455 Battersea Park Road, S.W. 11.

12. Election poster 1922

13. Clive Branson paintings. Above, *Engineering Factory*; below, *Workers' March*

14. John Archer, Pan-Africanist and Mayor of Battersea.
Painting by Paul Clarkson

15. Saklatvala with Charlotte Despard (second from right)

16, John Burns, Battersea's first socialist MP

17. Saklatvala with fellow communist MP, J. Walton Newbold, in 1922

18. Saklatvala with J.R. Campbell, one-time editor of the *Daily Worker*

19. Above, Saklatvala speaks in Trafalgar Square at the 1932 Hunger
March rally, and later in the same space

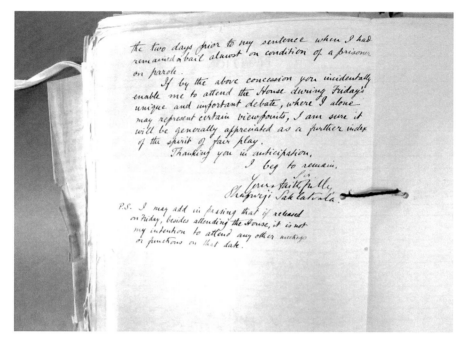

20. Saklatvala's letter from Wormwood Scrubs Prison, 1926

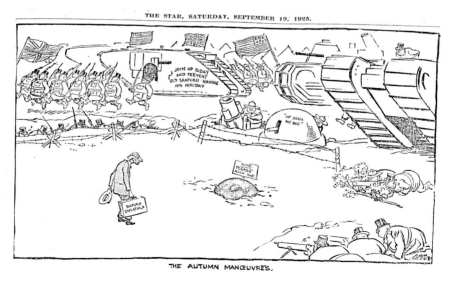

21. *The Star* cartoon on Saklatvala's exclusion from the USA, 1925

LEFT BEHIND

NO YOU DON'T!

Another "Rum" Runner Held Up.
The U.S. Government has revoked the passport visa granted to Mr. Shapurji Saklatvala.

22. *Sunday Worker* cartoons on Saklatvala's exclusion from the USA

ACTING-COLONEL SAKLATVALA, D.S.O.
(DISTINGUISHED SOVIET ORDER)
O.C. Battersea Internationals.

23. Caricature of Saklatvala from *Punch*, 1928

24. Anglo-Indian, David Ochterlony Dyce, elected as British MP, in 1841

25. Dadabhai Naoroji, first Indian Liberal MP in Britain

26. The Saklatvalas on their silver wedding anniversary, 1932

APPENDIX 1

Minutes of the Executive Committee, Labour Party, 7 December 1921
National Agent's Report

Organisation Sub-Committee meeting, held on December 1st 1921

BATTERSEA NORTH.

The Secretary and National Agent reported upon an interview they
had had with representatives of the Battersea Labour Party and Mr. S.
Saklatvala, who had been selected as the Candidate for the Constituency.
Considerable discussion ensued as to Mr. Saklatvala's association with
the Communist Party, his attack upon the policy of the I.L.P. in continuing
its association with the Labour Party, and his attempt to form a secessionist
I.L.P. Group favourable to affiliation with the Third International.
It was reported that Mr. Saklatvala, in accepting the candidature for
Battersea North, had indicated his acceptance of the Labour Party
Constitution, with its usual implications.

RESOLVED: 'That the candidature of Mr. S. Saklatvala for Battersea
North be sanctioned on condition that he accepts the Constitution of
the Party, agrees to receive the Labour Whips if returned to Parliament,
and to abide by the decisions of the Parliamentary Party.'

APPENDIX 2
Private and Confidential.

TRADES UNION CONGRESS AND THE LABOUR PARTY.
No.9 July 1924.

JOINT INTERNATIONAL DEPARTMENT.

ADVISORY COMMITTEE ON INTERNATIONAL QUESTIONS.
IMPERIAL SUB-COMMITTEE.

THE BRITISH LABOUR GOVERNMENT AND INDIA.
BY S. SAKLATVALA.

So far the Sub-Committee has discussed India from the point of view of what a *just* Government or what a *Generous* Government should do, by taking into consideration the sentiments or grievances of the ruled. But as among the ruled there cannot be a common agreement on all questions, especially in a large and varied country, political question for a foreign imperial ruler must retain their eternal difficulty, regardless of the personnel of the ruling class.

However it should not be assumed that the present Labour Government basing its moral reputation on socialist principles is not a Labour Government in its unpleasant task as an imperialist administrator.

It would be a calamity if such an assumption is persevered in to the end till the present Government went out of power, when it is well-known that the main purpose of the old imperialists has been economic exploitation. Also the Wage position of the British Workers is bound to be gravely affected by the 'coolie' scale of wages in the Eastern parts of the Empire in similar industries. Coal Mining, Textiles (Cotton and jute), Iron, Steel and Engineering, Ship and Dockwork are established instances.

The Labour Government can justly and even to the grave discomfiture of their capitalist opponents do a great deal in their Indian policy to abate this exploitation without affecting their administrative responsibility under the existing order of things.

Such measures will have a tremendous moral value on Western opinion ultimately in favour of Labour principles as compared to the past.

In India at first the present political leaders may perhaps be startled, they may even feel they went to complain against King Log and brought in King Stork. However, the good results of application of Labour Principles will be so apparent that they will shortly value and even embrace them. Whether they do or, not, the Labour Government will bring into existence a new mass party and mass psychology in India which will submerge the present

minority expressions of confused aristocratic and reactionary thought
passing under the name of national rights.

The Labour Party must give publicity to the two much forgotten facts:-

1. The Government of India are directly employers of Labour of a low
grade on a vast scale.

2. The Government of India is based on a tremendously restricted
franchise, and the masses who form more than 95% of the population and
have no direct voice in the choice of representatives can only be compensated by a Labour Government, and it is dangerous to assume that they are
under the benevolent protection of the 5% franchised population on score
of nationality when their economic interests are not at all common, and
when they are set back in economic pace by British policy in the past.

The Labour Government can immediately introduce the following
measures:-

1. WEEKLY PAYMENT TO ALL GOVERNMENT EMPLOYEES WHO ARE
EARNING LESS THAN 100 RUPEES (£6. 15. 0. NOMINAL) PER MONTH.
By this practice of Government in all departments industrial concerns
will be bound to follow suit without legislation. Where the population
is illiterate and large numbers are paid £1 or £2 per month, they continually
run into debts, and live on credit with shop-keepers or on money lenders.
Thus in actual practise the Worker as well as the peasant pays far more
for his food or taxes, when he submits to price as fixed by his creditor,
or when he pays enormous interest on cash borrowings.

2. RISE IN GOVERNMENT WAGES TO UNDERPAID LABOUR.
The Government are continually sanctioning rise in all higher services,
where wages are already the highest recorded in the world. The low
wage earner is neglected to a scandalous degree. In large cities like
Bombay, Calcutta, Allahabad, etc, Government figures show that a
laborious family requires 53 rupees per month for upkeep, and yet
the Government pays 30, 35 or 40 rupees per month, to postmen,
policemen, office peons, clerks, railwaymen, telegraph men, etc., when
their wives cannot go out and join their husbands in work as no operatives,
dock-labourers, etc., are doing.

ALL GOVERNMENT WAGES IN LARGE CITY AREAS MUST THEREFORE
BE MADE WEEKLY WITH A MINIMUM OF 15 RUPEES PER WEEK.
The surplus can easily be raised from higher income tax, because it is
still light in India on incomes higher than say 30,000 rupees (£2000)
per year.

3. LIMITATION ON EXORBITANT RATES OF INTEREST.
High rate of interest is a well known curse to the poor in India. Co-operative banks giving small loans on reasonable interest are helping the peasantry; however, where money-lenders can exact 35% to 150% by direct advances to illiterate persons, there is not much chance of deposit in Government Loan Banks. Protection can be given to the poor, and a maximum rate of interest of about 30% or one PIE per week per Rupee, should be fixed, by making non-saleable all claims above that on borrowers whose yearly earning is under 5000 rupees or whose business is under 5000 rupees per year, just as so many gambling or unconscionable contracts.

4. ABOLITION OF THE SYSTEM OF IMPRESSMENT OF LABOUR.
It is no use quibbling over words. A regular system exists by which Government officials simply seize persons to do work in their Camps when they are on tour. The same facilities are granted freely to representatives of large firms, mostly European, to seize labour for work on exploration, prospecting etc. The practise then spreads to regular agents going out on behalf of Companies into remote districts to fetch men for industrial work by doubtful methods. The Labour Government should abolish this custom at its source, namely, the touring government officials, and facilities of the police, etc., granted to private firms in this respect.

5. TRADE UNION ACT.
The Trade Union Act should no longer be held back. It should be put through, but certain safe-guards require to be adopted. Indian Labour is illiterate en masse, and they cannot read notices, etc, and they have always to be advised of all movements verbally. Peaceful picketing becomes far more necessary there than in any other European country, and the Government officials and employers of India are trying their best to prohibit all picketing by a clause in the Trade Union Act, thus obstructing the organisation of Labour. Similarly in the early days of Trade Unions educated young Indians must do the organising and other Committee work as they are doing now. The Masters and the Government Officials are introducing a drastic Clause by which no person outside Industry could associate with a Trade Union which means that in process of time, factory managers and favourite foremen under managers will act as the loading officials of their Trade Union Workers. It would be more like conscriptive Labour than Trade Union Labour.

6. LABOUR REPRESENTATION ON COUNCILS AND MUNICIPAL BODIES.
The best solution of the deadlock in the Councils is to introduce a
large measure of working class representation, both industrial and
agricultural. The Indian villager is from time immemorial accustomed
to some form of electoral right in order to work his village or his Caste
Committees. It was a short sighted policy to cut 95% of people from
their natural rights. The Labour Government should create some sort
of a franchise by delegation for the peasants and the workers and then
they can be assured of labour legislation being not only carried through
now but for the future, thus bringing India into line with other countries
of the world in the possibility of a genuine working class or mass democracy
coming into power.

7. APPOINTMENT OF A COMMITTEE TO FIX INCIDENCE OF LABOUR
COST.
The whole question of low wages in industry is not only responsible
for illiteracy, poverty, high death rate, in India but is soon going to
become a problem of first importance in the Western Countries as to
the allowable improvement of standard of life of Labour. The Masters
in India are wrongly arguing that the Industries in India are not able
to bear a much larger incidence of Labour Costs. Roughly speaking
the Indian skilled or unskilled worker would be producing about one-
third the output of his Western Comrade, and that mostly owing to
his underfed condition and insanitary surroundings. The wages generally
are one-tenth and even lower of the British wages in the self-same
industries. A Royal Commission on political issues may be appointed
by any government, but a proper Research and Investigation Committee
into the problem of wages can only be expected to be appointed by a
Labour Government. It would be a disastrous error if such a Committee
composed impartiallyof Industrial Magnates in India, of Industrial
Magnates in Great Britain engaged in the same Industries and
representatives of India Labour and representatives of British Labour
be not appointed as hurriedly as possible. Such a Committee would
bring out the truth and the British Masters themselves would help
improving if enormous profits are possible in rival industries in the
East where men in positions at the top as well as the shareholders receive
a far greater return than they do here. The present Labour government
can certainly constitute this investigation and then leave to a future
the question of minimum wages in industries to a future agitation which
is bound to follow.

8. ECONOMIC SERVICES TO MASS OF PEASANTRY.

India is a Country of peasantry with 286,000,000 of rural population and should be helped to remain so in the economic interest of the world generally. The heavy death rate in the villages, the prevailing ignorance and the insanitary conditions will not improve, when the Councils will think of spending revenues upon towns and cities and not upon agricultural areas, and thus save their own class from being taxed. Export Duties upon Raw Materials are coming into favour to place European Manufacturers at a disadvantage as compared to Settlers in India. The Government could cultivate in the interest of unrepresented rural people a system of tolls or duties on outgoing products from village areas regardless whether the purchaser is local or abroad. They should set aside these revenues, ear-marked for the particular district from where they are derived and to be considered as local or municipal revenues to be spent on education and on sanitation in these areas. These Revenues must not be allowed to go into the general National Revenues which can only help the rich people by saving them from further taxation. A system of general export duties for the benefit of Revenues is harmful to the agriculturalist.

9. A COMMISSION FOR A MASS EDUCATION.

The question of mass education may be studied although it cannot be immediately solved. For 100 years Britain has left the question of education alone taking it as something that will take care of itself in process of another century or so. Capitalist administrators and tax payers have never found the solution of it and are not likely to. The Russian Revolutionaries, who apart from all other disputed points are a working class administration, within seven years have attacked the problem of mass ignorance with remarkable success. The conditions in Russia were, if anything, more difficult and financial resources more unfavourable than in India. Still they have done it. British officials and Indian Capitalist Councils will not be able to evolve out of their brains a scheme which could apply to peasant life. The Labour Government should no longer show any bias in learning whatever useful lessons can be learnt from Russia. A Commission consisting purely of Indians and assisted by two or three experienced members of working class organisations in Britain prominent in Research and Educational work should be appointed. This Commission should travel especially in the agricultural villages of Russia and Siberia and study the method adopted there for quickly spreading mass education in an agricultural country. The present Labour Government should then leave this heritage to the future politicians and rulers in India for further practical action.

10. ENCOURAGEMENT TO T.U.C. OF INDIA.

Even in the absence of a proper organisation some enthusiastic Indians have in a laudable manner started a Trade Union Movement. The Government should give them every recognition and encouragement the same as they would give to other political organisations in India. At their last sitting the Indian Trade Union Congress have made certain valuable suggestions for Women and Child labour in Mining and Tea Plantations and with regard to a more genuine selection of their representative at the International Labour Conference, etc. which should be given consideration and negotiated with the Indian Trade Union Congress Office. Certain other sentimental suggestions, for instance, abolishing the word 'coolie labour' from the Government Reports, should certainly be respected as a matter of self respect demanded for the Indian Working Classes. Of course the right cure is to abolish the Coolie system instead of letting them go on as they are and calling them by a more ambitious nomenclature. However, these little attentions are bound to show to the people of India the difference of a Labour Government from other Governments.

11. JUDICIAL REFORM AND TRIALS BY JURY.

There are one or two Reforms badly needed in the judicial system of India which have been clamoured for for very many years. The Labour Government could easily introduce elementary reforms as the present injustice tells far more heavily upon the poor villagers than upon educated and higher classes. There are abundant educated Indians to act as judges and magistrates with restricted powers in outlying districts and the whole system of the Executive Officer acting alternatively as judge and frequently hearing complaints against his own executive decisions should be immediately abolished.

The Second reform is that Trial by Jury should be introduced wholesale exactly on the same footing as it in Great Britain. By instinct as well as by practice of centuries Indians are quite fitted to act as Jurors as they have always conducted their caste affairs and Village affairs by communal decisions.

APPENDIX 3

THE NEW LINE

7/10/25

The Political Bureau.

Dear Comrades,

I feel the extraordinary circumstances prevailing at the moment call for extraordinary measures to be taken by our Party. There is not much doubt in my mind that without drastic measures to build up our Party we shall be submerged into insignificance in Great Britain. Parliamentary customs and traditions still have a very great attraction for the masses.

In order to overcome this we must adopt merciless measures to fight the Labour Party. We will not succeed to the point of actually wiping it out but we do not require to do that. What we shall succeed in doing is to give a dangerous shaking to the Parliamentary position of all the right-wingers and it would then be their turn to patch a piece with the C. P. at any price and the left wing will be forced into an open fight against the right. We must appeal to the C. C. at Moscow to let us work temporarily along the lines we are suggesting. We must adopt the attitude that the L. P. has deserted its original function and turned itself into a Liberal reformist group like the Irish National Party and that the real political crusade for Socialism has been abandoned by the L.P., therefore the C. P. must now set itself up as the only avowed anti-Capitalist Party to take such action inside and outside Parliament as will lead to the taking over of the means of production and the abolition of Imperialist exploitation and the consequent blacklegging of British and European Trade Union conditions.

We should then in an open manner invite all T.U. branches that take this view to affiliate to the C. P. for the purpose of assisting in carrying out the politico-economic struggle of the workers.

With the consent of the Central Committee at Moscow we should deliberately leave the position of those T.U. branches to be of an indefinite and temporary nature. We should not even make it a condition that they disaffiliate from the Labour Party because the pressure of the Press will induce the L. P. itself to take such action. This affiliation would gently weaken the position of right wing M.P.s and would increase the chances of rival candidates. Most important it will provide a new recruiting ground for Party membership,

Yours fraternally

Shapuri Saklatvala.

APPENDIX: 4

SAKLATVALA-GANDHI CORRESPONDENCE

(A) SAKLATVALA'S OPEN LETTER

Bombay
8 March 1927

Dear Comrade Gandhi,
We are both erratic enough to permit each other to be rude in order to freely express oneself correctly, instead of getting lost in artificiality of phraseology.
I realise the khaddar movement as it stands is not entirely your virtue or vice, but poor, ardent, and enthusiastic followers have added much to or subtracted from your intended programme. However the world must guide itself by practical results.

The Charka Movement
Several of your enthusiastic supporters have assisted me greatly by criticising me openly in the public press. Unfortunately my present nomadic life with a very heavy programme of work in every town I go prevents me from carrying on my correspondence or journalistic work. However these several critics have effectively replied to each other and one has contradicted the other and each one has tried to prove a different case on your behalf. You may not be responsible in creating this confusion. But I consider you are in duty bound now to clear it. Let us understand, openly, whether the charka movement is or is not an attack upon machinery, upon physical science, upon material progress. If it is so, then it is a most damaging disservice to our country and must be stopped. If it is not so, then your ardent followers ought not to be allowed to believe so.

What Is Art?
Is it or is it not a protest against artistic development on up to date lines, irrespective of geographical or national considerations as to their source? What is art but a free display of human taste, both instructive as well as acquired? One of your critics maintains that your movement was to drive away western fashions, etc., and when I discovered that the khaddar production was doing nothing of the kind, another critic blames me as if I was suggesting that it should try such an impossible as well as harmful procedure. In view of this confusion, you ought to give a clear lead on that you would like in every modern article of life

in all forms, designs, eastern or western, or mixed to be produced in khaddar.

Khaddar Earning Power?
As to the economic argument that khaddar adds to the earning power of the agricultural worker, I consider this to be a feeble case altogether. It is pointed out to me by a newspaper correspondent that if I had seen the great ocean of khaddar in India in 1921 and 1922 and the tremendous enthusiasm of people at that time, I would not have ventured on the criticism that I am now doing. That is perfectly true, but this conclusively proves that my criticism now is fully justified, and that all that ocean of khaddar and all that enthusiasm has dwindled if not disappeared on their merit or demerit, long before I came here and offered my criticism.

It is the duty of every sincere public man in India to find out how and why this tremendous enthusiasm was created, how and why it died out and how far the fault and mistakes of your followers have been responsible for this state. The present condition of affairs demands a criticism and not a condemnation of criticism.

The methods adopted by other countries of organising labour and peasantry and guiding and leading the workers in factories or farms to obtain their rights have produced far more benevolent and efficient results in human life than the two-annas-a-day charka movement will ever do. The government schemes of canals, scientific manuring and carrying on agricultural work by machinery will add ten times more to the economic prosperity than the charka, but you have already described the government to be satanic. Let us have a clear idea as to your position in this matter. Is a person adding to the economic value of the poor peasantry a friend or an enemy of the poor?

I want you to put one question to your own conscience, irrespective of public articles – had you come out in this country after the general failure of your attempts to free Indians in South Africa from political and civic slavery, and after the mess you made with some young Indians in London, in drawing them into some direct or indirect service of war, would India have given you any importance, would India have allowed you to take political leadership, would India have poured in lakhs of rupees in response to your demands if you had said that you wanted all this only for the purpose of adding As. 2 a day to the income of barely three per cent of Indian peasantry?

Were not all these great powers laid at your entire disposal because you made a definite political promise and allowed the people at least to believe that you had some plan or method which would quickly, within a limited period of two years, give to the Indians political freedom from the British yoke? Now where do we stand with regard to the primary aim of the charka movement and its position today? Are you shifting your limit of two years to four years or to twenty years or to two hundred years? Do you suggest that a rise of As. 2 income, say of the whole population, is a process which is going to drive the British out of this country or do you believe that a still higher figure will have to be reached? Did you believe this government to be satanic because it brought poverty on the people, did you then believe that this poverty could never be cured before the satanic government was overthrown? Do you believe now that you can improve the economic condition of the people without removing the satanic government or without any reference to politics, or have you suddenly come to the conclusion that the immediate poverty of the people has touched your heart so much that you launch out into that problem of life and have made up your mind to ignore the problem of the existing political slavery of the country?

Economy of Charka
Reverting to the economic value of charka, it is the admitted experience of the whole world that out of all handicrafts in competition against machinery, handspinning is of the least economic value; handweaving, embroidery, carpentry, shoe-making or making any kind of footwear, etc. have a much greater value. If you would look at the Parsee Girls' Industrial Home in Karachi or a still more splendid institution of the Hindu Orphanage at Surat, namely Hardevran Vakil Hindu Orphanage, you will realise how the earning power of the helpless poverty-stricken people can be improved by one or two rupees a day. I clearly see that such crafts cannot be taken up on a large scale by all villagers, whereas handspinning can. But why do you persevere in handspinning with superstitious adherence, and why not introduce alongside of it other more profitable handicrafts for a few persons in each village if economic salvation is your present object?

'Robbing Peter to Pay Paul'
You are not teaching the people to wear more clothes than before, your own example would rather lead them to wear less. At the same time you are teaching more people to produce clothes, and how can you fail to realise that you are robbing Peter to pay Paul, and while you are improving the economic condition of some, you are doing it at the expense of others. Sensible economists, socialists and trade-union organisers have within a short period increased the economic earning of their followers by more than a 100 per cent; they have taught their followers to use more food, more furniture, more clothes; they have thus created great demand which has taken away the burden of man

from the land, and have left the land workers more prosperous than before.

You are afraid or unwilling to follow this natural and sensible course, which is of course very inconvenient to a few rich manufacturers, merchants and zamindars who grow rich by starving millions of people. You are freely receiving gifts from these selfish rich in order to carry on work in the opposite direction of increasing the economic value of workers in industry or on land. The poverty of the population on land can easily be remedied, instead of being played about with, by bravely fighting the causes which directly produce such poverty, such as the unnatural and unjustifiable rights of the zamindars over God-created land and low wages of agricultural labourers.

Thus I say that if you had not put forward political claims you would never have acquired the power and opportunities which you have, and if you had purely economic aims, you are standing against the economic interests of the masses and in favour of the interests of the wealthy classes by deliberately 'noncooperating' with, and indirectly obstructing the work of those who would bring about an economic regeneration of the people along lines that have proved successful in all parts of the world.

Entirely Wrong Theories

You have raised the objection against western methods of organising labour on your mistaken notion that such a process would introduce class war and that acute oppression of capitalists over labour does not exist in India. In both these theories you are entirely wrong. Those who organised labour had not created class war. Modern system of production, commerce and finance produces class war, the parties in which are the capitalists and the workers. Those who organised labour are doing nothing but the great moral work of helping and strengthening the weaker of the two parties in that class war. Those who organise labour always do so deliberately with a view to abolishing class distinction by making capital the common property of all, and by making manual or mental labour the common duty of all. This alone will stop class war, and you who would not assist in organising labour help in the continuance of class war, which is going on every day in all industrial countries of the world, among which India today occupies the fifth place and not an insignificant place.

'Class War So Acute in India'

The acuteness with which class war operates upon the wage-earners of India is more than in most of the advanced European countries where thanks to the organisers of labour, several of the cruelties of class war are being removed. Just look at the palatial houses of any millowner of Bombay, Ahmedabad, Nagpur or Calcutta and look at the disgraceful and diabolical one-room tenements of poor workers, devoid of all furniture, appointments or embellishments. Such acute difference between the dwelling conditions of the rich and poor does not exist in Great Britain, America, or any part of Europe where labour is well organised. It is unjustifiable defence of the rich industrialists of India to describe them to the world as endowed with special virtues, when all the facts of poor people's life proclaim loudly that these virtues are not existent. The personal obsequiousness of the poor worker towards their masters, the utter helplessness before arbitrary dismissals and the ill-treatment as it actually exists in India everywhere are unthinkable in Europe or America, where labour is organised, and your defence of the Indian master class is an unpardonable mockery of the poor suffering working class. The way in which zamindars, khotas and malguzaries claim by force the labour of their tenants at certain seasons for half an anna a day is a diabolical disgrace to humanity and does not exist in countries where modern agricultural trade unions are existing.

That is not all. The class war in India is literally murderous and more cruelly murderous because it is infanticidal. Just analyse the figures of death. The death rate of the adults, and especially of the infants, in large industrial towns is much in excess of the normally bad death rate in India. Now kindly follow me in still closer analysis of these figures obtained from municipal health officers of infantile mortality of well-to-do Parsee, Hindu and Mohammedan families in Bombay, Ahmedabad, Nagpur or Calcutta or other industrial towns. You will find that the mortality amongst infants under 12 months of age among the rich would be about 80 to 90 per thousand whereas the infantile mortality in the municipal wards where the factory workers live would be from 600 to even 830 per thousand. Such a damnable attack upon human life is unknown in those countries where the working classes are organised. To defend such a position is criminal but for anybody to go even further and to throw dust in the eyes of the world that class war is not operating acutely in India is monstrous and inhuman, and I have always felt that through your misguided sentimentality, you have preferred to be one of them.

Then take the other important elements of life – the dignity, the consciousness and the self-respect of man, and look at our unfortunate clerks, teachers, postmen, and railway station staff, etc. The treatment which they are made to suffer, and are almost habituated to, is a disgrace to human society, and the only salvation out of it is efficient labour organisation. Class war is there, will continue to be there till any successful scheme of communism abolishes it. But in the meantime not to organise the people and not to struggle against the evil effects from day to day is a doctrine which cannot appeal to any genuine humanitarian.

'Charka Does Not Make'

During my conversation with you at certain periods you did not seem to take a definite attitude with regard to the value of organisation of labour and peasants. You emphatically argued that the Charka movement was making organisation. I emphatically deny it. There must be conscious and deliberate work of organisation, to be carried out for its own sake in a proper scientific manner and for the purpose of our national object, with a straightforward and unconcealed imparting of political consciousness. The same similarity of the working of charka, with some vague idea, religious zeal or economic welfare or a great Gandhiji's command, does not and cannot do any effective organising work, and cannot create and has not created any political consciousness. For centuries together, millions of men and women in India have been boiling rice, utilising similar quantities of rice and water and conducting cooking operations of a similar nature, doing some industrial work when cooking it and producing food of economic value without buying ready-made food. All these operations surely have not produced any organisation, and the work of spinning can never do so any more than the work of cooking.

Psychological Value of Movement

Then we come to the psychological value of the movement. This was great. It all began well and it almost became wonderful at a certain stage. But why create a psychology if you do not intend to mobilise the spirit so created, and if you do not intend immediately to form men and women into an organisation for a definite material object while they are under a psychological influence and before that influence passes away? That is exactly my complaint, and the bitter disappointment of your world-critics against you. You missed an opportunity and you only opened the eyes of the political opponents of India, and by your inaction, after a certain psychology was aroused, you only brought India under a tighter grip of her opponents and made her enslavement a little worse than before. Not only that, but the position of India worsened that of Egypt and, for a time, of China, and at any rate became harmful in Turkey, Persia and Afghanistan. All these people have a right to complain against us if we bungle our affairs in such a manner as to have an indirect harmful effect upon them.

Whatever may be the feelings of some of your ardent admirers, I hope you and I are both agreed that we are both very common and ordinary persons. The political world that lives, works and struggles consciously can analyse you or me with the same completeness as dissecting an ordinary insect. After the year 1900 the world changed from what it was immediately before the year 1900. Before 1900 leaders who gave expression to submission and to legislative hypocrisy and worked to build up hopes of salvation on such instruments of legislation were popular leaders, as Gladstone was to the British, Bismarck to the Germans, or Parnel to the Irish, or Dadabhai or Pherozeshah and Surendra Nath to the Indians. By the year 1900 the masses of men got tired and sick and their hearts began to burn with fire. The change came on very rapidly and universally and only such individuals as expressed the burning fire of the heart and the revolt of the suffering human beings were taken as leaders.

The first task of these leaders was to express boldly and fearlessly the unexpected voice of the people. The second task of these leaders was, without waiting for the new, to obstruct the old with such efficiency as to make it absolutely impossible for the old order to continue to function. The third task was to reconstruct and slowly to build up a new life. Ireland produced De Valera. He did No. 1 and No. 2 and his people are now bravely carrying on his task No. 3. Russia produced Lenin. He did No. 1 and No. 2 and, though his life was short, he led his people on the right side regarding No. 3. Turkey produced Kemal. He did No. 1 and No. 2 and is fortunate enough to be living and vigorous to carry on his task No. 3. China produced Sun Yat-sen. He completed No. 1 and No. 2 and after his death his well-organised and well-disciplined followers are carrying on task No. 3. In Italy, though in contrary direction, Mussolini plays an individual part. India at that moment announced her world leader to be Gandhi.

You performed No. 1 and but you abandoned task No. 2, and so task No. 3 is out of question, and we are so overwhelmed with the disastrous defeat at the second stage of your struggle that our lot today is harder than before to attain success over the conditions of the past. Instead of making the past conditions inoperative, they have become more vigorously operative in India, and now worse still, the hopes of future struggle are being continually lessened even by the reversal of the psychological advantage that we had. Your own admission and that of your followers, as well as the facts of life, make it clear that the psychology and the enthusiasm of the early days has vanished and the readiness of the people to work for the rightful heritage is turned into hesitancy and fear.

It is from this point of view that we, who observe your mistakes and carefully study your further perseverance in them, make bold to demand from you in the name of the suffering humanity of India, as well as of other countries, that you give your services to humanity in consultation and cooperation with others so as to retrieve the lost position. Pray do not misunderstand me as 'attacking' you or wishing for your disappearance from public life. The purpose of this letter is to show you the faults and defects of your policy and acts, and therefore this letter contains only your defects, but it by no means argues that you do not possess qualities that are estimable and that can be yet of great value. These qualities require no enumeration.

The great psychological wave having once died away, the perseverance of yourself and your immediate disciples in the same direction automatically become a degenerate form of the original activities. Here again you must permit me to speak as man to man.

How to Make People Ready for Civil Disobedience
You have created a certain influence over our countrymen in the lowest strata of society wider and deeper than anybody else. However, what is your real object? If your object is metaphysical or religious, your policy should be to cultivate a psychology of obedience and reverence towards you and diffidence in themselves as compared to your great self. If your purpose is to give your share in the national and political work, your approach to the people should be on terms of absolute equality and your task must be to inspire confidence into them. From this point of view you must stop allowing people to address you as Mahatma. You have no doubt intimated to your friends that you have never wished this word to be used, and no one really expects you to do otherwise, but that does not mean that you should not or that you cannot suppress it immediately. You can easily refuse to receive letters so addressed, and you can easily refuse to attend functions where you are advertised with this appellation. You have only to declare your wish publicly, instead of whispering about it with a few friends and the thing will be done. With some experience of political propaganda and mass mentality, I am speaking to you in earnest that our first approach to the people must be based on the fact that our powers are not greater than that of others. If you go into a bunch of villagers and start out by being called and known as a brother, you create a source of confidence and self-reliance in them. If you go to them with a long story first spread by your friends about 21 days' fasting and then with discovery of yourself as a Mahatma, even though the villagers may think about your charka with superstitious awe, they acquire no confidence in themselves, and they will only believe that what you say or do is the task of such superior persons and high souls like yourself and not of ordinary mortals. Such a mentality spread wholesale over the country becomes most injurious in the long run.

You should rigorously stop crowds and processions of human beings, specially poor women and little children, passing you with folded hands and downcast eyes. Once you create this phase of abject submission of man to man, no wonder that you should yourself despair of obtaining civil disobedience from your own followers. You now complain that the masses are not ready for any such self-assertion, but even if that were so, your whole procedure is certainly not making them more ready for it.

Then there is one thing that I witnessed at Yeotmal which has hurt me greatly, and I had slight evidence of it before. Your work regarding the removal of untouchability is grand in its aspiration, and is not bad in its success as it is generally carried on. However, I strongly object to your permitting my countrymen and countrywomen to touch your feet and put their fingers in their eyes. Such touchability appears to be more damnable than untouchability, and I would sooner wish that two persons did not touch each other than any one human being should be touched by an another in the way in which you were touched.

The depressed classes were subject to a sort of general disability, but this new phase of a man of the depressed class worshipping the feet of his deliverer is a more real individual depression and degradation of life, and however much you may misunderstand me, I must call upon you to stop this nonsense. It is no use saying that you do not like it, it is a matter of your not stopping it when nothing is easier in the world for you than to stop it. You are ruining the mentality of and the psychology of these villagers for another generation or two. You are preparing the country not for mass civil disobedience but for servile obedience and for a belief that there are superior persons on the earth and Mahatmas in this life at a time when in this country the white man's prestige is already a dangerous obstacle in our way. Politically this career of yours is ruinous and from a humanitarian point of view its degenerating influence appears to me to be a moral plague.

Organisation of Industrial Labour

As regards the organisation of industrial labour, you are not ready to give your share, when we know that your cooperation would be of a higher value in inviting workers to the fold of Trade Union Congress. You do not realise that by such cooperation you would actually help in preventing many preventable deaths, specially of poor, innocent babies. Then you go one step further, and you use your influence by frequent declarations which discourage others from taking up this most necessary and urgent work. Then at times you go still further and you actually and deliberately fraternise and cooperate with the master class, so as to make the task of labour organisers not only difficult but almost unjustifiable in the eyes of poor workers. You may defend the process whichever way you like, but the experienced world can only say that it is the exploitation of the spirit of superstition and of ignorance among poor workers at the cost of human lives and their families and for the benefit of the bank accounts of the happy minority that rules the roost. I remember in London we all read the description of your royal reception at Jamshedpur and your acceptance of an address in a steel casket with a purse, as in that Jamshedpur underfeeding, bad housing, underclothing does not go on, as if deaths, which are preventable under modern scientific principles, are not daily taking place, as if men were never driven to resort to strike, through unreasonable obstinacy of their employers, and as if even military operations against workers had never taken place. I have confessed above that I have looked at this picture of your performance with disappointment from a long distance. Comrade, you have to take the world as it is, and you have to believe that all labour would have looked upon that picture with similar disappointment. Even with all your personal power and success you will not be able to change the great law of worldly life that those who are not with us are against us, and in the name of the working classes, I want to call upon you to remember it.

A Personal Appeal

I have put down my candid thoughts in the above paragraphs with a view to disburden my soul of personal grievance; I fully realise that I am courting great unpopularity in the eyes of my fellow countrymen whose good wishes and good opinion are as dear to me as to you. What I am really attempting to do is to disburden your mind of a lot of confusion and contradiction and to demand from you, in the name of all sufferers, not merely that you stop adding to their sufferings but that you come forward and live with us as a brother with brothers, and work with us in a manner and form which we all consider you to be most fitted and your service to be most valuable. I have already read to you my notes, in which I have mentioned what psychological, political and even revolutionary value can be attached to the khaddar movement. I have no prejudice against it, and I would even preserve and build upon whatever value it may have for a nation's liberty and life. I attach full copy of these notes again, which I am submitting to the Working Committee of the Congress for a preliminary consideration.

What I want of you is that you be a good old Gandhi, put on an ordinary pair of khaddar trousers and coat and come out and work with us in the ordinary way. Come and organise with us (as you alone by yourself have failed) our workers, our peasants, and our youths, not with a metaphysical sentimentality, but with a set purpose, a clearcut and well-defined object and by methods such as by experiment are making success for all human beings.

I am not a believer in slavishly obeying persons, prestige or organisations, but I always believe all past efforts and actions have their elements of good on which we can, if we will, build a stronger future. Instead of developing the vanity of making underclothing or overclothing a primary object of administration, and starting some traditions of a sage of Sabarmati, as an ordinary rough-and -tumble man making your food and clothing secondary and unimportant items that should not require any special thought of you, you would still be able to undo your great mistakes of the past, and to make up for the damage done to India and other Asiatic countries, and be one of the successful workers for India as other successful leaders have actually worked for their own countries.

Yes, when I have cast my eyes on you, I am not going to take any point-blank refusal from you. I know there will be the usual popular cry against me that I ought not to have used such language or such words, etc., etc., but I do not believe that in an attempt to use artificial polish in our language, we become as unfair to the addressee as to ourselves, and it is a much better policy to say the things as we think, as we talk among friends. Therefore, before I go, I should like you to get up one morning as from a dream and to say 'yes', and many of us can soon be put together in a good team, and set about putting an end to so many deplorable conditions of life in India, about which none of us has any doubt.

I remain,
Yours fraternally,
SHAPURJI SAKLATVALA

[*Amrita Bazar Patrika*, 12 March 1927]

(B) MAHATMA GANDHI'S REPLY

Ahmedabad
17 March 1927

Gandhi has written an article under the caption "No and Yes" in today's (17 March) 'Young India' in reply to Mr. Shapurji Saklatvala's open letter to him:

'Comrade' Saklatvala is dreadfully in earnest. His sincerity is transparent. His sacrifices are great. His passion for the poor is unquestioned, I have, therefore, given his fervent, open appeal to me that close attention which that of a sincere patriot and a humanitarian must command. But in spite of all my desire to say 'Yes' to his appeal, I must say 'No', if I am to return mere sincerity for sincerity, or if I am to act according to my faith. But I can say 'Yes' to his appeal after my own fashion. For underneath his intense desire that I should cooperate with him on his terms, there is an emphatic implied condition that I must say 'Yes' only if his argument satisfied my head and heart. A 'No' uttered from the depth of conviction is better than a 'Yes' merely uttered to please, or what is worse, to avoid trouble.

Against a Blind Wall

In spite of all desire to offer hearty cooperation I find myself against a blind wall. His facts are fiction and his deductions based upon fiction are necessarily baseless. And where these facts are true my whole energy is concentrated upon nullifying their (to me) poisonous results. I am sorry, but we do stand at opposite poles. There is, however, one great thing in common with between us. Both claim to have the good of the country and humanity as our only goal. Though, therefore we may be for the moment seem as going in the opposite directions, I expect we shall meet some day. I promise to make ample amends when I discover my error.

Satanic Civilisation

Meanwhile, however, my error, since I do not recognise it as such, must be my shield and my solace. For unlike 'Comrade' Saklatvala, I do not believe that multiplication of wants and machinery contrived to supply them is taking the world a single step nearer its goal. 'Comrade' Saklatvala swears by the modern rush. I wholeheartedly detest this mad desire to destroy distance and time, to increase animal appetites and go to the ends of the earth in search of their satisfaction. If modern civilisation stands for all this, and I have understood it to do so, I call it satanic, and with it the present system of government, its best exponent.

Its Baneful Effects

I distrust its schemes of amelioration of the lot of the poor. I distrust its currency reform. I distrust its army and navy. In the name of civilisation and its own safety, this government has continuously bled the masses. It has enslaved, it has bribed the powerful with distinctions and riches and it has sought to crush under the weight of its despotic regulations liberty-loving patriots who wanted not to be won over either by flattery or riches. I would destroy that system today, if I had the power. I would use most deadly weapons, if I believed that they would destroy it. I refrain only because the use of such weapons would only perpetuate the system though it may destroy its present administrators. Those who seek to destroy men rather than their manners adopt the latter and become worse than those whom they destroy under the mistaken belief that manners will die with the men. They do not know the root of the evil.

Movement of 1920

The movement of 1920 was designed to show that we could not reform the soulless system by violent means, thus becoming soulless ourselves. But we could do so only by not becoming victims of the system, i.e., by non-cooperation, by saying an emphatic 'No' to every advance made to entrap us into the nets spread by Satan. The movement suffered a check, but it is not dead. My promise was conditional. The conditions were simple and easy. But they proved too difficult for those who took a leading part in the movement. What 'Comrade' Saklatvala believes to be my error and failure, I regard to be the expression of my strength and deep conviction. It may be an error, but so long as my conviction that it is truth abides, the very error must, as it does, sustain me. Retracing of my steps at Bardoli, I hold to be an act of wisdom and supreme service to the country. The government is weaker for that decision. It would have regained all lost position if I had persisted after Chauri Chaura in carrying out the terms of what I regarded as an ultimatum to the viceroy.

South African Movement – A Failure?
My 'Comrade' is wrong in saying that the South African movement was a failure. If it was, my whole life must be written down as a failure. And his invitation to me to enlist under his colours must be held to be meaningless. South Africa gave a start to my life's mission. Nor do I consider it to be wrong to have offered during the late war services of my companions and myself, under my then convictions, as ambulance men.

Khadi Movement Not on Wane
This great M.P. is in a hurry. He disdains to study facts. Let me inform him that the khadi movement is not on the wane. It did last year at least 20 times as much work as during 1920. It is now serving not less than 50,000 spinners in 1,500 villages, besides weavers, washermen, printers, dyers and tailors.

Mr. Saklatvala asks what khaddar stands for. Well it stands for simplicity, not shoddiness. It sits well on the shoulders of the poor and it can be made, as it was made in the days of yore, to adorn the bodies of the richest and the most artistic men and women. It is reviving ancient arts and crafts. It does not seek to destroy all machinery, but it does regulate its use and check its weedy growth. It uses machinery for the service of the poorest in their own cottages. The wheel itself is an exquisite piece of machinery.

The Poor and Khaddar
The khaddar delivers the poor from the bonds of the rich and creates a moral and spiritual bond between the classes and the masses. It restores to the poor somewhat of what the rich have taken from them. Khaddar does not displace a single cottage industry. On the contrary, it is being daily recognised that it is becoming the centre of other village industries.

Khaddar brings a ray of hope to the widow's broken-up home but it does not prevent her from earning more, if she can. It prevents no-one from seeking a better occupation. Khaddar offers honourable employment to those in need of some. It utilises the idle hours of the nation. My esteemed comrade quotes with pride the work of those who offer more lucrative employment. Let him know that khaddar does that automatically. It cannot put annas into the pockets of the poor without putting rupees into the pockets of some, whereas those who begin their work in the cities, though they are no doubt doing good work, touch but a fringe of the question. Khaddar touches the very centre and therefore necessarily includes the rest.

Indian Conditions Ignored

But the whole of the impatient communist's letter concentrates itself upon the cities and thus ignores India and Indian conditions which are to be found only in her 700,000 villages. The half a dozen modern cities are excrescence and serve at the present moment the evil purposes of draining the life-blood of the villagers. Khaddar is an attempt to revise and reverse the process and establish a better relationship between the cities and the villages. The cities with their insolent torts are a constant menace to the life and liberty of the villagers. Khaddar has the greatest organising power in it, because it has itself to be organised and because it affects all India. If khaddar rained from heaven it would be a calamity, but as it can be manufactured by the willing cooperation of the starving millions and thousands of middle class men and women, its success means the best organisation conceivable along peaceful lines. If cooking had to be revived and required the same organisation, I should claim for it the same merit that I claim for khaddar.

My Work among Labourers

My communist comrade finds fault with my work among the labourers in Jamshedpur because I accepted the address in Jamshedpur not from Tatas but from the employees. His disapprobation is due, I expect, to the fact that the late Mr. Ratan Tata was in the chair. Well I am not ashamed of the honour. Mr. Tata appeared to me to be a humane and considerate employer. He readily granted, I think, all the prayers of the employees, and I heard later that the agreement was being honourably kept. I do ask and receive donations for my work from the rich as well as the poor. The former gladly give me their donations. This is no personal triumph. It is a triumph of nonviolence, which I endeavour to represent, be it ever so inadequately.

A Triumph of Nonviolence

It is to me a matter of perennial satisfaction that I retain generally the affection and trust of those whose policies I oppose. The South Africans gave me personally their confidence and extended their friendship. In spite of my denunciation of British policy and system I enjoy the affection of thousands of English men and women and in spite of unqualified condemnation of modern materialistic civilisation, the circle of European and American friends is everwidening. It is again a triumph of nonviolence.

Labour in Cities

Lastly about labour in the cities. Let there be no misunderstanding. I am not opposed to the organisation of labour, but as in everything else I want its organisation along Indian lines or, if you will, my lines. I am doing it. The Indian labourer knows it instinctively that I do not regard capital to be the enemy of labour. I hold their coordination to be a perfectly possible. The organisation of labour that I undertook in South Africa, Chamaparan or Ahmedabad was in no spirit of hostility to the capitalists and the resistance in each case and to the extent it was thought necessary was wholly successful. My ideal is equal distribution, but so far as I can see it is not to be realised. I therefore work for equitable distribution. This I seek to attain through khaddar – and since its attainment must sterilise the British exploitation at its centre – it is calculated to purify British connection. Hence in that sense khaddar leads to swaraj.

Charge of 'Mahatma'

The Mahatma I must leave to his fate. Though a noncooperator I shall gladly subscribe to a bill to make it criminal for anybody to call me Mahatma and to touch my feet. Where I can impose law myself, i.e. at the Ashram, the practise is criminal.

Amrita Bazar Patrika, 18 March 1927

(c) GANDHIJI'S LETTER
Nandi Hills,
10 May 1927

Dear Friend,

Srimati Anasuya Bai has sent me your letter to herself, and your joint letter to her, Gularizal and Desai. I have read them carefully. I had your letter also. I could not reply to you earlier for want of your address. As soon as I heard from Anasuya Bai, I put myself in communication with Motilaji. I am daily expecting his reply. You shall know it as soon as I receive it. I thank you for the confidence you repose in me and it will be a joy to me if I can render any personal service to you; but I am afraid my longing and ability to render service have to stop there. So far as our ideals are concerned, we stand apart. Whilst Anasuya Bai and Shankarlal Banker, as also Gulzarilal and Desai, are absolutely free agents, they have exercised their choice of accepting my guidance in framing their labour policy and administration. I must therefore shoulder my share of the responsibility for what is happening about labour in Ahmedabad. I have certainly advised them to keep Ahmedabad labour aloof from the other labour movements in India so long as Ahmedabad chooses to remain under their guidance.

My reason is exceedingly simple. Labour in India is still extremely unorganised. The labourers have no mind of their own when it comes to matters of national policy or even the general welfare of labour itself. Labourers in various parts of India have no social contact and no other mutual ties. It is not everywhere wisely guided. In many places it is under selfish and highly unscrupulous guidance.

There is no absolute cohesion amongst provincial labour leaders; and there is little discipline among the subleaders. The latter do not uniformly tender obedience to their provincial chiefs. Leaders in different provinces have no single policy to follow. In these circumstances, an all-India union can only exist on paper. I hold it to be suicidal, therefore, for Ahmedabad to think of belonging to it.

My own conviction is that Ahmedabad is rendering a service to labour all over India by its attention, or, as I call it, self-restraint. If it can succeed in perfecting its own organisation, it is bound to serve as a model to the rest of India and its success is bound to prove highly infectious.

But I am free to confess that there is as yet no assurance of success in the near future. The energy of the workers is sorely tried in combating disruptive forces that ever continue to crop up. There is the Hindu-Muslim tension. There is the question of touchables and untouchables in Hinduism, etc.

Add to this the extreme ignorance and selfishness among the labourers themselves. It is a marvel to me that labour in Ahmedabad has made the progress it has during the last 12 years of its corporate existence. If then Ahmedabad remains isolated it does so not selfishly, but for the sake of labour as a whole.

Labour and Capital
One word as to the policy. It is not anticapitalistic. The idea is to take from capital labour's due share and no more; and this not by paralysing capital, but by reform among the labourers from within and by their own selfconsciousness; not again through the cleverness and manoeuvring of nonlabour leaders, but by educating labour to evolve its own leadership

and its own self-reliant, self-existing organisation. Its direct aim is not in the least degree political, but is internal reform and evolution of internal strength. The indirect result of this evolution, whenever it becomes complete, will naturally be tremendously political.

I have not therefore the remotest idea of exploiting labour or organising it for any direct political end. It will be of itself a political power of first class importance when it becomes a self-existing unit. Labour, in my opinion must not become a pawn in the hands of the politician on the political chess-board. It must, by its sheer strength, dominate the chess-board; and my aim can be achieved if I can retain the intelligent and voluntary cooperation of workers in Ahmedabad, and if our joint effort ultimately succeeds.

This is my dream. I hug it because it gives me all the consolation I need, and the policy I have outlined, you will recognise, is a direct outcome of my implicit belief in and acceptance of nonviolence. It may be all a delusion; but it is as much a reality with me as life itself so long as I do not see it as a delusion, but see it only as the only life-giving force.

You will now see why I cannot, even if I had the power, respond to your appeal for dividing the funds collected by me in accordance with your suggestion. But I may tell you that I have not even the power. The funds have been collected purely for khadi work, and it would be a misappropriation on my part to direct them to any other use.

This letter may not please you. I shall be sorry if it does not. But I regard you as a fellow-seeker after truth and if my reading of you is correct, there is no reason why my having told you the truth and nothing but the truth should not please you immensely. It is not given to all of us to agree with one another in all our opinions; but it is given to every one of us that we tender the same respect for the opinions and actions of our fellows as we expect for our own!

Yours sincerely,
M. K. GANDHI.

(D) SAKLATVALA'S REPLY

1 July 1927
Dear Comrade Gandhi,

I am in receipt of your letter of 10th May, and I see that you have written it from the Nandi Hills, where I presume you are recuperating from your illness. I trust you will be restored to health by the time this letter reaches you.

Let me say in my usual blunt way that I am returning to my attack upon you. Of course, you understand the meaning and nature of my 'attacks' upon you, namely, that recognising in you a man of indomitable spirit, with a real propagandist's heart and qualities, I want you to deal with the various Indian movements in the way in which success is made for such movements in other parts of the world.

I am not coming to you in the midst of your success, in the midst of great defeats and setbacks to our imperialist oppressors, with merely a fanciful appeal to you to adopt some new method. I come to you, rather in the time of great reverses for our country, When on every front – political, economic and social, we are suffering reverse upon reverse, are being pushed back everywhere, are disorganised, disunited and dispirited in all departments of public life, and our insolent antagonists are launching attack after attack upon us.

I still want you to recognise that the forces within a nation do not depend merely on relative numbers. Now one small section of a nation and now another becomes an important factor, occupying a key position at some critical moment in the affairs of the country, and counting as a national force even though in itself a minority. The peasants and the villagers may become at times the most successful factor in defying the tax gatherers; the soldiers and the fighters may become at times an important factor to reckon with, when in their own mind and consciousness, they are unwilling to launch out upon an unholy campaign such as the one carried out by the Government of India in China. And at times the industrial workers, however small in numbers, may become for a country the all-important factor of life, and may bring about a paralysis of the most powerful activities of the imperial exploiter or of a dominating class.

Need for All-India Trade Union Movement
Because our country is largely agricultural, it does not follow that in the economy of modern life our organised workers shall be of less value or shall become a less important section of the community than in any other country which is more industrialised and less agricultural, under similar circumstances. If a large country has to depend upon a small number of industrial workers as compared to agriculturalists, the power of the industrial workers does not become any the less on that account.

It is with the above observations that I have been constantly attempting to direct your mind to the necessity and importance of an organised industrial labour movement within our national activity. Such a movement, in the first place, must be national and embrace the whole country. It is not for you and me today to devise new and fantastic organisations when we see the value of the existing trade union movements in all the advancing and powerful countries of the world. We must have an All-India Trade Union movement.

I am not at the present moment arguing about your methods or about your ideals. I am only denouncing your idea that the organisation of labour should be sectional, should be communal and should be limited to a little spot like Ahmedabad. Did you ever try to have an Indian National Congress for Ahmedabad alone? Did you ever try to have the National Education movement confined to Ahmedabad? Why, then, should you try to restrict you ideal labour movement to Ahmedabad?

You are not weakening the political movement, the khaddar movement, or the National Education movement by encouraging Ahmedabad or any one important district to fall away and stand aloof from the whole national movement; then why should you do so in the case of the large national labour movement by asking and encouraging an important industrial centre like Ahmedabad to stand aloof and alone? Let me examine your reasoning at some length.

The State of Indian Labour and the 'Remedy'

You say labour in India is extremely unorganised. Do you not say, therefore, that I am right in appealing to you to employ your great power in organising labour on an adequate national basis? You cannot argue that our numbers are unwieldy, for many western countries have larger number of workers to deal with; nor can you find fault with the vastness of the area of our country, for both Russia and China have overcome their greater difficulties in the respect.

You complain that Indian labourers have no mind of their own on matters of general policy or even of labour policy. That is exactly where the value and need of propaganda comes in. Had our workers their conscious policy, I would not have been driven to urge you to help them and to preach to them in order to organise them.

For khaddar and for noncooperation, you fearlessly carry out a whirl-wind campaign all over the country amongst villagers and workers who had no conception of your ideal before your propaganda reached them. You, with your colleagues, confessed to carrying out a labour propaganda in Ahmedabad, all I ask is that Ahmedabad should be merely a part of a whole and that your services should be given unreservedly to the whole move-ment.

You say in your letter 'Labourers in various parts of India have no social contact and no other contact and no other mutual ties.' That is where you ignore and overlook the most powerful common factor of life that has unfailingly united men and women in other countries despite their hun-dred and one, and sometimes very bitter, differences on religious, social or clan questions. No man has ever succeeded nor shall one now succeed in

stopping modern industrialism, and the economic factor is the one common factor that applies to, and that unites, men and women of various
social, national, religious and communal textures. Hours, wages, standards
of life, political and legislative needs of the workers are on the whole so
uniform that when organised to battle around those wants they have
invariably forgotten and drowned their internal dissensions. The absence
of labour unity and trade union discipline is a more serious loss to the India
of today than we have yet learned to observe.

Position of Ahmedabad Labour
On the one hand, you blame Indian labour for being sectarian and
communal, and on the other hand, when the All India Trade Union
Congress is struggling to build up national and international labour
unity, you feel tempted to induce Ahmedabad to stand separate and
apart, you say 'It is not everywhere wisely guided.' Does that not rather
support my argument that you and other popular congress and swaraj
leaders must take up the work? Then you describe various factors making
for dissension and disunity amongst labour organisers. All that merely
strengthens my appeal that all the sane and truly selfless persons in
public life should devote themselves to the task of organising the industrial
and agricultural workers.

The persons who have been organising labour in Ahmedabad may be
doing well owing to the fortuitous circumstances that they possess more
means than most other Indian groups could possibly have. There is a mild
form of welfare work carried on and conciliation is established between
individual complainants and their bosses. This is all. That is not modern
trade unionism which is struggling for justice and the right of the workers
to possess in common what they produce for the common good, and to
control and regularise their own destiny.

What has Ahmedabad labour done? What can Ahmedabad labour do, if
it is torn away from the all-India trade union movement? It can certainly
never aspire to be either a pattern or a model. Can Ahmedabad labour
secure better hours, better wages, better education, a better franchise and
the right of the workers to compensation in industrial accidents, unemployment allowances, old age pensions etc., unless and until labour in the
whole Bombay Presidency and in all India obtain the same? Ahmedabad
district by itself, as a district, even of well-organised labour, cannot possibly
do anything for itself, whereas by holding aloof it can weaken the labour
movement in the rest of India and can strengthen the power and opportunities of the master class to oppress the working class.

No Need for Ahmedabad to Stand Aloof
Ambalal Seth from Ahmedabad showed me a commendable welfare

scheme of his own, but I soon discovered him to be the exception and not the rule. I say unhesitatingly that 90 per cent of the labourers in Ahmedabad are living under conditions much worse than the conditions prevailing amongst the employees of some European firms that I observed in Cawnpore and Calcutta. I put it to you unhesitatingly and without exaggeration, that 90 per cent of the children of Ahmedabad workers are made to live by their masters, whom you consider so virtuous and patriotic, under condition which would be condemned and punished as criminal if dogs, horses or other domestic animals were kept under them in most parts of Europe and America. The standard of wages in Ahmedabad is, on average, lower than prevailing in Bombay.

Despite all this, nothing will hinder Ahmedabad labour from carrying on its experiments, merely because it is affiliated to the All India Trade Union Congress. All over the world Trade Union Congresses of various countries contain within them labour federations and trade unions of different trades and provinces pursuing different policies, and yet united together for national demands and general standards. That neither the All India Trade Union Congress nor any federation of textile workers can afford to remain for ever without its branches in an important industrial city like Ahmedabad is quite obvious, and your policy is only forcing a division in Ahmedabad itself.

We had in Britain a very unfortunate example of a miner's organisation in Fifeshire, attempting such aloofness to the detriment of both sides, but they have at last seen the wisdom of working for unity. I do not see that any of your reasons prove that the circumstances in Ahmedabad are peculiar and necessitate its holding aloof to such an extent as to justify a damaging breach in the All India Trade Union movement. The best that Ahmedabad can do is to agree to the affiliation to the TUC. The question of Ahmedabad policy being a model of help and assistance to other unions can arise and be of political value only after such affiliation. Your personal decision as to whether you should confine your interest in labour to Ahmedabad alone, or should extend it to the larger national movement, can remain the same even if the Ahmedabad labour union becomes affiliated to Congress.

Question of Labour Policy

Now with regard to you labour policy, which you explain so clearly, do let me submit at once that whatever your individual views may be on policy and whatever may be acceptable to the workers of Ahmedabad, all that has no bearing on Ahmedabad's affiliation to the TUC of India, and all that provides no justification for Ahmedabad's aloofness from and splitting of a large national movement.

Your idea of a policy for labour, as you explained, would in reality put you outside even those who are regarded as the 'friends of the workers', never mind the champions of their cause. However you confess that you are still in a dream, and even that it may all be a delusion, you show the ordinary confusion of thought of all apologists for capitalism by not sharply distinguishing between capital, capitalism and the control of capital, and you do not clearly see that in order to avoid any clash between labour and capital, the ultimate stage must be one of the control of capital by labour, which produces the entire one hundred per cent of capital, and that society itself must be composed entirely of labourers by hand or brain serving one another as a common duty and not for the sake of making something out of it for individuals who would not labour, but who would exercise their legal rights of confiscating the fruits of other people's labour.

The one great thing to me is that you so readily and frankly admit that labour should be so organised as to remain self-conscious, self-reliant and self-existing, evolving its own leadership and aim, and that such evolution, when developed, would be tremendously political and would dominate the chess-board of national polity. This outlook of yours satisfactorily defines the confusion, the timidity and the limitations of labour's rights that you seem inclined to impose upon the earlier stages of labour development.

Whilst Indian labour is illiterate, underpaid, underfed, mercilessly exploited and legislatively outplayed, it needs the help and assistance of outside people like yourself and those who are valiantly struggling to build up a Trade Union Congress and also a Worker's and Peasants' Party for India. Black sheep there will always be, especially when society is fired with an evil zeal to make economic, political and social progress along the lines of an individualist competitive system, but I have really met and seen in India some fine men and women working in the cause of labour, who would be equal in trustworthiness to any European organisers, although perhaps less experienced. Hence my second request to you personally, which I still press for, viz., that besides, securing the affiliation of Ahmedabad to the AITUC, you personally give your valuable assistance to that body, especially in the matter of organising industrial workers and peasants on a large scale all over India.

Despite your failing health, you are an active and truly all-India propagandist capable of covering enormous areas in a short time. Your popularity and charm enable you to capture the mass psychology and would render easier the otherwise stupendous task of organising an illiterate, overawed and semistarved population of many millions; your inspiring cooperation would give zest to the other voluntary workers in labour's cause, and I may even frankly say that your own new activity would give a suitable opening for practical work to the thousands of our youth who once enlisted in your movement and then cooled down in the absence of a practical and convincing programme.

Our Immediate Task

I do not consider it necessary to discuss the various reactionary sentences that you use against the full economic and political rights of labour. During the last month, during the debate in the House of Commons, on the diabolical Trade Union Bill, we have heard Tory and Liberal capitalists use almost identical sentences and arguments, but all the intelligent working class would realise such sentiments to be but a cloak for the unholy death of a rapacious and murderous employing class. In your case you merely lay it down as your speculative idea of what the early stages of labour organisation would be, and it is not worth while quarrelling over so long as I can see that in the ultimate outcome of labour organisation you are not drawing any close line of unnatural limitations.

You may think it must be twenty years hence before this final stage can be reached, and I may think it can be reached within two years, but it is not a question to be decided by you and me. It can only be decided by events. Our immediate task and duty is to unite together and to start vigorously on this great work.

I also do not share your views regarding the use of public funds entrusted to you. By calling it a Khadar Fund, you are warping your own vision and limiting it in terms of yarn and cloth, but I do feel sure that the public who subscribe funds to you are doing so with the idea of working out the emancipation and liberation of their country and are not sending you instalments as shareholders in a primitive company with circumscribed duties in their Articles of Association. Every national movement must fail, and will fail, if under modern conditions of industrialised life and capitalist power the labourers and the peasantry are not organised. As much of my future programme depends upon your present decision I shall be grateful for early consideration of the matter by you.

Yours fraternally,
SHAPURJI SAKLATVALA

APPENDIX 5

SOCIALISM & 'LABOURALISM'

A Speech in the House of Commons by S. Saklatvala
ONE PENNY

TWO OPINIONS

'No contribution to the debate had such a stirring and stimulating effect as Mr. Saklatvala's, and for some time afterwards the enquiry was everywhere made when two persons met within the walls of Parliament, 'Did you hear Saklatvala?' – *Manchester Guardian*, 22-3-28

'When Saklatvala rose the House rose too. A few who had already had tea remained... The dark mahatma poured forth a volume of continuous monotonous soporific sound. Several fell under the spell and sank into dreamless slumber' – Mr. Neill Weir, M.P. in *Forward* 31-3-28

Published by the Communist Party of Great Britain
16 King Street, Covent Garden, London WC2

INTRODUCTION

Since the Labour Party has gone closer to Liberalism in its programme and policy the House of Commons has become less and less a public forum for debates on socialist principles. Obsessed with the responsibility of being His Majesty's Opposition, preferring the role of advisers to His Majesty King George, and demonstrating their bourgeois conscience and respectability, and exercising themselves for another term in office, the Labour Party has ceased to concern itself with the propaganda of socialism.

When, therefore, that Diehard Tory of Tories, Sir Harry Brittain, thought to rub it in to the Labour Party, which he confounds with the Communist movement, and, incidentally force the Labour leaders to further confessions of impotence in readiness for the General Election, Saklatvala seized the occasion to rescue socialism and Communism from the dishonourable hands of the Labour Party and to be its standard bearer. The result is a speech, giving a clear exposition of the elementary things the socialist movement stands for, in such simple language as will be understood by every worker. Bearing in mind that Saklatvala stands alone in the House, hated and detested by the entire bloc of Labour members, from whom he got nothing but jeers during his speech, his effort limited as it was to forty minutes was a great achievement.

In his speech comrade Saklatvala sets out to repudiate the time-worn confounding of State capitalist enterprise with socialism, using the classic example of the Post Office and municipal trams, which are dear to the hearts of our 'Labourals' (as a contemporary wit defines them). In rapid succession he takes trustification and nationalism, war debt, Capital Levy, Surtax, and the living wage and lays bare the difference between the 'Laboural' policy and the real working-class policy. His pointed rejoinders on how the capitalists will contrive to evade this Surtax, and how impossible it is to hope for a living wage under capitalist imperialism should stick in the mind of every reader as illustrations of the manner in which the Labour Party is trifling with the working class.

Saklatvala's bold defence of a revolutionary policy and Workers' Councils of Action, and his open declaration that socialism means the end of the British Empire and the liberation of the colonial peoples, settles, once and for all, the distinction between Labour imperialist policy and the policy of the Communist Party. Labour imperialism stands for the continuation within the colonies of subjection to British military rule. The Communist Party stands for complete independence.

Comrade Saklatvala has done his job well. A wide distribution of this pamphlet will be a fitting reward for his efforts, and will surely help forward the exposure of the Labour leaders now masquerading under the mask of socialism. It is necessary to add that, in order to assure this wide distribution by issuing the pamphlet at one penny, the speech has been abridged.

SIR HARRY BRITTAIN'S RESOLUTION

'That this House, recognising the grave dissensions which exist amongst leaders of the Socialist Party and within the party itself on vital issues of public policy, considers that the formation of a Socialist Government would be a source of danger to the nation.'

MR. WILLIAM GRAHAM'S AMENDMENT

(Labour Party)
'To delete from the word 'House' and add:
    "Is of the opinion that, in view of widespread change in industry in the direction of syndicate, combine and trust, side by side with material insecurity affecting large numbers of people, there is no foundation for the fear of an economic system based upon the principles of public ownership and control."

MR. S. SAKLATVALA'S PROPOSED AMENDMENT

The following is the amendment prepared by comrade Saklatvala, but not moved on account of its being ruled out of order.

It should be noted that, in accordance with custom, amendments must only contain commas or semi-colons for punctuation. Hence the apparently involved manner of its presentation. Moreover, it should be borne in mind that the resolution or amendment must ask or urge the House to do something.

Amendment to Sir Harry Brittain's Resolution on Socialism

'Omit all words after 'House' and insert:
   "Considering that the private ownership of land, industries and means of producing wealth engenders the struggle of competitor against competitor of nation against nation, of class against class, thus leading to powerful commercial trusts within nations, fierce class struggles and the enslavement of foreign and colonial peoples by imperialist conquests, has failed and must fail to secure and maintain a full standard of living for the workers, to foster their mental and physical development and to secure international peace, this House whilst condemning the capitalist system as responsible for the aforementioned circumstances, at the same time sees that the Labour Party is rapidly deserting the worker's struggle for social emancipation and is adopting policies on finance, unemployment, imperial and foreign affairs such as the Surtax, living wage, nationalisation by purchase, imposition of British conditions for the rule of India, Ireland, Egypt, China and Africa makes necessary the perpetuating and strengthening of the capitalist system united with the militarist supremacy of the capitalists of Great Britain; and this House declares that the achievement of the social emancipation of the working class, the producers of the wealth of society, can only be secured along the lines of bona fide socialism, and urges the subversion of the capitalist system through the inevitable social revolution establishing the dictatorship of the working class during the process of transference of all land, houses and industrial undertakings from private ownership to the working-class State, and, during the period of bringing about the necessary and consequential changes in the judicial, military and administrative machinery, and in securing the independence of all those countries under British subjugation."

SOCIALISM & 'LABOURALISM'
Mr. Saklatvala: I wish to put a point of view, which I believe to be the only possible point of view, for any genuine form of socialism. The right hon. Gentleman the Member for Central Edinburgh (Mr. W. Graham) rightly charged the right hon. Member for Acton (Sir H. Brittain) the mover of the motion with not defining socialism, and with not making clear what it was that he was attacking. The mover did refer to the fact that, in one of the responsible Labour publications, he found the reproduction of about 40 different definitions of socialism. Misunderstanding has been created by the right hon. Member for Central

Edinburgh by the instances which he gave of industries which are under so-called public or municipal control, as if they could be a substitute for socialism. Socialism and capitalism are two entirely antagonistic forms. It is possible for capitalism to extend and expand ownership from one individual to several individuals, as in the case of limited liability companies. It is equally possible to extend that ownership, that partnership to the citizens of a whole borough, town or city, as the case may be, in owning something through a municipal council. It may be equally possible without at all disturbing the capitalist character of society, and without coming near socialism, to extend the ownership of any particular enterprise to all the citizens of a country or a nation.

I beg the House not to be misled into thinking that the ownership of the postal service, or a system of tramlines or transport, or the Broadcasting Corporation has any real bearing on genuine socialism. It is merely an enlargement of the number of shareholders. Let me take, for illustration, the Post Office. It is the height of absurdity to say that the Post Office system, within a capitalist country and a capitalist form of society, is a socialist organisation. It is nothing of the sort.

Mr. W. Thorne: Is it private enterprise?

Mr. Saklatvala: It is private enterprise as it is; it is not a socialist organisation in any shape or form. The only difference is that the shareholders are all the citizens of the nation, but it is a capitalist form and system. When the Post Office wants to erect buildings, it goes to a profiteering contractor. That is not socialism. It fills the pockets of private profiteers. If it wants mail vans, it again goes to private profiteers. If it wants pillar boxes it goes to another private company. If the Post Office wants postage stamps, it goes to a private company and buys the paper and gives a printing contract. There is no socialism about a post office in a capitalist country. There is certainly the compensation that the shareholders are so expanded that everybody within the state stands to lose or gain by its losses or profits. That is the difference, but that is not socialism. The postmen working in the Post Office are no better off than men working for a private corporation or company. It is entirely wrong and misleading to say that this is a form of socialism. This is where we differ in the Communist movement from the so-called socialist movement, which looks at these forms of capitalism as socialism. Though they have a socialist form, they have a capitalist soul. The postmen have no voice in the control of the Post Office. Instead of a board of directors appointed by shareholders, it has a board appointed by the State.

There may be a little difference between private enterprise owned by a few individuals in a nation and an enterprise owned by all the individuals in a nation, but it is misleading to say that private ownership by all persons in the State makes it a socialist organisation. It is far from being a socialist organisation. I read last Sunday an article which the mover of the motion did not mention, though he was very copious in his references to literature. The article was in the 'Sunday Graphic' and it was by the leader of the Opposition, who launched a severe attack on Communism and Communist methods, and tried to speak of socialism in terms of capitalism, or in terms that would confuse everybody and lead to no clear issue at all. What was the gist of that article? What is the real problem before the country and between socialism and capitalism? It is not merely the question of extending the field to a larger number of shareholders; it is a question of overthrowing the system of private ownership and introducing public ownership. It would become criminal for an individual to own land or houses or places of industry. Such a society would be quite a different society. If such a society were introduced it is a futile and absurd to argue that the whole of the social structure of the nation would quietly remain what it was and that the relationship of man to man within the State would continue to be what it was. It is deceptive even to put forward such a proposition, and again I suggest, especially to my comrades within the Labour movement who aspire to be socialists to take the example of the Post Office or the Broadcasting Corporation or of municipal tramways; the capitalist state of society has not been altered by merely widening the ownership. The position of the workers within these industries is absolutely the position of workers who are under the dictation of somebody not appointed by themselves. It is the capitalist system.

Mr. Graham gave many points for serious thought with regard to trustification, but there again I want it to be understood that competition by itself has never been the object of capitalism. The object of capitalism has been the increase of the profits of the individuals in an industry. Competition has been used as a means to achieve that object. For example, somebody for a time is making a profit in a particular industry; another individual or corporation enters into competition, not for the benefit of the consumers, not out of a desire to oblige the world by producing a cheaper article, but to make a higher profit. Competition in itself has never been the object of capitalism and individual ownership. It is a means which is used at certain times only. When the opposite takes place, when unregulated and uncontrolled competition endangers the profits of a particular corporation or several corporations or individuals, quite justifiably and without any inconsistency, the capitalist controllers of these industries combine to get rid of that instrument of competition in order to secure the ultimate object, namely, the safeguarding of their profits. The mere abolition of the element of competition is not the victory of socialism at all. It is still another power at the disposal of private capitalism, either to use that competition or to submerge that competition, to reach the main objective, namely the increase of the individuals profits. From those points of view I submit that within this capitalist country there has never been an experiment with socialism at all. It is a mistaken notion to imagine for a moment that socialism can be introduced alongside capitalism, side by side, and gradually. Such a thing would never happen; such a thing cannot happen. The Member for Central Edinburgh gave us an example drawn from the coal industry to which I would specifically direct the attention of genuine socialists, not only here but all over the country. Is it really satisfying to the socialist conscience to say that the coal industry of this country ought to be so pooled together and controlled as to secure for it a certain trade in coal in somebody else's country, doing this by measures and tactics which will create unemployment amongst the coal miners in Poland, Germany, Belgium, or elsewhere? Such a proceeding would not be socialism, but merely nationalisation. To put under State control a particular national industry, with the same objects as the capitalist owned and controlled, does not bring us any nearer to the attainment of socialism.

If we were to apply the real principles of socialism to the coal mines, the first consideration would be to secure the control of the miners themselves over their own industry. The first consideration of the miners who took charge of the British coal industry would be the welfare of the miners in the coal industry in Poland, in Belgium, in Japan, in India, in Africa, and elsewhere, and the first socialist step would not be to pool the British coal but to pool the world's coal, and arrive at such a position that all miners in all parts of the world would be employed and all the coal produced by them would be of some use to all the nations of the world. The nationalisation of the coal industry in one country does not take us nearer socialism, but may even strengthen the capitalist atmosphere and the capitalist structure of society, in which this sort of nationalisation is practised.

To come back to the argument used by the right hon. Leader of the Opposition in last Sunday's 'Sunday Graphic' in his futile attack upon Communism. What does he mean to say? I have no hesitation in saying that he is not in a position to say what he wants to say. (Hon. Members: 'Why?'). Because he has to attack the Communist Party, because he has got to attack the one country which has achieved socialism, and has also to keep up the appearance of preaching socialism.

We as a nation, and all other nations, are concerned not merely with the theory of socialism; we are concerned not with expressions of pious hopes of what socialism will do and what public ownership will lead to, but, as practical politicians, we are in duty bound to say how it is to come about. The Leader of the Opposition says in that notorious article in the 'Sunday Graphic' that it will come by the democratic will of the majority of the people, by learning lessons in socialism. That is exactly the charge of the Communist Party against the right hon. Leader of the Opposition, that instead of educating the electorate, and instead of telling them to adhere to socialism, year after year, he and his party are receding from and going against socialism.

There is no difference between Communism and socialism – take any ordinary dictionary and see. There is certainly an ever-growing difference and divergence between the Communist Party in Great Britain and the Socialist Party. I admit it quite candidly, and I do not suggest for a moment that in that ever-growing difference we are always the faultless party – we may be committing our errors and our individual faults. But the general picture is this, that since the revolution in Russia the Communist Party are standing firm by one and the same programme. we are not adding anything to that, and the divergence does not occur because we want something more year after year but because the Socialist Party wants less and less socialism year after year. At one time the Labour Party of this country were agreeable to forming the Council of British Workers and Soldiers. At that time the Communists were agreeable to that proposition, and there was no difference of opinion between the two. To-day the fault is that the Communist Party still demand that this country should be placed under the control of a council of workers and soldiers, and the Labour Party does not want what it once wanted. The Council of Action was established by the Labour Party in this country. There was no divergence between the Communist Party and the Labour Party on that subject in those days. There is divergence today. To-day, the Communist Party says that during the Chinese Expedition, during the Simon Commission, during the hundred and one struggles of the workers, there ought to have been councils of action all over the country amongst working class organisations. (Laughter.) My Labour friends laugh at it. They did not laugh at it in 1921, and to-day they want to go away from the only method – the only method – which will introduce socialism, and then allow the people to imagine that socialism is to come in some unknown and mysterious way.

There is the question of war debts. There was a time when I, as a member of the Independent Labour Party, had learned my lesson, with the Independent Labour Party, that the whole war debt of this country is blood money, and should be repudiated by every socialist.

When that was the cry of the Labour Party, the Communists and the Labour party stood together – nearer than to-day. Then the Labour Party receded from that position, through the exigencies of Parliamentary vote-catching, and brought it down to disallowing half the debt instead of the whole of it. Then they came to the Capital Levy. Then the Labour Party withdrew from the Capital Levy. To-day our objection is that when the country is appealed to, democratic support is sought not for socialism, but for subterfuges and substitutes for socialism.

The Surtax! I know it is rather a sore point. I have been bred and brought up in a capitalist business life myself, and I know Surtax is never going to be a reality. If you impose the Surtax to-day, I can vouch for it that at least one firm have got their plans ready in the City of London to have dummy shareholders in Buenos Aires, Calcutta and Hong Kong in whose names large numbers of shares will stand, and there will not be many capitalist mugs who will allow all the shares to stand in their own name.

In the Amendment which I had hoped to move, but which I am not permitted to move, I point out that apart from the impracticability of the Surtax there is no socialism in the Surtax. The principle of the Surtax is, 'I will take 2s. in the pound out of your unearned profit, and I will then permit you to make 20s of unearned profit.' The government have therefore become shareholders in the unearned income of people who do not work and who exploit the working class, living as parasites upon them. The Labour Party says, 'I will square my conscience if you give me 2s. out of 20s., and I will call it socialism.'

Then comes the living wage. The living wage is not socialism. How can a living wage be produced within a capitalist society? A living wage within a capitalist society cannot be produced as long as there is international competition. Lancashire cannot afford to pay £4 a week to spinners when capitalists can erect cotton factories in Shanghai and get people to work at 6d. or 8d. a day of ten hours. In such cases Protection is no good at all. The people who sent out a Chinese Expedition to Shanghai took away every protection from the Lancashire workers, and now no protection is possible. At the jute mills in Dundee the workers are not earning half a living wage, but how can you help that happening when the same fraternity of financiers are erecting jute mills in Calcutta, and paying miserably low wages to their workers?

The workers in Great Britain should realise that God has not created man to be ruled dictatorially and autocratically by another man. Through self-determination and mutual consent we should elect somebody to rule who is not a socialist boss, but a helper and adviser. If that is our essential belief, how can the people of this country believe that God has created the British Labour Party to rule the Indians and the Africans in the way that they are being ruled? The leaders of the Labour movement say to the Indians and the Chinese, 'We are ruling you; we are sending Commissions to your countries because you are less experienced and we are more experienced, and we want to be kind to you and tell you how you should live your lives.' That is exactly what the capitalist masters and bosses are saying to the workers in this country. They say to them, 'We are more experienced in directing industry than you are, and we keep an Army, a Navy, and an Air Force to protect you, because you are less experienced than we are.' Socialism believes that that sort of incapacity is not inherent in human nature. How can the Labour Party say that they are preaching socialism and collecting the majority of voices in favour of socialism when they are pursuing such a policy as I have described? The Labour Party supports expeditions to China, the Colonies and the old Coast: in fact, one member of the Labour Party has gone to visit one of those countries. How can those things go on?

I believe in socialism, because in my view all the devices adopted by the workers in the development of industrial life through individual owner- ship and capitalist control have ceased to produce any good for the workers. This has caused much degredation of human life and character within capitalist countries, and it is still more degrading and crushing as far as human life is concerned in the countries which have been conquered for the benefit of the capitalists. For those reasons, I do not believe in Tory politics, because there is no socialism at the back of conservatism. Capital- ism and individual control only create misery and do more harm than good. We hear a lot of people talking about their hard-earned wealth and savings, but what does it all mean? The capitalist society to-day is unjust. Consider the case of an honest man doing well, educating his children in a first-class institution and maintaining his wife in a luxurious manner. That man gets run over by a motor car and becomes incapacitated. Under the present state of society, that man will be forced immediately to sell up his home and withdraw his children from the university, and his family is crushed once and for all. That form of society is so unjust and cruel that I understand the justification of that man having savings in the bank, so that, when he meets with an accident, there is enough in his bank to enable his family to go on.

I will give another illustration. Take the case of an acknowledged criminal. Your present state of society says, 'We punish him because he is dangerous to society,' and you lock him up in a prison: but you take care that three times a day he is fed, you take care that once a week he is medically examined, you take care that he has open-air exercise once or twice a day, you take care of many things, realising your liability to human life, even though it be that of an acknowledged criminal; and yet you disown all responsibility and liability to the innocent wife and children of the same man, and throw them on the scrap-heap to starve – you are no longer responsible for the women and children who have not been criminals and who have committed no fault. In these circumstances, that wife and children would certainly be happier if, out of the stolen property, some provision were set aside for them.

We have seen that there have been some rich criminals lately, and, when they have gone into prison, their wives and children have never had to go to the Board of Guardians or be locked up in workhouses; they were amply provided for.

The very first principle of a Communist State, the essential and funda- mental principle, is that the State first assumes full liability and responsibility for the honourable and comfortable maintenance of all men, women and children as long as they honestly carry out their task; and, as long as society as a whole relieves the burden of these accidental catastrophes to individuals, that State is morally justified in denying the right of private ownership and private saving, which are no longer needed, and for which there is no moral justification. Therefore, I take it that, if socialism, genuine and bona fide, is ever to be introduced, it can only be introduced with the immediate deprivation of the right of any individual to possess or own private land, private houses, places of industry, and, above all, human labour.

That being so, we know what will happen. It is our nature to struggle against that. We do not give up our own Parliamentary position so easily, we do not give up our little individual advantages which we create around us, and we are not under the delusion that a large powerful, resourceful well organised class of capitalists, with its agents in all parts of the world is going to say, 'From to-morrow morning we give up all our posessions.' It is not the Communist mind, it is not the Communist mentality, it is not the socialist creed, but it is the individual capitalist greed that makes a revolution inevitable. On that account we say, without any delusion, that those who demand socialism, if they are true to their convictions, must first demand it by making it unlawful for any man to possess private property. If they sincerely mean to make that unlawful, then they must be prepared to back up their legislative effort by a socialist revolution. And that is not all.

It is no use imagining that we shall suddenly have to-morrow morning a state of society in which there will be no private ownership, in which all industries will be nationalised, and in which the social structure will yet remain the same, so that a clerk will walk into the office and take his cap off as his master passes by and hide round the corner. We cannot for a moment imagine that the policy of private ownership, and of power in the hands of one individual to say, 'You obey me, or I starve you, your wife and children,' will remain; and, with that power gone, it is a complete delusion on the part of anyone to say that society will still remain as it is, because we shall have destroyed private ownership through the ballot-box, and there is not the slightest doubt that there is going to be a complete revolution from that moment in the relationship of man towards man.

You may consider that the Russians were mad in reorganising their army and turning it into a Red Army, instead of a capitalist army, but the Red Army, its construction, its principles and its formation, the equal rights of the soldiers to political votes, their right to select their own officers, the right to pay their own officers the same wages as are paid to the ordinary man who risks his life, all these things are absolutely unavoidable consequences of establishing socialism, and it is no use for a socialist party to say that, because we are going to alter the law through the ballot-box, there is no need for the workers to be prepared for a socialist revolution, there will not be a complete reversal of the present discipline of the army, and it will not be followed by a complete destruction of what you call the British Empire. Of course it means the destruction of the British Empire. Of course, in all the colonies, and in India and China, with the assistance of the workers, there will be the formation of the workers' organisations in those countries: there will be the overthrow of the zemindars, the landlords, the mandarins, the mill-owners, and all of that class in those countries. There is not the slightest doubt that, if you mean to pursue socialism, you will have to pursue it by the first step of declaring capitalism and individual ownership to be illegal.

The second step will be the inevitable socialist revolution, not because a revolution is dear to the heart of the Communist or the socialist, but because it is inevitable in the final struggle of those who possess individual property. There is not the slightest doubt that there will be a complete reversal of what you call law, order and discipline. Within offices, within factories, within the army, within the police, within the navy, within the colonies, and the relations of this country to the colonies and to the conquered countries, everywhere the workers will organise themselves into their own organisation, the peasants will organise themselves into their own organisation, and they will not only say, 'This is possessed by the nation, and the Postmaster-General is ruling us,' but the postmen and the miners and the railwaymen will say, 'We have no Postmaster-General except the one that we appoint, and, if he goes on making obnoxious speeches, and recommends private enterprise in the Post Office, we will dismiss him within 24 hours.'

That is the system, that is the control, that is socialism. Whether the Labour leaders foresee that such a thing will scare away the voters or not, we say that the teachings and the lessons of the Labour Party were responsible for what happened in Russia, and that the events of 1917 in Russia would have been impossible but for the great fraternal backing and support which the British working-class organisations gave to their suffering Russian comrades from 1902 right up to 1917. The Russian revolution would have been impossible but for that, and we say, similarly, that no pact, no contract, no wishy-washy phraseology in Parliament, is going to keep the workers of Britain in this perpetual slavery. The example and progress of the socialist movement in Russia and the neighbouring countries –

Mr. MacLaren: And in Battersea!

Mr. Saklatvala: And in Battersea, in spite of the Labour Party's attempts now to drive Battersea out of existence – those very examples will create a genuine socialist movement and a genuine socialist revolution even in this country.

APPENDIX 6

WITH THE COMMUNIST PARTY IN PARLIAMENT

EXPOSURE OF PARLIAMENTARY HYPOCRISY

SAKLATVALA'S GREAT SPEECH ON KING'S ADDRESS
NOVEMBER 7TH 1928

Communist party of Great Britain, 16 King Street, London. W.C.2

Amendment Moved by Comrade Saklatvala to the King's Speech

> 'But this house regrets that, whilst His Majesty's Government have
> encouraged and entered into pacts with imperialist Powers like the United
> States of America, France, Japan etc., with a view to a new grouping of
> forces for future wars, no serious steps have been taken by themselves
> and their allies to consider the Russian proposals for total disarmament
> or the limitation of the Imperialist aims of European and American Powers,
> this House regrets that His Majesty's Government still pursues the
> unpopular policy towards India of forcing on that country a Parliamentary
> Commission instead of allowing the people of India to frame their own
> constitution; further, His Majesty's Government have made attempts,
> without the consent of Parliament, to curtail the liberty of British subjects
> carrying on political or trade union work in that country; this House
> also regrets that His Majesty's Government have not yet seen fit to withdraw
> all British forces from the Chinese territories, as the presence of foreign
> forces is the root cause of all trouble in China; this House deplores,
> that while unemployment and under-employment is devastating millions
> of homes of workers in Great Britain in ever increasing measure, His
> Majesty's Government has not yet sought powers to take possession of
> the mines, factories etc., at present standing idle and kept so by their
> present owners, who shut out millions of workers from their legitimate
> rights to work regardless of the suffering and misery caused thereby.'
> (Hansard, Nov.7,1928)

Mr. Saklatvala: With regards to the Gracious Speech, I can only recall
the policy of the Tory Government before a previous General Election
when they tried to hypnotise the country on the slogan of tranquillity,
and I believe the present speech is also an attempt to restore tranquillity
as if nothing is happening in the country or in the world. However I
find that while the speech permits of a little verbal wrangling between
members of different parties here, it provides to all parties that common
platform of Parliamentary hypocrisy which keeps from the ordinary
man in the street the truth about the realities of life. I unhesitatingly
say that it devolves upon me, not only as a member of the Communist

Party but as representing the voice of all those who are not here charged with hypocritical parliamentary democracy, to point out where the reality stands. The hon. and gallant Member for North Aberdeen (Captain W. Benn), who by the way has wiped out his past and swallowed a new monkey gland and become rejuvenated to deliver his maiden speech, was hinting at the very numerous subjects I had to mention in an amendment of mine. I am not now referring to the Amendment in particular. But I would point out that the party to which the hon. and gallant Member now has the good fortune to belong, being a little more numerous than my party in this House, has got 14 hon. Members to divide the subjects and to put down Amendments on many topics under different groups, and has set up a division of labour on many different topics. I, being less numerous than any other party, just ask the House to realise that I am not trespassing on their indulgence in any way, but that I find myself called upon to take up all the topics and to speak of them.

The Kellogg Pact

There is the reference to the Kellogg Pact. I am very sorry that I cannot share the bubbling enthusiasm about the Kellogg Pact as an instrument of peace. It is a definite and deceitful American type of instrument of conspiracy against peace. Where is the peace about the Pact? Where is the renunciation of war? When Kellogg landed in France, American soldiers were shooting Nicaraguans and interfering with their affairs. I shall not go into details. The right hon. Gentleman Leader of the Opposition objected to the British attitude. It is not that I want to defend that attitude. I submit that every Big Power that signed the Kellogg Pact signed it with a militarist reservation. Some may have been honest enough to express that, but others were cunning enough not to do so. Did America sign the treaty without any reservation about the Monroe Doctrine? Did she sign it without reserving herself to enough murderers, in the shape of an army, to bully the people of Nicaragua and the Philippines? She signed it with the distinct reservation that her disarmament was to leave an armament sufficient to bully the less powerful nations around her, but she entered into a conspiracy with other powerful nations that they were not to hurt one another.

France signed the Treaty while in the Rhine area French Troops were occupying German territory. Did France sign without reservation? She signed with the reservation that her disarmament would leave a sufficiency of murderers to terrorise the Moroccans, the people of Indo-China, and of all the colonies belonging to France. Did Japan sign the treaty without reservation? That was another hypocritical deceitful State which put its signature to the Renunciation of War while at the same time Japanese

soldiers were killing and murdering Manchurians day after day and terrorising the Koreans in order to make wealth out of the exploitation of Korea.
The Japanese signature is subject to reservation, and the Japanese renunciation of war only means that the big brothers will no longer quarrel
among themselves but will keep sufficient military power to bully and
terrorise the helpless peoples under the false and hypocritical pretence of
safeguarding their Imperial interests.

Has England Renounced War?
The Kellogg Pact is nothing but an attempt to deceive the public that
it means a renunciation of war. Does this House believe that the country
has renounced war? Our honourable colleague who moved the address
to the King for his Gracious Speech, is himself, as one could judge
from his clothes, still a military officer and in this House we have colonels,
majors, captains, brigadier generals, admirals and rear-admirals, scattered
about in all parties. Yet Members of this House would tell us that this
country has renounced war and that certain parties were never in favour
of war. But not one single party has taken the attitude that if that
renunciation is to be a reality no one of their members ought to hold
a commission in the Army and that the Army is not wanted. They have
all renounced war but they all want officerships in the Army.
    Mr. E. Brown: Are you not a Colonel in the Red Army?
    Mr. Saklatvala: So far I am not. There was one enthusiastic colleague of
mine who did become one and who felt very proud of it, but he has found
it more convenient since then to retire to the Labour party.
    Hon. Members: Name!
    Mr. Saklatvala: Mr. Newbold. We are emphatically of the opinion that
this Kellogg Pact is nothing but a secret conspiracy of the powerful armed
nations to keep in abeyance their own quarrels, in order that they may be
strong enough to suppress those countries which each one of these
bullying, murderous nations is exploiting. There is not the slightest doubt
that when all these people were signing the Treaty they were equally
preparing for war on Russia, an attack on China if China turned Bolshevik,
for an attack on India if the Indians tried to evict the British intruder and
turn him out of their country. They were all making their own preparation
and at the same time pretending that this was some great act of peace.
    All these disarmament theories neglect one important point. All the
armies armed in the modern and efficient way represent only about
450,000,000 human beings, out of the population of the world, but there
are another 900,000,000 human beings who are not armed at all, or who are
very imperfectly armed. These 900,000,000 people have no consolation
whatever if they are shot down by means of a fewer number of machine-
guns instead of a larger number. What is the consolation to the Egyptians

if the British bully destroys Alexandria and bombards their coastal towns with six cruisers instead of sixteen? What is the consolation to the Arab of Iraq if you bomb his villages - as members of all parties in this House have done - and destroy innocent women with babies in their arms by means of bombs thrown from the air, if you say that the aeroplanes employed in killing those people numbered 12 and not 20. If you keep that in mind, that 90,000,000 of the people in this world are living in an unarmed condition and an unprotected state, for a few nations to arm themselves with small cruisers or big cruisers, or with few or many bombs, is immaterial; the fact remains that you are carrying on your murderous game against some section of human beings, and that is only to be put to an end when you begin to consider more honestly the Russian proposal of complete disarmament, instead of playing about with deceitful games.

Anglo-Japanese Relations
Then comes the satisfaction about the Japanese Emperor being enthroned and so on.

'The historic friendship which for so many years has united Japan and my country has always been a potent factor in the maintenance of peace in the Far East.'

What does that mean? After the Anglo-Japanese Alliance, Japan was definitely made able to carry on war on Russia and on China, The Anglo-Japanese Alliance, has not led to peace in the East, but it has led to wars, to murders, to destruction, to fire to arson, to crime, to inhumanity. After the Anglo-Japanese Alliance, what did Japan do? She crushed the Koreans; she sapped their life-blood. She put forward false deceitful claims on the innocent people of China, and it was the British militarists who taught the first nation of Asia, took her in partnership and taught her the same murderous game that Britain has always been famed for in this world. Yet you claim that the Alliance produced peace. It produced terrorism, murder, war; it destroyed the peace that did continue when Japan was not encouraged by her British ally to cut other people's throats and take other people's lives.

There is now again the same flattery of Japan going on, not because the British merchants love the Japanese merchants, but because they find that perhaps it is possible to use Japan to bully and terrorise the Chinese. This house is asked to congratulate itself over the new atmosphere of peace and settled government in China, and you have all denounced war; you are no longer going to carry on war, but why has nothing been done to completely withdraw all the foreign forces from China? There have been disturbances in China. Would there have been no disturbances in Great Britain if German Troops were occupying the British Isles? There are disturbances in China because of the presence of foreign troops and of foreigners

demanding in their country unjust and unequal rights and treaties. I submit
that there are more Chinamen in Limehouse, Liverpool, Glasgow and
Newcastle than there are British citizens in Shanghai. Will you permit the
Chinese people to keep a few Chinese battalions and Chinese battleships
for the protection of their citizens in Great Britain as you presume to keep
yours for the protection of yours? It is a game of cowardice and not of
statesmanship, and you know it in your heart of hearts. There are more
British subjects living in France and America than in China, far more.
Would you dare to keep British soldiers and British battleships in American
and French soil and waters? You dare not. You are keeping them in the
pretence of protection simply against weaker nation whom you can rob and
plunder, and you put on the hypocritical garb of protecting them and
keeping the peace in those countries.

Export Credits
The Speech refers to the extension of export credits. I have not heard
a word, as formerly we used to hear from the Opposition, as to whether
even now the Government will give up their policy of cutting their
noses to spite their faces, and extend these credit facilities to traders
with Russia. You will not do it. Why? Because the Worker's Soviet Republic
was founded through bloodshed. There was a civil war, a revolution,
and human beings were killed, so you will have nothing to do with
them. Was the British Empire founded without bloodshed? There was
a hundred times more human blood shed in the founding of the British
Empire than was ever spilled in Russia during the years of the Revolution.
Look at all the wars from 1805 to the last German war. This country
has shed a hundred times more blood of people of all nations in the
world. You have slaughtered Frenchmen, Spaniards, Dutch and Russians,
you have slaughtered Turks, Persians and Afghans when they had not
the least chance to fight you. You killed in their own homes the Punjabis,
Bengalis and the Mahrattas and the Ceylonese, the Burmans, the Malayans
and the Chinese. You murdered poor, primitive races, people who did
not know geographically where your country was situated, as the Sudanese,
the Zulus, the Bantus and the Swazis, and you had not the remotest
excuse that they were going to attack you and kill you. You have butchered
them and killed them in a wholesale manner. You have killed them in
their own country. There is no nation in the world, no institution in
the world, which has devoured more human lives and created more
murders than the British nation and the British Parliament. Yet the
Government of this Empire, which was founded on murder, armed
bloodshed, armed loot, armed destruction and confiscation of other
people's property and other people's land, has the insolence to say that
we do not trade with Russia because they founded their State on bloodshed.

You can tell that tale somewhere else, but the world is growing wiser, and the Government would be wiser not to carry on this sort of falsehood any further.

India
We have come to the one great omission, India. India makes the Empire. It is India that even gives the legal technical title of Empire to the British Empire. The Colonies do not constitute the Empire. If India were dropped tomorrow, the British Empire would not be known as the Empire. There is again a complete omission of any mention of India at a time when the outrage is being committed by this nation of thrusting upon the people of India representatives of this Parliament to go and terrorise over the people of India, and of keeping soldiers there to extort a good opinion of this Commission from the people of India. There is no mention of it at all. It is all very well for you to get into a frenzy about enslaving and robbing other nations, but you are forgetting your own destiny. In the constitutional development of this nation, - in the days of King John - in the days of King Charles, in the days of Queen Victoria - what has been the method followed? The people wanting their liberties and their freedom formulated their demands. We did not see the powers representing the Crown telling the people what liberties and what freedom they should demand. In the development of a nation it is the people who have the right to formulate their constitution and to make their own demands upon the Crown and the agents of the Crown. It is a ridiculous farce that the Crown and the Crown's agent should keep soldiers bullying the people and say to the people, 'You will demand as your measure of liberty and freedom what we tell you to demand.'

I am sorry to say that the Opposition has neglected its sacred duty towards India, and made common cause with the Government in running that slavery abroad. I am sorry to say that in your frenzy you are surrendering great principles of British life. Save by the express vote of Parliament, no Government officers, no agent of the Crown – not even the King of England himself – has the right to deprive British citizens of those liberties which their ancestors won for them, once as I have said under John and once under Charles and his successors. When creating a new legislative machinery in South Africa, in Canada, in Australia, in the Irish Free Sate, and also in India, we expressly laid it down that local legislatures there should have no right to deprive British-born British Citizens of the liberties which have been won from the Crown, that is, without an express and clear decision of the British House of Commons; but now agents of the Crown by the exercise of arbitrary and autocratic powers such as would lose the Crown the Throne if they were tried in this country, are seeking to deprive British-born British citizens in India of their one liberty, of their right to a fair trial before being punished. Under the law as it is they could be punished if they had done wrong, but the Crown is to-day seeking powers against British Citizens in India such as Abdul Hamid lost his throne for, such as the Tsar of Russia lost his life for, and for which the Kaiser of Germany lost his throne for, and such as are no longer tolerated in any country, great or small. The British Crown, through its agents, is seeking to destroy the liberty not only of the enslaved people of India but of British-born subjects, under the false and hypocritical pretence of what they call the Public Safety Bill.

The Public Safety Bill is to deal with those Britishers who go to India and say to the people of India that their fellow countrymen have no right to rule India. They are to be deported without trial, their liberties are to be cut away. If the Crown attempted to do anything of that sort in this country the Conservative Party would immediately organise a revolt against the Crown. This nation has already organised a revolt. The hon. and gallant Member for North Aberdeen referred in the Debate to the black soldiers of France, and pointed out the danger to Europe of employing those black soldiers. What about your brave Gurkhas, Mahrattas and the Negroes employed in the Army in British Africa? Are they not black soldiers? Is France the only country which has employed black soldiers? We have heard some hair-splitting arguments from the hon. and gallant Member for North Aberdeen and from the leader of the Opposition. I have not forgotten the hypocritical and diabolical utterances of the right hon. Gentleman the Member for Carnarvon Boroughs (Mr. Lloyd George) on this question. What did the right hon. Gentleman say when he was discussing the subject of peace? He represented this country as consisting of peace-making angels, and he told us that the cause of the great loss of human life was the system of conscription.

'Angels Without Wings'

The right hon. Gentleman the Member of Carnarvon Boroughs described the people of this country as angels without wings and as a peace-loving nation because we have not a system of conscription. That is what the right hon. Gentleman said in the Debate about peace, but surely he is aware what a mockery the British system has been in the past. It is true that you had no conscription in peace time, but in war time the Government adopted full-blooded conscription in a few weeks' time. Under these circumstances how can you expect the world to believe that England is a peace-loving nation? What is the lesson of the last Great War? What is the meaning of having hon. Members of this House who are officers, and who are now out of military practice? Those hon. Members are now in civil life. They sit in this House and some of them write articles in the newspapers. During peace time they appear as innocent as doves, but when war comes – [interruption.] The last War was a great lesson to us, especially as administered by the right hon. Gentleman the Member for Carnarvon Boroughs, who condemns conscription in foreign countries but who is clever enough in war-time to adopt conscription in this country in 24 hours. It is all humbug and moonshine for anyone to write the sort of King's speech we are considering, and for the Labour party to offer a namby-pamby opposition to it. France has black troops on the Rhine, and Britain has black troops in the Himalayas; therefore the French are decried while the British are angels. The times are past when the workers, in this country or abroad, are going to swallow this sort of political logic. It might work very well in a general election or a by-election, where people are half thinking instead of fully thinking, but, in the cold, calm study of their daily life, people are not going to accept this sort of hypocritical arrangement of statesmen and Parliamentarians as touching the realities of life.

Greenock

I was a little disappointed when our Scottish champion stood up to speak of Scotland. May I ask the Prime Minister why he has not allowed this House to know what His Gracious Majesty's agents are doing in Greenock, where a chief constable, or magistrates, are issuing orders with regard to public meetings? If anyone does anything wrong in a public meeting, there is a court of law; but here, although the Parliament of the people has fought for centuries for liberty, one twopenny-halfpenny chief constable or magistrate comes down and says that meetings shall not be held. To such a scandal has it extended that even in the case of borough council elections, when meetings were organised, the men who organised them have been arrested and put in prison. The liberties of the people are not observed in this fashion, and I am really surprised at the calm, cool way in which Scotland takes, lying low, this rapacious enslavement by officers of the British Crown. It is really amazing how people are getting accustomed to Fascism under the soothing name of Parliamentary democracy. I ask the Prime Minister whether he is prepared to say on his oath that borough council elections carried on in Greenock under these conditions are at all legal and valid.

Mr. Maxton: Ask the Lord Advocate.

Mr. Saklatvala: I would have asked the Lord Advocate, but I know that he is a Parliamentarian, and does not know what the subordinate officers are doing. If he knew, perhaps his own sense of decency would revolt, but the very fact that there is a Lord Advocate, and the very fact that this is going on, shows that the Cabinet Ministers are puppets, and that the country can be run by Fascist battalions outside.

Mr. Maxton: He is responsible.

Mr. Saklatvala: I will put down a question to him on Tuesday, when I suppose we shall see what sort of responsibility he has. Having wandered, as the hon. and gallant Member for North Aberdeen said, over a vast area, let me come down to the very grave situation with regard to unemployment. Here again there are on the carpet so many pairs of boxing gloves, so that men of different parties may have a sham fight among themselves, but that does not bring us to the realities of life. With regard to migration, this country, with its vast empty Colonies like Australia, New Zealand and Canada, ought to have had continuously a migration policy completely dissociated from the problem of unemployment. I think it is an immense shame that a country which has genuine healthy room for a scheme of continuous, independent migration to its Colonies, should have confused the issue and subordinated that problem to party tactics by associating it with the problem of unemployment. I appeal to the Ministers of those Dominions to compel the Prime Minister of this country not to associate the problem of migration to the Colonies with unemployment at all. Even if this country were fully employed, the need of regular, systematised, healthy, open clean migration would still exist, and to have dragged in the unemployment issue, and made the misery and suffering of the people a handle for a party politics display, was not only a piece of meanness towards the unemployed of this country, but a great injustice to the colonial and migration requirements of the Dominions.

Emigration and Unemployed
You have so completely mixed up the issue that only the unemployable and the unfit of this country are going to be encouraged to go to the Colonies. You have done the greatest possible harm to a problem which has quite a clean and independent position of its own. I urge the Ministers yet to take immediate measures to completely dissociate the problem of migration from that of unemployment. If you do not do so you are doing the greatest possible harm to the people in the Colonies and adding injury to insult to the unemployed in the country and at the same time you are producing no result of any value whatsoever. You must pull yourselves back out of the mirage of using the unemployment problem for migration. Leave the unemployment question as a local question to be settled by yourselves in this country, and leave the migration question as an independent question for the Colonies, remembering that here you have a country restricted in its area, and growing in its population, and there you have vast lands available in the Colonies.

That is my first remark, and now I come to my second remark. The Employment Exchanges and the Government authorities are ready to pack up the Reds and send them to different places so that they may not organise a campaign against the government before the General Election comes. That is not being done for the benefit of the workers, but is trickery to preserve the Conservative vote and the position of the Government.

Mr. E. Brown: The Reds are against the Labour party, too.

Mr. Saklatvala: They are like the Conservatives and the Liberals. The whole machinery is created for the purpose of removing the Reds when they are organising themselves among the unemployed workers locally. I ask the Prime Minister one serious question. What guarantee does he give to these men and women that they will be put back into their own constituencies at the expense of their Government when it comes to be their right to exercise their vote at the next General Election? Are thousands upon thousands of voters to be fraudulently and dishonestly transferred from their legitimate areas in order to make it convenient for Tory candidates by removing their votes? I want to know because during the last municipal elections hundreds of cases of realisation of this great deceit upon the working classes has come upon these men and women. They have been transferred to areas where they have no vote. The last municipal elections have disclosed that circumstance, and I ask the Minister to say how they are treating this particular subject of the liberties of the people before the General Election comes, without making it a matter for joking. With regard to unemployment, if all these schemes are going on and these debates are going on, as they are, and if the results are concealed from the people we must warn His Majesty's Ministers of the consequences which may befall them and their position and authority. How long are the people going to keep away from expressing their anger? Not very long, for the cup is getting full.

Unemployment

There was a lot of talk by the hon. Member for Broxtowe (Mr. Spencer). He delivered a speech like a bull in a china shop. The position is this, a quarter of a million miners have lost their jobs. That means that 60,000,000 tons of coal taken out of Britain are not wanted. You do not tell the world that British capitalists are settled in Africa, India and Southern China, and are paying labour 7d. for a day of 10 hours underground. You are concealing the fact. You do not tell the jute workers of Dundee that unemployment has become permanent in Dundee, that about 30 per cent. of the looms and spindles will never work again, and at the same time you have 75 jute mills in Bengal, where you are paying 3s. 8d. a week of 60 hours to the girls in the spinning department. By the process India is devouring more than 60 per cent. of the total jute product of India, there is not sufficient raw jute left now for all the spindles and looms in Dundee. You are not telling the textile workers the truth as to how your Imperial policy in China and India, with labour exploitation, the enforced illiteracy of the people, enforced slavery and the denial of political life to the workers is creating a mass of unemployed workers in this country.

These are the causes of unemployment. Now with all the criticisms I would still disagree. Unemployment cannot be cured by building houses and this, that, and the other. Unemployment can only be cured by the Government passing an Act, and, without any compensation, taking possession of all mines, factories, dockyards, and places of industry. That is the only way of creating normal employment where capitalism is creating unemployment. Make friends with Russia, give up your game of murder in India, treat them as you treat France and America and withdraw your troops from China, and there will be more than enough demand for all that you will produce by seizing these failures, and carrying on your work without any compensation to the owners.

APPENDIX 7:

THE CLASS STRUGGLE IN PARLIAMENT

S. SAKLATVALA
(Communist M.P. for N. Battersea)

ON
Communism. Egyptian Indemnity.
The Supplementary Reserve.
The Prince's Tour. The Air Force.

PRICE - 1D.

Being Speeches by S. SAKLATVALA, M. P.
and Reprinted from Hansard

KING'S SPEECH.

Mr. SAKLATVALA: I have to explain to the House the reason for which I have to stand up now more or less in connection with the Amendment, that stood in my name, to the Address. Though I may have to put forward a new point of view arising out of a new situation, I do not for a moment want the House to understand that it is in any spirit of wanton interruption or dragging of the proceedings at this time of the night. It may seem rather out of proportion for an individual to stand up and say he represents a party which claims to put forward its views, but I appeal to the House to realise the position. We have heard about the great fondness this House has for its traditions, and I can well understand that it would take some time to adjust itself to some new feature that arises here.

I represent a proper, well-organised, well-formed, and rather too loudly acknowledged political party in this country now. I am not one of those international Socialists who take offence at having friends in Moscow, Berlin or Delhi. As a member of the International Communist Party, I submit that our movement does extend from Moscow to Battersea, and much beyond that. It is as well organised a party as any other party in this State, with its machinery, its Press, and its branches all over the country. I would point out to hon. and right hon. Gentlemen opposite – I do not know if it was put on, or if it was their sincere belief, – that right up to the last election we were saying that our party was the vital tail that was wagging the whole Labour dog. We do not count by numbers, but what we lack in numbers, we make up in solid importance. Our friends of the Liberal Party only succeeded in returning to the House one member for every seven and a half candidates, whereas our party succeeded in returning one Member out of seven candidates.

Considering the change that is going on, and considering the rightful place that the Communist Party is taking in Parliaments all over Europe, the House might now grant to us our justifiable claims, and put us in the time-table. I do not for a moment claim that our party should have a whole day, or a couple of days allotted, but surely, now, the House can begin to allot to us, say, an hour, when other parties can have a full day to themselves. I have looked over the debates for the last four or five days, and it seems to me that my party would be the only one that would stand in real difference without getting mixed up at times. We find it very difficult to find a line of strong demarcation. the last time that I was a Member of the House, our friends of the Labour Party were fighting tooth and nail against the very scheming wording of the rent Restrictions Act, which was likely to endanger its existence. Yesterday we heard from the same Labour Party that the Rent Restrictions Act was standing, and will stand, in the way of building new houses. We have heard during the last few days of the Debate many point of agreement between the Tory Party and the administrators of the Labour Party, and we have seen very few points of disagreement. We have seen in to-night's Debate the party believing in Protection pointing out instance after instance where the parties believing in Free Trade were indulging in Protection and almost asking for it at times when it suited them.

We have heard to-night even the example quoted about the Capital Levy having disappeared, and looking at it all I submit that it is for the good of this nation and not for its harm that one party should stand up boldly to say that it always says what it believes in, and believes in what it is prepared to say, and to act up for it. We represent that section of the working class that does not believe in continuity of policy. We represent a section of the working class that does not believe in saying at one time that your employers are your enemies, that individual capitalism is the source of all your evils, and yet that we should sit down with them, make friends and form a joint club so that these evils may disappear from time to time.

With regard to the wording of my amendment, I remember that when I was in the House in 1922 the first King's Speech I heard was read and debated. My hon. friend for Westhoughton was reported to have said this:

'I was proud to have come to the House because I did not during the war send any young boy to his doom, and the Labour Party, I feel sure, will echo every word when I say that their advent to this House, if it means anything at all, means goodwill among all peoples of the earth. I am glad to learn that the people of India rejoice because our numbers are growing, and the people of Egypt fell better towards this country because they know that the Labour Party means international goodwill.'

I offer no comment, but I suppose everyone is agreed that, foolish as the Egyptians may be, I do not believe that today they entertain the belief which was attributed to them last year. With regard to the Amendment of which I have given notice, I submit that it is based upon the teachings and doctrines preached to the working classes from one end of Great Britain to the other for the last 30 years. We are still telling the working classes that their struggle is a class struggle, that their emancipation lies in the complete extinction of the individual ownership system, and that their only salvation in international affairs is not based upon Imperialism and protective tariffs, and armies, bombs and insolent letters to Zaghlul Pasha, saying, 'My soldiers and bayonets will remain where they are, but still we are pacifists,' and telling everybody, 'We believe in a certain philosophy of life, but we do not practice it when it is a question of the democratic Parliament of the British Empire .' In this respect i put before the House that the things I would have placed before it would not have been in any hostile spirit, but would not have been presented to this House and the country at large as the viewpoint which will have to be accepted some day or other as the only sane and honest view of life.

(Hansard 17/12/24)

EGYPT.

Mr. SAKLATVALA: May I point out that even a wise use of this money is not going to satisfy the constitutional point involved in the whole issue. We were informed at the beginning that a cheque was demanded and promptly paid. The promptness of payment does not at all prove either the justification for the demand or the willingness with which the payment was made. I have in mind two cheques amounting to a total of £300,000 which were also paid by an eminent gentleman, and I think that the British Government have applied exactly the same tactics, and the promptness with which the £500,000 was paid was due to the same fear under threat of intimidation and blackmail. The Secretary of State informed us that the matter incidentally comes before the House because the British Government, rather than the Sudanese Government, happened to collect the cheque. The right hon. Gentleman knows that if the Sudanese Government had put forward such a preposterous claim upon the Egyptian Government there would have been no chance of the Egyptian Government being blackmailed, and that the Sudanese Government was never entitled to this cheque.

The right hon. Gentleman seems to speak as if it were some amount due to the Sudanese Government, and that the British Government were merely collecting it in a spirit of benevolence. That is not so. The British Government are now using the name of the Sudanese Government just as a matter of convenience. The cheque was extorted from the Egyptian Government in a manner which is discreditable to the whole history of international relationships between two Governments at any time, and it was because of the mailed fist of Britain that this cheque was forthcoming. Then we have got some account of it. We have got a play upon the words 'fine' and 'indemnity.' The Government themselves have used the words fine and as my hon. Friend has shown the iniquity of it, that the plaintiff goes and imposes a fine upon the defendant and collects it without any trial. The justice at the back of it were your gunboats and your bluejackets. Then they say it was not a fine, it was an indemnity. The British Government had to pay after all what appeared to them to be justifiable sums to the extent of £50,000 and not £500,000 and the Egyptian Government might be looked to to indemnify the British Government for this £50,000. But the margin of safety for the British Government is not in a proportion to the superiority of their brute force over a helpless nation. And they have demanded ten times the money which they paid and now there is talk of benevolent purposes.

Whether the Rt. hon. Gentleman consults the leaders of the Opposition parties or not would again make any difference. He seems to think that there is a Sudanese Government. What is the Sudanese Government but a military tyranny of a foreign Power imposed upon the innocent people of Sudan? Who are the Sudanese Government? How many Sudanese have created the Sudanese Government? When the Germans entered Belgium and they created there the new Belgian Government every man in this country said that it was not a Belgian Government, but that it was a German tyranny. In the Sudan to-day the Briton is a robber who is sticking there by force of arms. The Sudanese Government is a military officer paid by the British Government to tyrannise over the people of the Sudan. I say in the name of the Communist party – (*Laughter*) – which makes you laugh in the House and dread in your homes, in the name of the Communist party which makes you jeer here and makes your Brigadier-Generals go to Trafalgar Square and enlist thousands of young men as Fascisti to go and fight them, that this House is going to be now a party for the first time to this blackmail. We have applied to France to deliver up Captain Arthur, and at the same time we are trying to justify to-day in the name of this House the misappropriated cheque of the Egyptian Government.

Are we to understand that this nation is not even entitled to recover its common sense and sense of justice a little later on when the angry mood has passed away? Are we to understand that the sense of justice of the British Foreign Office, the British Prime Minister, the British House of Commons and the British nation on this particular question is lost for ever, and that we are going to misappropriate this loot in perpetuity? Is there no possibility even now of referring the moral point involved in this exaction of £500,000 and of handing back to the Egyptians whatever balance an impartial tribunal may say you wrongly took from them? Instead of talking loudly about benevolence to the Sudanese, cannot you ascertain that the Sudanese are more self-respecting than you are and would refuse to touch this blood-money and use it for benevolent purposes?

These are points which are far more pressing than the talk of schools and hospitals and the possibility of consulting the leaders of the opposition as to how you should make benevolent use of this money. It may look a benevolent use, but it is not, however benevolent it may be in appearance. It is for your own selfish purposes that you will use this money. You extorted this large sum from the workers and the peasants of Egypt, and instead of spending your own money, you put on airs and make false representations to the people of Sudan that you are so kind that you are spending for benevolent purposes the large sum of £500,000 which you have obtained by blackmail, and all the benevolent institutions will be nothing more than monuments to British injustice and British robbery in Egypt. I will still appeal to the House that instead of talking nonsense about consulting with the Leaders of the Opposition as to dividing the loot it would be far more honourable, even at this stage, to see the whole matter settled by referring it to an impartial international tribunal, and if the decision be against you to observe it than to attempt to be unjust by spending this money obtained by blackmail from the Egyptian people.

(Hansard, 11/2/25.)

PRINCE OF WALES' TOUR
Mr. SAKLATVALA: I stand once again to speak as a member of the Communist party and I suppose, hon. Gentlemen of the Opposition will accept with some amount of equanimity the sincerity of myself and my party in saying what we think of this matter. I quite approve of the Amendment which has been moved, but I am equally touched at the defence set up by the Financial Secretary. The more my colleagues and friends in the Opposition are trying to come to a compromise in outward form, the more they are assailed, and the more they will be open to the charge of being insincere persons. What is the truth about it? Certainly we object to this use of public money. At the same time, if my hon. Friends opposite want Royalty, if they want Royal ambassadors, I quite agree that they cannot have ambassadors without business capacity at

the same time. If they want luxury they must pay for it. If you want an Empire with a Royal nob at the head of it – [Hon. Members: 'Withdraw!'] *The CHAIRMAN*: I did not catch the expression. [*HON. MEMBERS*: 'Royal nob.'] If I had caught it I should have dealt with it.

Mr. SAKLATVALA: If this country or if hon. Members of the Opposition want an Empire, want a Royal head over that Empire, want a Royal ambassador to go about even the streets of Buenos Aires, then I agree that they must pay adequately. Therefore, as a Member representing the out and out working class view I oppose it. I oppose it definitely on the ground that this whole expenditure is the usual trickery of the minority helping themselves at the expense of the majority. It is class expenditure. It is all camouflage to talk about commercial activities and His Royal Highness the Prince of Wales discussing with any appreciable intelligence the possibilities of this trade or that trade. Nothing of the sort happens. To put forward the invitation coming from Africa and America is one more sham in this House of many shams. [*HON.* MEMBERS: 'Order!'] This is a complete sham.

I have in my mind millions of persons in South Africa and Argentine and East Africa who are not associated with this invitation. These games are played in the name of the people. I may give you as an illustration that some time back we were told His Royal Highness the Prince of Wales had received a cordial invitation as a Royal Ambassador from India, and the people of India had to say that they did not want His Royal Highness there, and the Government had to empty out gaols and to pay money to spectators. [HON. MEMBERS: 'Order!']

THE CHAIRMAN: The question dealt with in the Vote relates to Africa, and the hon. Member's remarks relate to a wider area than that. Asia does not come into that discussion.

Mr. SAKLATVALA: I am saying, with due deference, a little as to the want of sincerity in these invitations. The invitations are minority invitations. They come as class invitations. They come from certain class interests. They are social invitations from a particular section, which is the smallest section in every country and society, and they are not invitations of a genuine character coming from the working classes and the masses of the people in these countries. I put it to the Committee. There are large numbers of the population in Africa, in Argentine, in Brazil, and in many other countries desiring to go out as ambassadors to the masses, and there is a larger section of people in this country. Take trade union leaders, for instance. You would not pay their expenses; you would make them pay and put obstructions in the way of their going by hindering passports.

These invitations sound very well, but to talk about them being in the name of the people is to make a wrong use of the name. The insincerity is not on this side of the House. The insincerity is completely on the other side of the House. You are talking in terms of Nations when you know very well it is a sham. I would suggest that this money could be utilised with far greater advantage in this country. But I would not even then accept entirely the suggestion made that we should spend £2,000 in getting His Royal Highness to pay a visit to some of the slums here, there and everywhere. That amount would not carry him far in all the slums here. I would use the £2,000 in my constituency in a different manner. I would take some of my slum dwellers and enable them to stay for a week in the palatial surroundings in which the Prince lives and give them experience of another class of life. There would be greater unity of knowledge and a greater communication of thoughts in the Empire by the poor, struggling, starving, ill-fed masses being made to see and realise and experience the life which other people are leading entirely at their cost.

I submit that the whole of this money comes from the poor, underpaid and degraded workers of this country, and from nobody else. It is all very well to talk about mathematics and political economy, economies of budgets and the headings in the tables of the budgets, but, after all, the rich who pretend to pay their taxations would not be able to pay their taxes before they made their incomes, and the incomes which they make, every farthing of them are earned by the workers, who are robbed of their living to get possession of it. If after robbing the workers in this country, after robbing the workers of Africa and Argentina of the wealth they have produced, the rich man wants to use a slice of it for this sort of show, for this sort of grandeur, by which to capture trade for this country, I fail to understand how a visit from the Prince of Wales can enable you to sell to Argentine any article which you are not capable of selling with the sound workmanship of the British workers at a reasonable and competitive cost. If your workers are not producing good work, if the cost of their work cannot stand competition, 100,000 visits from Royal ambassadors cannot produce trade. Trade is produced by the honest work of the workers.

THE CHAIRMAN: The hon. Member is going into political economy and building far too large a structure on a slender basis.

MR. SAKLATVALA: I am attempting to point out that this sum of £2,000 is coming from sources which the hon. Members opposite deny. It is coming from the workers. This proposal is put forward as one for assisting trade. You cannot send Royal ambassadors to any country if your workmen are producing bad materials and try to induce trade through splendour of Royalty. I would challenge hon. Members opposite to take any shoddy material produced by workers and effect a large trade in it by sending Royalties abroad as salesmen of this country. All the sham is on the side of those who are trying to charge Members on this side with frivolous obstruction. In the name of my constituents I oppose this grant.

(Hansard, 12/2/25.)

AIR FORCE

Mr. SAKLATVALA: Once again I feel happy to stand up as a member of the Communist party who does not possess any front bench. The hon. Member for Shoreditch (Mr. Thurtle), in introducing this Amendment, said that he did not like Mr. Facing-both-Ways. I am not in a position to-night of having a party facing two ways. I put it seriously to this Committee that we are not here to afford to the country some amusement every night. It does not mean doing patriotic duty simply to jeer at minorities in this House. We are here to discuss problems which, in the hands of the older parties, have failed and have brought on the world misery, ruin, murder, degradation, unemployment, starvation and everything else that is evil. We are here to review the policies of the past and to apply to them a new outlook, a new vision, and a more daring thought than you were accustomed to in the past. It is no use talking of the Air Force Estimates in the terms of a patriotic duty as you understood it in the past, and I also agree that it is no use merely blindly voting against it without showing the new way, without disguise and without putting a cloak of phraseology upon it. We must be perfectly clear and honest in our future vision when we are out to destroy the policies of the past.

Hon. Members have spoken of the alliance with France. Hon. Members opposite protested, and perhaps sincerely, that we were never going to be enemies of France, that France was never going to be an enemy of Great Britain. If they were as intelligent and as logical as they claim to be sincere, I would then put it to them that if France, being your friend, inseparable and in all perpetuity, has already got 120 squadrons of an Air Force that is quite enough to protect you as their friends, and you will not require any more. If the French Air Force is the biggest Air Force in the world, if France is only 20 miles away from you, even not as far away as some of your aerodromes in Scotland, then, if you believe sincerely in the friendship of France, we should have no Air Force at all, but we should simply have an agreement with France so that they should assist us in our time of need. But it is not so. As the hon. Member for Bow and Bromley (Mr. Lansbury) pointed out, history will repeat itself. It was Germany and Great Britain destroying France 100 years ago. It was France and Great Britain destroying Germany in the late War. Now in the cycle of events it may be France and Germany attacking Great Britain and destroying us. One can never tell.

11.0 P.M.

Right hon. Gentlemen are so very confident, so trustful of France. Then they are doing exactly the opposite of what they ought to do in building up an independent Air Force instead of relying on the Air Force of France. You do not look upon the Air Force of France as your protector, but you do look upon it as your future enemy, and that you are submitting to the Committee to-night.

It is said that we of the Communist party are the enemies of the Christian Church; that we are out to destroy all Christian Churches. I submit that the foundation stone of the Christian Church is, 'Thou shalt not kill.' You who pretend to be the supporters and faithful upholders of that Church, come and tell the nation to-night that the biggest function of the Government and of the State is to organise the most efficient weapons for murder and killing. Organised murder, you say, is the duty of the State, and preaching 'Thou shalt not kill.' is the duty of your Church, and you pretend that the Church and the State are the best friends of each other. They are nothing of the kind. You must wind up either the Church or the State. We would request that you wind up the present form of state rather than to wind up the Church. The right hon. Member for Platting (Mr. Clynes) was trying to mislead the country, through this House to-night, that the voice of Labour and of the working-classes is not in favour of abolishing warfare and armaments. I would mildly put it to my right hon. Friend that he should present himself either in his constituency or in mine, and put to the vote the question of the opinion of the working-classes on the subject. I confidently believe that the right hon. Gentleman would not gain his point in any working-class audience. He read to us a resolution of the Labour Conference of 1923. We know that these resolutions are framed with one meaning on the surface and another convenient meaning to suit the future moment when it becomes necessary to use it. The resolution that was put to the Labour Conference, and was understood by the Labour Conference, contains distinctly the words that the Labour Party and the country desired a conference for immediate and universal disarmament. I would like the right hon. Member for Platting to explain the force of the words 'immediate and universal disarmament.'

Of course, since that conference the right hon. Member for Platting and his colleagues have been responsible for going back on that Resolution and acting contrary to it. Surely, the construction of the five cruisers was not a step towards immediate and universal disarmament. Surely the use of the Air Force in Iraq to bomb Arabs, who did not possess even a long range rifle, was not a process of calling together a conference of British and Arab workers in order to have immediate and universal disarmament. Surely the

insolent letter to Zaghlul Pasha stating that the British sword would remain
fully drawn in Egypt –
THE CHAIRMAN: It is intended that the Debate should be wide,
but it must have some relevance to the Air Force.
MR. SAKLATVALA: The Air Force is a wing of armaments. The right
hon. Gentleman the Member for Platting read a Resolution of the Labour
Conference demanding immediate and universal disarmament which
included and covered all the various wings of the Army. I wish to point
out to the right hon. Gentleman that his leader the right hon. Gentleman
the Member of Aberavon (Mr. Ramsey MacDonald), speaking at Swindon
the other night, said, in the usual dramatic fashion, that whatever was
won by the sword, and attempted to be kept by the sword would be
perish by the sword. Was he intentionally sending the British interests
in Iraq, in Egypt, and in India to perdition when he was trying to defend
them by the British sword? We have to study the question of disarmament
in the new light of conscience that we should possess, and not in the
light of party wrangles, party dicta and party dogma, which can be interpreted
either way to suit the convenience of the moment. The argument which
we put to the Committee is proved by illustrations from history. If you
go one inch along the road of armaments, there are others to go six inches
further still. To-day we argue that we must increase our Air Force
immoderately because France has increased hers immoderately. That is
not a communication to France asking for immediate and universal
disarmament. It is a gesture to France that she may now go another mile
on the road. The history of armaments is that, in this way, they increase
numerically and multiply in variety, and become more intense in their
deadlines. The vote which we are discussing does not lead towards
disarmament, but leads towards the growth of armaments. I wonder how
the right hon. Gentleman the Member for Platting can say to us that
though the Labour party intends complete disarmament, it is by acting
in support of this Vote that he is going to achieve that end.

We have had from the Government one serious argument to which I am
prepared to give serious attention. There is a fear in the minds of men and
women, which we cannot discard as of no account, that if you had no Air
Force somebody else would pay you back the same coin which you are
accustomed to deal out to other nations in the world. What are we to do
then? What is the position? Hon. and right hon. Members who are
supporting these Estimates, and who are not even fully satisfied with the
full measure, dictate the view that there is nothing annihilation, destruction, and demolition in store. [HON. MEMBERS: 'Agreed!'] We do
not agree. You cannot laugh away the convictions of men whose convictions are as strong as yours. If you have not that knowledge now, from next

week you will begin to acquire it, if you read the new 'Lansbury's Workers' Weekly.' Perhaps there are in this Committee very large numbers of Members who hold the conviction that it is mere nervousness that sees shadows of destruction in disarmament, when historic facts prove that murder and destruction are visiting the nations of Europe through armaments. The hon. Member for Bow and Bromley gave a list of 11,000,000 slaughtered human lives amongst the nations that were armed and not among the nations who were not. Switzerland, Denmark, Scandinavia, the poor Negroes of Africa – those who are not armed so madly never show destruction in their national life. We have large masses in this country among the working classes, in spite of the diffidence of the right hon. Member for Platting, who are quite prepared to take life calmly, without seeing ghosts or shadows of war, without air forces, battleships and armies.

MR. SEXTON: What about the Red Army?

MR. SAKLATVALA: My hon. Friend is a prophet; he has read my thoughts. I was coming to the Red Army. The Red Army raises ghosts and makes uneasy the minds of those who are believers in piling up armaments [AN HON. MEMBER: 'With its Air Force.'] – the Red Army, with its Air Force, with its composition, and with its purpose, does not frighten a few million workers of Great Britain and Europe as it frightens the hon. and the right hon. Members on all sides of the House who are believers in armaments. You are simply determined to believe in armaments, and in order to buttress up your belief, you want to point to the examples of those who have got to arm in defence against yourselves, just as you find an excuse to arm yourselves in defence against someone else, and that is exactly the race of armaments which we who talk of complete disarmament want to stop, and we are not disturbed by the apparition of the Red Army or the Blue Army or the White Army.

Here we have the product of human brains like the aeroplane and the airship. There is famine in Ireland to-day, and no aeroplanes are going over to the West of Ireland immediately with food for the little children and scattering and showering that from the air. There are so many uses to which the Air Service could be put, and we all know it, but the first and immediate use to which all nations want to apply it is the use of destruction and killing one another. Why? Because you insist on maintaining your system of Imperialism, of Imperial trade, of Imperial Trade routes, and your hereditary and God-given right to raw products growing in other nations' countries; your right to cotton in Rhodesia and Mesopotamia, your right to oil seeds in India, your right to cotton in the Sudan, and to rubber in Malacca. Therefore, you want an efficient Air Service because you believe that the mode of killing human lives and of terrorising human lives through a sea Service is no longer up-to-date and efficient.

We suggest to you that you now begin to think out ways and means of how to employ scientific progress and how to employ growing human knowledge in reversing those systems. Hon. Members on this side who are opposing this Vote, see that one excuse for to-night's Estimate is that other nations are arming themselves. It becomes the duty of this nation, just as clearly towards Great Britain as towards any other country, to begin to preach to the peoples of other nations, just as well that aerial forces and armaments are not for the happiness of nations, but for the misery and disgrace of nations. But when somebody does that, you say it is the Russian and Communist Government foreign propaganda. Yes, if we want to live in a human world like human beings, it is our bounded duty now to have international propaganda just as much as anything else. In stead of spending £20,000,000 on arming yourselves for the air against your neighbours and against the helpless, unarmed Arabs and negroes of the East, if you could spend that money on what you term foreign propaganda for peace and goodwill and international relationship and brotherhood and equality, you would be making better use of that money; but you hold to your old-fashioned ideas of the last hundred years and consider it is a great crime to take care of yourselves and not allow international jealousies to make you increase your air forces. The hon. and gallant Member for Mid-Bedford-shire (Brigadier-General Warner) gave voice to another note that is alarm-ing. I hope that my right hon. friend the Member for Platting (Mr. Clynes) will seriously consider the significance and implications of that new note. He appealed to the universities and to the public schools – I do not know, Mr. Hope, whether I may be permitted to speak of 'these *nobs* of society' – to start their aero clubs and to perfect themselves in the art of flying. I can visualise my constituency and other constituencies in Great Britain where there are millions of working-class boys and girls who will not have the opportunity of being experts in flying. This is the new class that is going to assist the ruling class. (*Interruption.*) It is all very well to try and drown the voice of the speaker. But it is bound to come out in the next few months when the nations of the world through the working classes are going to get closer and closer together in opposition to armies and air forces; and they will take, rightly or wrongly, though it may not be the intention of hon. and right hon. Gentlemen opposite, an attitude of opposition to the Air Forces, the Naval Forces, and the Armies of Europe. This gathering together of the working classes, especially within Great Britain and Russia, will have its unavoidable influence upon the front benches of parties generally. A study of armaments and national forces will take place, and these various schemes will be looked into in a different spirit and from a different angle from that which we are taking up to-night, and it would then be realised that the Vote which you are asking for to-day, and the additional force that you are creating to-day, will be, rightly or wrongly, put under the microscope and examined quite differently from how you are trying to look at it to-night. It would be found out by working-class conferences, or gatherings, or committees that the armaments of the future are so devised that by a handful of persons, the controllers of the working class, large masses of the working class in Great Britain and Europe could be controlled and kept in check, as well as kept under terror, and kept in the right place; and when that view begins to spread, I put it to the House that this House will not be as joyful and as cheerful and light-minded as it is to-night.

APPENDIX 8

Labour Monthly
December 1930

SOME TRIBUTES TO SAKLATVALA

JAWAHARLAL NEHRU: 'I wish to pay my tribute to the memory of Shapurji Saklatvala, who throughout his life was a brave and intrepid soldier of freedom.'

GEORGI DIMITROV: 'The Communist International lowers its fighting banner over the coffin of our true comrade, Shapurji Saklatvala, a worthy son of the Indian people, a true friend of the working class and a tireless fighter in the cause of socialism.'

S. A. BRELVI: 'Accept my heartiest condolences of your sad and irretrievable loss which is also the loss of the entire Indian nation, for whom the dead leader was also a fearless fighter.'

SUBHAS CHANDRA BOSE: 'Your loss is India's loss. Please accept heartfelt condolences from Indian community and from myself.'

GEORGE LANSBURY: 'Through the death of Comrade Saklatvala the whole international labour movement has lost one of its very best comrades and workers. India has lost one of the best of her sons; he will be missed very much indeed in the struggle for Indian freedom. I can only express the hope that the fact we all mourn his loss as a comrade and friend will in some way help his wife and family to bear their loss. 'I should like to say that although Saklatvala and I often found ourselves in disagreement on questions of method and organisation, we always remained true friends.'

CLEMENT ATLEE, M.P.:'Mr Saklatvala was a devoted worker for the causes in which he believed. he was always a pleasant man with whom to have dealings. He was ever courteous and was gifted with a very vivid sense of humour and personality. I always got on well in personal relationship with him. His loss will be felt by many.'

HERBERT H. ELVIN (Gen. Secy. National Union of Clerks; Member, General Council of TUC): 'I have known Saklatvala for many years, both as a member of the NUC and in public life. Although in late

years our path has diverged I have always had the utmost respect for
him. I had a firm belief in his sincerity of purpose, and it may be because
of my sojourn in India for many years, I always had a profound admiration
for him in his championship of the depressed and distressed classes
of that great country. The Indian workers indeed have lost a strong
advocate, and one who was prepared to sacrifice personal interest for
the workers' interest.'

REGINALD BRIDGEMAN (International League Against Imperialism):
'The sudden death of Comrade Saklatvala comes as a great shock to
all the thousands who have been personally associated with him.

'His tireless efforts on behalf of Indian freedom have told on his
remarkable vigour and it may be truthfully said of 'Sak' that he has
sacrificed his life for the struggle for the freedom of India from foreign
denomination.'

BEN BRADLEY (British section of the League Against Imperialism):
'In comrade Saklatvala's death the working-class movement has lost
one of its most sincere and courageous revolutionary fighters.

'The Executive Committee of the League Against Imperialism has lost
not merely a valuable member, but a staunch friend whom it will be
impossible to replace.'

WILLIAM GALLAGHER, M.P.: The death of Shapurji Saklatvala will
leave a gap in our ranks that can never be filled. He, more than any
man of our age, cemented the ties binding the toilers of Britain and of
the colonial countries together.

'Wherever I have gone on propaganda work in England, Scotland and
Wales, I have found Saklatvala respected, loved and honoured by the
workers, who appreciated his sterling worth, his utter selflessness, his
devotion to duty.

'The workers of West Fife learned to know him well during the recent
elections and the more they new him, the more they loved him.
'In parliament and outside, loyal and devoted was Saklatvala, the friend
and champion of all who were oppressed. Physically frail, he had
tremendous courage, both physical and moral. The utmost that any
of us who are left behind can hope to do is to carry on the struggle
with the same untiring faith and devotion that inspired Saklatvala
throughout his life.'

R. SAWYER (Negro Welfare Organisation): 'It will be a great shock
to all the Negro peoples throughout the world to learn of the death of
Shapurji Saklatvala.'

THE COMMUNIST PARTY OF THE USA: 'With the revolutionary workers of the world we share your loss. Let the world mark the significance of the fact that Saklatvala, a native of India, and battler for the liberation of that oppressed land from British imperialism, was the spokesman of the Communist Party of Great Britain in Parliament.

'He was the forerunner of greater victories of which a new series is opened with William Gallacher's election to Parliament.

'We salute Comrade Saklatvala and accord his memory an eternal place in our midst.'

THE COMMUNIST PARTY OF IRELAND: 'Irish workers are deeply moved at the death of Comrade Saklatvala, valiant fighter for Indian liberty and for all oppressed people, and the unwavering supporter of the struggle for Irish independence.'

PAT DEVINE (Belfast Communist Party): 'Sak was a fine fighter and will be greatly missed. As a communist fighter he raised a lone voice in parliament in 1923 against the partition of Ireland. Convey our heartiest sympathy to his family. Our party expresses its heartfelt regret at his passing.'

CONGRESS SOCIALIST PARTY OF INDIA: 'The death of Shapurji Saklatvala has removed a great champion of the submerged and exploited classes all over the world. He was a stalwart among the communists outside Russia and was an active member of the British Communist Party at the time of his death. He was an ex-M.P. from the constituency of North Battersea. In him India mourns the loss of a fearless champion of her cause in England.'

TOM MANN: 'I desire to express my heartfelt sympathy with our dear Comrade Saklatvala's family in their terrible bereavement. Our capable, loyal and lovable old comrade has been snatched from us with awful suddenness; his devotion and zeal for the movement were of the highest order, and we shall honour him by ourselves working with greater zeal.'

TWO MEN:TWO FAITHS

Two men are being buried today, each in his own way a great national figure. They will both be buried in London, though one of them is not an Englishman. They are Saklatvala and Kipling.

Saklatvala, frail, passionate, intensely courageous, the revolutionary who devoted his whole life to the struggle for the liberation of the Indian people from British imperialism, who fought for the right of the oppressed to life in every country, will be remembered forever not only by his own countrymen, but by the best of all countries.

Kipling, the poet of imperialism, the great artist who was the involuntary prisoner of his own caste and class traditions, is being exploited after his death by all the most reactionary and vile elements in British imperialism as a means for whipping up jingo sentiment and class and racial hatreds.

Saklatvala saw the future of his great country, with its rich and splendid civilisation, as lying in the hands of its millions of workers, peasants, artisans and poor intellectuals. He saw it as a struggle against the struggling forces of medieval feudalism and capitalist imperialism, forces which had destroyed the national life of his country and reduced the masses of his fellow-countrymen to abject poverty.

The British rulers of India, the civil servants, magistrates, army officers and businessmen will use the name and work of Kipling in order to perpetuate those forces and deepen that poverty.

Saklatvala fought to restore elementary human rights to millions of humanity. Kipling used his genius to defend the men who had taken these rights.

There should be little difficulty in judging between the two. If Kipling is to leave anything to the common treasure of humanity it will only be because men like Saklatvala have lived and fought. East and West meet in Saklatvala, but it is through the common cause of humanity and the great battle for its liberation.

In the end it will be a victory in that fight which sorts the dross from the gold in the work of Kipling.

[*Daily Worker* editorial, 20 January 1936]

APPENDIX 9

ELECTION RESULTS

1922 – General Election (North Battersea) Turnout - 56.6%
1. Saklatvala, S. Labour   - 11,311   - 50.5%
2. Hogbin, H. National Liberal   - 9,290   - 41.6%
3. Albu, V. Liberal   - 1,756   - 7.9%

1923 - General Election (North Battersea) Turnout - 62.4%
1. Hogbin, H.   Liberal   - 12,527   - 50.4%
2. Saklatvala, S. Labour   - 12,341   - 49.6%

1924 - General Election (North Battersea) Turnout - 73.1%
1. Saklatvala, S.   Labour   -15,096   - 50.9%
2. Hogbin, H.   Constitutional -14,554   - 49.1%

1925 - St Pancras Borough Council (Ward 4)
1. Alliston, E.   Municipal Reform   -   2,787
2. Johnson, J.   Municipal Reform   -   2,782
3. Masterman, F. L.   Municipal Reform   -   2,684
4. Miles, A. R.   Municipal Reform   -   2,651
5. Robinson, C. C.   Municipal Reform   -   2,571
6. Dobbs, W.   Labour   -   2,067
7. Kennett, H.   Labour   -   1,987
8. Sharpe, S. E.   Labour   -   1,904
9. Shapter, M.   Labour   -   1,843
10. Hoy, J. R.   Municipal Reform   -   1,793
11. Saklatvala, S.   Labour   -   1,785

1929 - General Election (North Battersea) Turnout - 69.7%
1. Sanders, W. S. Labour   - 13,265   -   37.8%
2. Marsden, A.   Conservative - 10,833   -   30.8%
3. Saklatvala, S. Communist   - 6,554   -   18.6%
4. Brogan, T. P. Liberal   - 4,513   -   12.8%

1930 - By-Election (Glasgow, Shettleston) Turnout - 59.2%
1. McGovern, J.   Labour   - 10,699   -   42.9%
2. Templeton, W. P. Conservative - 10,303   -   41.2%
3. McNichol, J. M. Scottish Nat. - 2,527   -   10.1%
4. Saklatvala, S. Communist   - 1,459   -   5.8%

1931 - London County Council (North Battersea)
1.   Sainsbury, B. A.   Municipal Reform   -   4,781
2.   Clarke, V.   Municipal Reform   -   4,647
3.   Ganley, C. S.   Labour   -   4,107
4.   Douglas, F. C. R. Labour   -   3,969
5.   Saklatvala, S.   Communist   -   728
6.   Usher, E.   Communist   -   535

1931 - General Election (North Battersea) Turnout - 67.6%
1.   Marsden, A.   Conservative   - 18,688   - 55.4%
2.   Sanders, W. S.   Labour   - 11,985   - 35.6%
3.   Saklatvala, S.   Communist-   3,021   -9.0%

1934 - London County Council (North Battersea)
1.   Douglas, F. C. R.   Labour   -   8,334
2.   Ganley, C. S.   Labour   -   8,325
3.   Vincent Clarke, A.   Municipal Reform   -   4,549
4.   Sainsbury, E.J.   Municipal Reform   -   4,459
5.   Saklatvala, S.   Communist   -   577
6.   Johnson, W.   Communist   -   526

1934 - St Pancras Borough Council (Ward 4)
1.   Coombes   Labour   -   2,148
2.   Davies   Labour   -   2,112
3.   Evans   Labour   -   2,035
4.   Headland   Labou   r   -   2,014
5.   Lake   Labour   -   1,968
6.   Menon   Labour   -   1,928
7.   Alliston   Municipal Reform   -   1,679
8.   Bellman   Municipal Reform   -   1,663
9.   Coggan   Municipal Reform   -   1,615
10.   Day   Municipal Reform   -   1,596
11.   Lawrence   Municipal Reform   -   1,559
12.   Jack   Municipal Reform   -   1,548
13.   Carter   Communist   -   237
14.   Saklatvala Communist   -   106
15.   Fink   Communist   -   102
16.   Powell   Communist   -   92
17.   Williams   Communist   -   91
18.   Thornton   Communist   -   73

INDEX